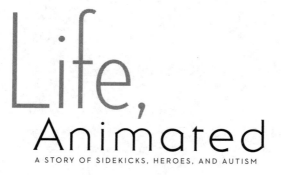

Life, Animated

A STORY OF SIDEKICKS, HEROES, AND AUTISM

ALSO BY RON SUSKIND

Confidence Men
The Way of the World
The One Percent Doctrine
The Price of Loyalty
A Hope in the Unseen

Life,
Animated

A STORY OF SIDEKICKS, HEROES, AND AUTISM

RON SUSKIND

WINNER OF THE PULITZER PRIZE

👑 | **KINGSWELL**

New York • Los Angeles

For more information address Kingswell, 1101 Flower Street, Glendale, California 91201.
ISBN 978-1-4231-8036-4
G475-5664-5-14057

Printed in the United States of America
First Edition
10 9 8 7 6 5 4 3 2 1

SUSTAINABLE FORESTRY INITIATIVE   Certified Sourcing
www.sfiprogram.org
SFI-00993

THIS LABEL APPLIES TO TEXT STOCK

To our son, Walt,
a real life hero

As you will learn in this book, my son Owen relied heavily on turning dialogue and song lyrics from Disney animated movies into tools to shape his identity and emotional growth.

I am grateful to The Walt Disney Company, which agreed to exert no influence whatsoever over the content of this book, even though it involves assessment and appraisal of their core line of business. The company has judiciously honored that agreement.

In this case, the independence of this work is also a matter of mutual interest, in that Disney is in no way endorsing the use of its materials for any matters related to autism.

What follows is the story of one family's experience across twenty years, and what we discovered.

contents

chapter one

GROWING BACKWARD

There's a videotape I have a problem with.
It's of a toddler running through fallen leaves with a
Nerf sword. The time code is OCTOBER 1993. The boy runs
like kids do at that age, about two and a half, with a reckless, headlong wobble that will soon be gone. We know this because, by late in
the image-drenched twentieth century, we know how things are *supposed* to look, and can read all manner of inference into the moving
landscape, most of it spot-on. He's a wide-eyed, curly-haired boy,
clad in green cords and a brightly colored winter jacket; tree types
and topography suggest the northeastern United States; the leafy
yard is behind a smallish home, though the swing set is elaborate—
grand and spanking new, a sign of young parents trying too hard.
The kid is being chased by a boyish, dark-haired man who's laughing
and holding a small stick as he knee-slides into the leaves, prompting
the boy to turn, smiling and ready to fight. As they cross swords, the
man says, "He's not a boy, he's a flying devil!" in a passable imitation
of Captain Hook from Disney's *Peter Pan*.

That the man and boy are reciting dialogue from an animated
movie made in 1953 bespeaks the ubiquity of the VCR, the then-
latest step in the electronic capture of sound and image begun a
century before by Thomas Edison with his first recording. Rather

than traipsing to the movie theater, one could then watch movies countless times in a free feed. So they did. Disney began releasing classics, like *Dumbo*, *The Jungle Book*, and *Peter Pan* on video-cassettes; movies baby boomer parents once loved that they could buy and share, afresh, with their kids. It was a commercial bonanza that helps explain this artifact: a video of two people reciting from a video.

Now take these specifics to the universal. This appears, after all, to be a father and son playing the roughhouse games that tend to nimbly carry volumes of hidden emotions: the boy, with each step, grows into the hero of his fertile imagination; meanwhile, the dad, knowing, in some deep recess, that the boy will grow to someday replace him, considers the many creative ways to perish. All played out, effortlessly, as the boy offers his best, most elegant thrust and the man falls—as dead as the crunching leaves—before pulling the giggling child on top of him.

•   •   •

I'm the father in this nice if unremarkable little video. That's my son. I've watched it a hundred times, as has my wife, until we couldn't bear it anymore.

It's a last sighting of him, captured mercilessly and forever on the magnetic tape.

A month later, the boy vanished.

•   •   •

Her name was Cornelia Kennedy—from a large Irish-Catholic clan in Connecticut—before we were married. She now uses Suskind. I'm her husband, Ron, a Jewish guy from Delaware. The older of our two sons, Walt—named after my father, who died when I was a kid—is now five. Our younger son, the boy with the foam sword, is Owen. The starter home with the leafy backyard is in Dedham, Massachusetts. I've spent three years in the *Wall Street Journal*'s Boston bureau. We're bound for Washington, DC, where I'm to be a national affairs reporter for the paper. The video is shot the day before the moving van arrives, and we're all still firmly ensconced in the land of *normal.* I never thought much about that word, how it's one of those definitions by default, shaped not so much by what it is as what it's not—a circle defined by everything outside of it.

• • •

Cornelia sees it first a few weeks after we get to Washington. She's with him all day, every day.

Something's terribly wrong.

Owen is unglued. He cries, runs about, stops, cries some more. When he pauses to catch his breath, he just seems to stare into space.

That is, when he isn't staring at Cornelia with searching eyes. She cups his wet, red face in her hands and asks what's wrong. It appears he can't tell her. Owen has never been quite as chatty as his talkative older brother, but chatty enough—the usual going-on-three vocabulary of a few hundred words, there, at the ready, to make his needs known or express love, or even tell a little joke or story.

We have moved to a rented house in Georgetown and everything transpires within a flurry of ambient activity: boxes to unpack, a new school for Walt, and a new job in a large, noisy news bureau for his father. So the loss of speech isn't noticed until Owen is down to a few words. A month after the moving vans depart in November, Owen has but one word: juice.

Sometimes, though, he won't drink what's in the cup—a sippy cup. He graduated to a "big boy's cup" nearly a year ago. But in Georgetown he's spilling, as though he's lost his bearings. He has.

He's whirling and weaving. So Cornelia holds him, as much as she can, sitting in the gliding chair, as her mind races across the months. Did something happen, something she missed?

It's like reviewing clues to a kidnapping. There was that one time, on a trip to Southampton last August, when he cried inconsolably for much of a day, though he'd never been much of a crier—not ever. Then there was the day the moving van was being loaded in late October, when a close friend had taken the kids for the day and, dropping them off, told us Owen had slept the whole time. He still took naps, but half the day? Unpacking a box, Cornelia finds a video from that very day, moving day. The sun was setting and Walter led a tour of our half-empty house. He was gleeful. A big trip to Washington. His goldfish, Artie and Tyler, named after his two best buddies, were already in a sealed bowl, ready for the journey: "My fish are coming with us, too!" And then a glimpse of Owen, briefly on camera, saying softly, sleepily, "This is my crib and all my things."

She finds another video in that same box—the *Peter Pan* sword fight. That night, she and I watch. It makes no sense. *Look at the way he moves, the ease of his speech.* We rewind, watch it again. And again, looking for clues.

Come mid-December, Cornelia finds herself lying with Owen in his lower bunk, Walt fast asleep up top. A small lit tank hums on the bookcase, where Artie and Tyler swim silently through bubbles. It's three A.M. Owen is rolling side to side, mumbling nonsense. Cornelia holds him as tightly as she can, to calm him down. In the dark night of desperation she now prays, whispering through tears to her baby, hoping God can hear: "Please help us. Whatever is going on I'm going to love you so much that I'll love it out of you. I'll keep holding you until all this is over."

• • •

The holidays are approaching—there are gifts to buy and Washington is alive with events, the season of giving.

It should be a time of great expectations. On the surface, it seems to be all coming together, our life plan, years in the making. Cornelia and I had become friends after college, running a political campaign. She read my law school application, sitting on my desk, and told me it didn't sound much like I wanted to go to law school—which I didn't—but that it was well crafted and I should consider being a writer. She already was one, a youthful prodigy, and I immediately liked the idea. Before my father died of cancer at forty-six, he wrote a letter to my older brother and me imploring us to do "something worthwhile" with our lives. Journalism seemed to fit, opposing authority, searching for bits of truth, building a readership. Our candidate lost, but we became a couple, with her landing a job in New York as a reporter at *People* magazine and me off to Columbia University Graduate School of Journalism, followed by two years as a news clerk at *The New York Times,* while she moved up as a New York magazine editor; a year and a half reporting at the *St. Petersburg* (Florida) *Times,* where we married; then the editorship of a small business magazine in Boston and, in 1990, a slot at the *Wall Street Journal's* New England bureau, a stone's throw from Boston's Old South Meeting House. I'd been crafting stories since I could barely talk—at the behest of my fiercely prideful Brooklyn-bred mother—and even turned them into stand-up routines during the difficult years after my father's death. But I was learning, year by year, to write them, long form, for the paper's signature front page. I was transferred to Washington to do that full-time—a dream job.

So in the evenings we try to focus on all the positives—new friends, deals on used furniture for our rented three-story Federal-style row house, neighborhoods where we might someday buy a home—before Cornelia reluctantly mentions a story from her day, some troubling thing Owen's done. "Everything will be all right," I say before trying out some plausible explanation: Owen is experiencing some sort of distress, maybe gastric, maybe, even, some hearing loss—and we'll get to the bottom of it.

"No kid loses what they've already attained. You don't grow backwards."

•　•　•

The pediatrician asks to see our son for a moment, by himself. He tells us to sit in the waiting room. We're extraneous. He wants to see how Owen interacts with a stranger, without us there. Because kids are trusting little people, they tend to look at strangers. They're curious. They suck in information like small vacuum cleaners. They make eye contact and express themselves. At least, that's what they're supposed to do.

After a few minutes, the doctor calls us into his office. These things aren't happening. We say, yes, we know, that's why we're here. Cornelia briefly describes what she's been seeing, the nature of our worries, how our lives have been upended.

He listens. "If something is causing this much of a disruption in the life of the family," he says, "then it is definitely a problem." When pediatricians aren't sure what they're seeing, especially with small children, they default to "mother concern."

He says he wants to take a blood sample for two genetic tests. One is for fragile X syndrome (a neurological condition, we find out later, with a detectable genetic marker and devastating outcomes). The other test is for Tay-Sachs. I know what that one is: a disease that causes mental and physical decline in babies and usually kills them by the age of four. It's especially prevalent in Jews of Eastern European descent. That'd be me. This is something you learn about in Hebrew school, along with the Holocaust. And then he refers us to a center—a place in Rockville, Maryland—that might be more helpful.

By February, we're sitting in a very different kind of waiting room, inside the Reginald S. Lourie Center for Infants and Young Children. It's attached to a playroom, visible through a one-way mirror. Inside are large, multicolored blocks, swings, and mats for children to play with . . . while they are being observed.

We're shown to an office where a tall, severe-looking dark-haired woman waits. She greets Owen, whose hand Cornelia is holding with the firmest possible resolve. In her office where she talks to us are more items to play with. Owen ignores them. Minutes pass. Then she has him walk down that long hall, from me to Cornelia. Letting him go, I want to say, "Walk nice and straight, like back in Dedham, just this once." He doesn't. He's moving his arms, veering, catching himself, a zigzag, like someone running with their eyes closed. Cornelia scoops him up. Then we return to the woman's office. "It appears he has a pervasive developmental disorder, affecting most of the traditional areas of development," she says, and, "It's clear in his gait, among other things." She continues to talk in a removed, antiseptic way, barely looking at Owen, sitting on the floor, fussing with his fingers. We're not really present at this point. Cornelia and I both are somewhere else, floating off, looking down at the young couple frozen in their chairs, nodding every few seconds, next to a child who's intently studying his hands. Which is why I'm not sure precisely what point the doctor was making when she said the word "autism."

Denial is a powerful force. Years later, a close friend's father, an old psychiatrist, said something wise to me: "Respect denial. It's there for a reason: a way we cope with what we cannot face." At thirty-four, I didn't respect it; didn't even recognize it.

Driving home, Cornelia and I sit silently, while Owen thrashes behind us in his car seat. There is no way that woman is right. We know about autism what most people do in this time period. We saw *Rain Man*, like everyone else in America. Our son is not Raymond Babbitt, that guy Dustin Hoffman played. No way in hell.

A month later, we find a new doctor: a young developmental pediatrician in a booming Bethesda practice who looks uncannily like Cornelia's longtime high school friend—a guy I befriended in college, who first introduced us. This feels much better.

Dr. Alan Rosenblatt takes Owen on his lap and says, ever so softly, "Hey there, buddy." This time, Owen looks back. They do a few exercises—touching fingers, watching, together, as the doctor moved his hands—and then they get down on the rug. Owen seems comfortable. They build little houses using blocks, Rosenblatt starting one, seeing if Owen adds to it.

He doesn't. There isn't much interaction. Owen gets up and begins to wander. Rosenblatt calls his name. And then Owen crawls under a chair and glances back at the doctor with a "come and get me" look—a brief expression, there and then gone—beckoning a chase. Rosenblatt jots something on his clipboard.

Back in his chair, he says, "I'm afraid that Owen has what we're nowadays calling pervasive developmental disorder, or PDD, with the addition of NOS, for 'not otherwise specified.'" That means Owen has some "autistic-like behaviors" but also others—like that "let's play" look—that don't fit the current definitions of classic autism.

He goes through a regimen for Owen that he feels we should start immediately. Intensive speech and language therapy, occupational therapy, play therapy, and the immediate hunt for an appropriate school for the coming fall, for which he has some suggestions. "Early intervention," he says, "is crucial." He adds, "Families who have religion or some faith community in their lives tend to do a bit better," which chills us both—that catastrophe awaits—but is something Cornelia, raised Catholic, will soon draw strength from.

·That Owen was not labeled "autistic" is a relief, as is Rosenblatt's characterization of Owen's problems as a "delay." We'll learn more later about the connotative cover these terms offer us. The important effect: it keeps us from running out of the office and driving home feeling like we've both just had our arms and legs cut off.

We make small talk with Rosenblatt walking toward the parking lot that day in April and get a bonus in building our defenses. We mention our wonderful pediatrician in Boston, a Harvard doctor named Bob Michaels. Rosenblatt does a double take. From Pittsburgh? Yes, we say excitedly—raised in Pittsburgh. "Do I know Bob Michaels? His father was my pediatrician. A great one. He was a major reason I became a pediatrician!"

As soon as we get home, we call Dr. Michaels at Harvard to tell him of this extraordinary coincidence and—not incidentally—elucidate what we've been seeing with Owen since leaving Massachusetts. He puts us on hold and gets Owen's charts. He scans them but hardly needs to. "I just examined him in the summer. He was completely fine. I don't see how this could be."

Neither do we. Yes, something went haywire, but something that is confusing even to the doctors. He is "atypical"—Rosenblatt's word—and his problems are assorted delays. They can be corrected. We sleep that night in a wash of relief. We will save this boy, rebuild him—rebirth him!—every waking hour of every day. *Fools.*

• • •

The next morning, Cornelia takes Owen by the hand and walks Walt the seven blocks to Hyde Elementary, down the street from our house in Georgetown. Walt is thriving there. Other than a slight disciplinary issue—for playing the harmonica to announce his presence at a morning meeting on the first day—he's enjoying school, making friends; playing, learning, growing. That day, after drop-offs, Cornelia, Owen in tow, meets with a small group of parents.

Hyde isn't quite measuring up to some of the elementary schools in other Northwest DC neighborhoods, but it's aspiring to—an effort discussed in that morning's coffee klatch about the upcoming Hyde Spring Fair. It can, and should, raise plenty of money for the school, and Cornelia—as the fair's co-chair—has been busy lining up sponsors, donated goods, and the like.

All of which makes the day—a Saturday in early May, two weeks hence—a big one for a new family in a new community. The large fenced-in playground alongside the school is starting to fill up by late morning as the ride managers hustle to get the moon bounce pumped. It feels like what we hoped to find in DC—what anyone would want, really—the company of happy warriors, building a little bordered world of fun and food, where equal, matching armies of parents and children gather and cheer for a good cause.

We've taken great care, of course, in planning the day for Owen so he can attend with us. There's only one gate to the playground, managed by parent volunteers who know him and are on guard against him slipping out; and that isn't even an issue, considering that either Cornelia or I will be with him every minute. And we are, over hours, as the frenzy of running a fair like this ebbs and flows: more ice; does anyone know where the power switch is; are we out of hot dogs!

It's hard to pinpoint the exact moment. Generally, Father Error is to blame. Mothers probably have hard-wired neurological equipment, dating back to roughly the Big Bang, for instantly knowing the coordinates of offspring. It's well along into the afternoon when I let go of his hand to shove the remainder of a hot dog—Owen's lunch was the other half—into my mouth and then grab a Coke can I'd rested on the ground. When I turn, the patch of swing-set gravel a foot to my left, where he just stood, is empty.

Fathers have equipment in these situations, too. But the circuits fire differently. First rule: don't panic. Scan the perimeter, steady and swift: 90 degrees, 180, 270, 360.

Then panic. I start to run, first a slow trot, toward the gate and ask one of the dads at the gate: "Did you see him—did Owen slip by?" It's astonishing how much attention a running man can draw. I turn to see a small crowd of parents already behind me . . . led by Cornelia.

I don't have to say he's gone; that, she can see, so I jump to pertinent facts. "I was with him at the swing set thirty seconds ago. He didn't get out of the gate!"

It helps that the fair is winding down—there are fewer people to block our lines of sight. After five minutes, he's still nowhere to be found. Cornelia and I, running and panting, are tamping down the same, shared memory: a year before at a school fair in Wellesley, near our home in Massachusetts, he was briefly lost. We filed it away: two-year-olds get lost. It happens. Actually, it doesn't happen all that often. They tend to have at least a remnant of separation anxiety—a match of the mother's radar—and a dawning awareness that no parent is nearby. That's the moment they realize they're lost and start crying. Whether or not Owen once had that equipment, it is now shut off . . . and this isn't verdant Wellesley. It's a patch of fenced concrete in Georgetown, with cars weaving down cobblestoned O Street and, half a block away, speeding down Wisconsin Avenue—one of Washington's main thoroughfares.

At ten minutes, panic spreads. Parents start fanning out into the streets. Cornelia and I run into the school—off limits for the fair, but a door, through which some of the power cords run, is open. It's a turn-of-the-century brick box, huge and empty, with crumbling cornices and two hallways we run down—I, down one hall; she, the other. There's honking outside—sounds like a wreck on Wisconsin. My heart stops beating—*Please, God, let that not be him.* Cornelia is now moving like a spirit—silent and swift, breathless—her feet skimming the ground. Not really in her body. She's in his head, looking around and then out through his eyes, the two of them meeting in there, talking softly: "Where would you go, honey . . . where would you want to go?" Most classrooms are locked. A door is ajar.

And there, next to a wide window, partially open onto the playground where everyone had been shouting "Owen, Owen!" he's standing, quietly, next to a sand table. Outside, parents move in fearful unison while Owen intently watches grains of sand run through his fingers.

•   •   •

Seats in the jammed ballroom just north of Washington are already scarce by eight A.M. on a very hot June morning. The air inside the Crowne Plaza Hotel in Rockville, Maryland, is electric, all clipped conversations and eager looks, this way and that.

Cornelia spots a lone seat at a crowded table as Dr. O. Ivar Lovaas—gray-haired and energetic at sixty-seven, with a wide smile, blue eyes, and only the slight trace of a Norwegian accent—takes the stage to raucous applause.

He's come east from his offices at UCLA and his growing California operation, to encourage the faithful, but also to win converts. He'll do that by putting on a show. Soon the stage is alive with a kind of psychodrama—therapists working with the Lovaas Model of Applied Behavioral Analysis, or ABA, on autistic children, and Ivar, himself, presiding.

His technique is, at its core, bracing, whereby an ABA-trained therapist sits across from a small child and, with rewards and verbal "aversives"—stern language and sometimes shouts—forces changes in the child's behavior. It's pure behavior modification. Lovaas is a disciple of B. F. Skinner and his use of rewards and penalties to condition responses: in this case, how to reduce interfering behaviors, how to build the child's attention span, how to use succinct instructions, how to use effective consequences for behavior, how to sequence the teaching materials to shape more complex behaviors, and so forth. It looks to the untrained eye like animal training. To build eye contact, for instance, the ABA therapist will put the reward (M&M's being a favorite) on the bridge of the child's nose to make them look up toward the therapist's face. If, after succinct instruction—"Look at me"—eye contact is made, the M&M is popped into the little mouth. Crisp instructions, like "Quiet hands" (autistic kids often flap their hands) or "Mouth quiet" (no self-talking), are backed up with some grabbing and manipulating, moving the child's hands into their proper place. Lovaas's selection criteria for an early quartet of autistic kids he worked on in the 1970s included the request that they have a healthy appetite so the withholding of food would have maximal effect.

A master of one-liners, Lovass implores the audience to get children into one of his intensive, forty-hour-a-week programs before they turn four for optimal outcomes.

"Once they reach four, it becomes more difficult—so please don't wait," he says before offering inspirational stories of how lives have been turned around through the use of his method.

Lovaas presented startling results in a 1987 research paper regarding nineteen children. His finding—that nine of the severely affected autistic children were "cured" by his technique and went on to successful lives in mainstream settings—has not yet been replicated by early 1994.

But there was no shortage of those willing to try.

• • •

We've furiously run up a learning curve since meeting with Rosenblatt. There's a lot more to know than *Rain Man*, of course, a history going back to the late 1930s, when Leo Kanner, a child psychologist at Johns Hopkins, first tested eleven kids and wrote up his findings:

of a particular boy "drawing into a shell and living within himself" and being "oblivious to everything around him." The kids generally had difficulty with expressive language, treated objects with a care typically reserved for people, threw tantrums when routines were changed, but often had strong yet narrow memory capabilities and, Kanner wrote, "could not be regarded as feebleminded in any ordinary sense."

Around that time, half a world away, Hans Asperger, an Austrian researcher, was doing original research on four boys whose behavior and capabilities showed "a lack of empathy, little ability to form friendships, one-sided conversations, intense absorption in a special interest, and clumsy movements." Asperger, who never met Kanner, dubbed these children "little professors," hyper-verbal at a young age, deeply focused on their particular affinities, but still "autistic" in that they lived lonely, socially isolated lives—much, in fact, like Asperger himself.

In the decades to follow, there were battles over causation, including Kanner and later the celebrated Bruno Bettelheim attributing it, falsely, to so-called "refrigerator mothers"—a theory that finally collapsed when genetic testing in the early 1980s showed a high prevalence of autism in twins and siblings who had been separated at birth.

But the numbers kept growing. By the early 1990s, children with a wide array of profiles, from those who spun, self-stimulated, and never spoke to the hyper-verbal and hyper-focused, were finding a diagnostic home somewhere along the shoreline originally mapped by Kanner—defining what eventually would be called "classic autism"—and Asperger, whose "Asperger' syndrome" wasn't even discovered until his lost papers were translated by German child researcher Uta Frith in 1991. Somewhere in the middle was PDD and PDD-NOS, for kids who didn't fit neatly into either category.

In the latest *Diagnostic and Statistical Manual of Mental Disorders,* or *DSM*, published in early 1994, all of them are listed, and a few doctors, including our Dr. Rosenblatt, are already calling it a *spectrum* of related disorders. Why the numbers seem to be growing is a mystery, as are effective treatments. The two that seem most promising are Lovaas's behaviorism and a technique developed by a George Washington University professor named Stanley Greenspan called "Floortime," a system of basically following the kids—driven by their intense self-directed urges—wherever they go, and in whatever they utter, and try, with various methods, to draw them out. Very different therapies—almost polar opposites—that share a one-on-one model of intense engagement and a goal of bringing these kids into the world.

Because Owen is "atypical" in some of his features and, at that point, ABA is more the destination of "classic autism," presenting at birth or soon thereafter, Rosenblatt suggests we go with Floortime. Owen has already been to a few sessions with one of Greenspan's longtime adherents, a middle-aged woman who doesn't seem to have much of a knack for getting on the floor. Mostly, she gets Cornelia on the floor and coaches her about how to follow Owen around to pick up motions she could imitate, sounds she might repeat, or looks—at whatever object might be in his path—that she can mirror. Exhausting, but no discernible progress. Cornelia figures she should at least see what Lovaas had to offer, which is what brings her to the hotel this morning. At the lunch break, she chats with a dozen or so other attendees sitting at her round table, loaded with piles of ABA materials, and realizes they are almost all teachers and therapists from Montgomery County, looking to get certified as ABA trainers. This session is a first step. Once certified, they'll be ripe for hire as, in essence, a member of a family with a burdened child. The protocol is to spend forty hours a week in someone's house, to stay on top of the child all day, and then train the parents to carry forward conditioning on evenings and weekends. The key is to totally shape the environment. It is expensive, but desperate families are willing to try anything.

Cornelia listens, quietly, to the excited chatter, not saying much. After a moment, she realizes she's a rarity in this ballroom: a parent.

She lets on . . . and their faces flush with sympathy. Tell us about your child, how old? Three. Does he have any speech? No, not really. One asks if the ABA training is difficult to watch. She nods and forces herself to smile. If she's looking to hire someone, a therapist mentions, she'd be happy to travel each morning to DC. Cornelia doesn't let on that we're drifting toward the opposing camp.

It isn't until late afternoon after picking up Walt from school, putting Owen in his car seat, and racing north from DC to Rockville, Maryland, that I meet up with Cornelia. She's already waiting outside the hotel and slips silently into our Volvo station wagon— our only car—looking shell-shocked. "It was like spending a whole day, eight hours straight, with the Ice Queen," which is what we now called that first autism doctor. She describes the day and then offers her summation: "We don't have to do this monkey training, because Owen isn't like those kids."

I nod. We both nod. It's just a matter of reaching him, of figuring out what caused this storm to envelop him, so we can clear away the clouds and let the light back in. It also costs about forty thousand dollars a year for Lovaas. I figure that's a lot of cash, well over half of my after-tax income, *that we just saved*. To celebrate, we decide on dinner out on the Rockville Pike—a repeating Hanna-Barbera landscape of every franchise created by the wit of man. We end up at the Silver Diner, one of a chain of restaurants crafted with admirable precision to look like genuine, home-grown neighborhood diners—a favorite of our kids and their beleaguered parents: a perfect place to vanish, where they serve ice cream sundaes all day.

• • •

A Georgetown video store has a life-size cardboard standup of Walt's new favorite movie, *The Sandlot*, 20ᵗʰ Century Fox's recent hit about a group of neighborhood kids who forge friendships as a ragtag baseball team. As September 1994 arrives, our months of pleas and cajoling pay off: the manager, ready to swap it out for another movie studio giveaway, hands it to us. So, for his sixth birthday party at a park near our house, Walt's buddies crowd around their cardboard *Sandlot* doppelgangers—Bertram Grover Weeks, Mike "Squints" Palledorous, Benny "the Jet" Rodriguez—with Walt front and center, making for a thin line between the imaginary and the real. We snap pictures—lots of them.

A year before, this fairly conventional scene would've barely elicited a shrug. So, he's got lots of friends, is at ease in the world—*of course, and why not . . . to be expected.* That's the way it was back in Dedham. We didn't make a fuss over what was expected. Now it fills us with a sense of the exceptional.

And a wash of relief that Walt, smiling away, doesn't seem to notice that the rest of us are barely keeping our heads above water.

A few days after the birthday party, we put Owen in the car for the forty-five-minute drive to Rockville, Maryland, and the Ivymount School, which, with two hundred students, from kindergarten through high school, is the largest and best school for kids with disabilities in the area. When the school was started in a church basement in 1961, there was no place for children with serious disabilities like Down syndrome or those with most developmental disabilities to go. Before Eunice Kennedy Shriver started Special Olympics in 1968, and public awareness began to grow, most were either kept at home or institutionalized.

It is a long way from there to this large Eisenhower-era school building, once a public elementary school, with its painted cinder blocks, blond wood, a library, gymnasium, and student artwork taped to the walls of long hallways. There are two children waiting in

Owen's classroom—a Down syndrome boy named Eric and another boy, Julian, very much like Owen, with a PDD-NOS diagnosis and no speech. Owen makes three. The teacher, Lucy Cohen, explains that the school recently had more kids, but in the past year many decamped to receive Lovaas-style ABA training at home. It will just be the trio, with Lucy, a speech therapist, and an aide. We're asked to sit on floor mats against the wall to observe. And we do, as Lucy attempts to get the children to do simple tasks. Owen and Julian spin, murmur to themselves, and look about as Eric draws a figure on a page, per the teachers' instruction.

Sitting on a mat, my back to the wall, I find myself thinking, in a kind of rueful amazement, how many wild-eyed expectations you carry around about your kids, especially when they're young. Presidents? Nobel Prize winners? Global celebrities? Super Bowl quarterbacks and prima ballerinas? *It could happen.* Or, more soberly, millionaire philanthropists or, at the very least, graduates of the finest colleges, Harvard or Yale, then graduate school stars, most-recognized professionals in their field. *More likely, certainly than the Nobels . . . and, thereby, certainly likely.* Their enrollment in school—where they meet other children and start slotting into lines, receive test scores, make teams or get cut—starts the process of wrestling those unspoken fantasies toward abiding reality. And even then, those fanciful notions are surprisingly resilient. After all, as long as that kid's on the field of play, in the tournament's main draw, *it could happen.*

How many of these breathless expectations—also called dreams—constitute the traditional allotment? Best way to figure that is to extract them, one by one, and smash them in the corner. The pile is quite high. And that's what we do, minute by minute, sitting on the floor mats, backs pressed against the cinder blocks. Owen spins and murmurs next to the sweet blond boy. We haven't seen other kids like Owen before. Here is one who could be his twin. But Eric? Someone my age, growing up, knew those Down syndrome kids—spotted, peering from the window of the "short bus." No, they weren't in the game. Damaged goods. Ripe to be mercilessly ridiculed. Why? They wouldn't even know they were the butt of the joke. It was a free kick. That was the reality of it—just as ugly as it gets.

And that's where Owen has landed. Of course, we know nothing at this point—we've just landed on this planet—like the way Down syndrome folks often have highly evolved sensory equipment. There's something about the way one area of challenge, a blockage, often creates compensatory skills somewhere else. No different than blind people with powerful hearing, but, in this instance, in subtler areas of emotion or expressed sensitivity.

Suddenly, Eric is standing in front of me, his eyes at the same level as mine. He looks at me, his brow furrowed, then at Cornelia. He can see we are sitting there frozen in misery. He reaches his small arms around my neck, hugs me, and says, "I love you." I'm not sure if he hugs Cornelia or not—all I know is I'm in a daze, my world upended. Then he walks back to finish his drawing.

• • •

Cornelia needs someone to talk to.

She can't get me on the phone. None of her friends really know what the hell's going on. Little bits, maybe—yes, trouble with Owen—but not the real deal. All that, she figures, should remain private, at least until we figure out what we're dealing with.

She dials the number to her childhood home in Fairfield, Connecticut, and, as the phone is ringing, she realizes she's not exactly sure what she's going to say. Her folks don't really know what's been happening, either. It's November 1994. We've been in DC a year. But being far away from family and old friends means there aren't regular visitors to the house.

She's about to hang up when her mother's voice comes on. "Hello?"

"It's me, Mom."

"Oh, Lily, how's your day been?"

That's her old nickname, Lily. *And how's her day been?*

A disaster. She drove Owen to school, picked him up at midday, and drove him to intense speech and language therapy and then occupational therapy. None of it seems to be doing much good. He's still acutely agitated, unable to make his needs known, crying from time to time, and just a few minutes ago, he threw a wooden step stool down a long flight of stairs at her. He was frustrated—he didn't seem to want to hurt her—but she's shaking.

And none of this she tells her mother. She tries to make small talk and not cry. But her mind starts to race, looking for a way out of this solitude. We still don't ever use the "A word" in the house, and Owen's many therapists don't either. But she's thinking about one of her mom's first cousins, who had a son named Tommy, whom Cornelia saw a lot when she was a child. He had no speech and was sometimes hard to control, though more out of agitation than anger. He ended up living up in a state home. Cornelia's mother, a woman of headlong and unfettered compassion, was close to her cousin and had regularly visited him there.

Now, hesitantly, Cornelia asks her mother an out-of-the-blue question wrapped in "oh, by the way" casualness, about Tommy's diagnosis. "They said he was retarded," her mother says. "But I always wondered if he wasn't autistic." Cornelia takes a deep breath and pushes forward, telling her mom about some of the things that have been going on of late, right up to the worst of it: that day's throwing of the wooden stool. "I feel like I'm with Johnny!" she blurts out, a fireball rising from her gut.

The phone line seems to go dead. It hasn't. From the silence, her mother says, "Did I tell you I bought a new quilt for my bed today?"

•   •   •

At this moment, Owen is upstairs in the one place where he always seems calm, at ease, even content: in our bedroom watching his Disney videos.

In the first year in Washington, that's mostly what Owen has done on his own and what the boys have done together. What they can do. They watch on a television bracketed to the wall in a high corner of our smallish bedroom. They'd pile up pillows on our bed and sit close, Walt often with his arm around Owen's shoulders.

It's hard to know all the things going through the mind of a six-year-old about how his little brother, now nearly four, has changed. But we can't help wondering if this is a big brother's way of holding the world in place, holding on to what he knows.

After all, Walt's been sitting in front of a screen watching Disney movies for a healthy share of his own short life. That's the way it is with most kids around his age. A year after Walt was born in 1988, Disney, following a few decades in the doldrums, roared back to the fore of popular culture with *The Little Mermaid*. Families flocked to theaters and even more bought the video—it was the top-grossing video of the year. The same happened with *Beauty and the Beast* in 1991, only more so—that one was the first animated film nominated for a Best Picture Oscar. Then there was *Aladdin* in 1992, which was that year's highest-grossing movie. People our age were building up video libraries for their kids. Not just the recent hits—which critics dubbed Disney's "new golden age"—but videos from the original golden age starting in 1937 with *Snow White and the Seven Dwarfs*, *Dumbo*, *Fantasia*, *Pinocchio*, and *Bambi*.

We watched them all, sang the songs, danced to them.

All this to the mild disdain of some of our graduate-degreed, baby boomer friends. They had a world-wise, right-minded riff: that Disney was a voracious, commercialized, myth-co-opting brainwasher, using primal tales to shape young minds into noxious conclusions about everything from dead mothers (forget about step-mothers) to what happens to thrill-seeking boys (Pinocchio's Pleasure Island, as donkeys *forever*) to how a princess ought to look (utterly unattainable!), all before the tykes knew what hit them.

Many of them, though, didn't have kids. Cornelia and I weren't huge fans of Disney, but the comfort and convenience of these videos was overpowering. The movies were an instant babysitter, a group activity, something parents and kids could do together, and always within reach. When Owen arrived, Walt learned to use the remote on self-serve.

And soon enough, his little brother slotted right in. It was the house he was born into. And we were just about average on the video front with a few special restrictions. The year before we left Dedham, we limited viewing time and, at one point, even stored away the TV. We were surprised Walt wasn't more upset. After a few weeks we realized why: he was watching the Disney movies at houses of other kids. They all had them.

•　•　•

All that, though, was before the move and the change. Now, seeing the two boys on the bed, pillows piled high, *Peter Pan* or *Aladdin* flashing on the screen—we want to freeze time.

Of course, by six, Walt is being drawn away. New friends. New everything. He taught Owen how to use the remote control last summer and began to slip out. Not that his little brother has that many hours free. We "program" Owen as much as we can. Cornelia has him moving, carpooling to this therapy session or that, taking him to the market, the park, on errands. By the time they get home, she's exhausted and letting him watch some movies doesn't seem like a terrible crime. So, often he's up in our bedroom with the remote control. Movie after movie he watches. Certain parts he rewinds and rewatches. Lots of rewinding. But he seems content, focused.

We ask our developmental specialists, doctors, and therapists about it. They shrug. Is he relaxed? *Yes.* Does it seem joyful? *Definitely.* Keep it limited, they say. But if it does all that for him, there's no reason to stop it.

So we join him upstairs, all of us, on a cold and rainy Saturday afternoon in late November. Owen is already on the bed, oblivious to our arrival, murmuring gibberish . . . "juicervose, juicervose." It is something we've been hearing for the past few weeks. Cornelia thought maybe he wanted more juice; but, no, he refused the sippy cup. *The Little Mermaid* is playing as we settle in, propping up pillows. We've all seen it now a dozen times—more for Walt—but it's one of the best parts: where Ursula the sea witch, an acerbic diva, sings her song of villainy, "Poor Unfortunate Souls," to the selfish mermaid, Ariel, setting up the plot in which she'll turn her into a human—allowing her to seek out the handsome prince—in exchange for her voice:

> *Poor unfortunate souls*
> *In pain, in need*
> *This one longing to be thinner.*
> *That one wants to get the girl.*
> *And do I help them?*
> *Yes, indeed! [. . .]*
> *Now it's happened once or twice*
> *Someone couldn't pay the price*
> *And I'm afraid I had to rake 'em 'cross the coals.*
> *Yes, I've had the odd complaint*
> *But on the whole I've been a saint*
> *To those poor unfortunate souls. . . .*
> *Have we got a deal?*

That's what I hear every day, I tell Cornelia, from corporate public relations departments. She laughs and says, "Right, we've had the odd complaint, but on the whole I've been a saint."

On the screen, the song's over. Owen lifts the remote. Hits REWIND.

"Come on, Owen, just let it play!" Walt moans. But he doesn't go back to the start of the song, just twenty seconds or so, to its last stanza, with Ursula shouting:

Go ahead—make your choice!
I'm a very busy woman
And I haven't got all day
It won't cost much
Just your voice!

He does it again. STOP. REWIND. PLAY. And one more time.

On the fourth pass, Cornelia whispers, "It's not *juice*."

I barely hear her. "What?"

"It's not *juice*. It's *just* . . . just your voice!"

I grab Owen by the shoulders. "Just your voice! Is that what you're saying!"

He looks right at me—first real eye contact in a year.

"Juicervose! Juicervose! Juicervose!"

Walt starts to shout, "Owen's talking again!"

A mermaid lost her voice in a moment of transformation. So did this silent boy.

"Juicervose! Juicervose! Juicervose!" Owen keeps saying it, watching us shout and cheer. And then we're up, all of us, bouncing on the bed; Owen, too, singing it, over and over—"Juicervose!"—as Cornelia, tears beginning to softly fall, whispers, "Thank God . . . he's in there."

•   •   •

Three weeks after the "Juicervose" dance, we're at Walt Disney World.

We'd already scheduled a trip to Florida, with cheap flights booked months ahead, to visit my brother, Len, and his family—two boys, same age as ours—in Hollywood, Florida, where my mother also now lived.

The joke in the family is that Len never read the deathbed letter from my father about seeking the "worthwhile" life, which is why he is now raking it in as a financial manager. The easy lore is that I am more like our aesthetic, head-in-the-clouds father, an insurance executive who dreamed of teaching or writing; my brother, more like my ferociously pragmatic mother. It is, at best, half true.

As we became parents, we could see that—just like our kids— we were mixtures of both of our parents' traits, along with plenty of untraceable origins. What didn't change through the years—back then to right now—is that, at day's end, there're just the two of us, two brothers, having to figure it all out. Late that night, after everyone has gone off to sleep, he asks me how things are going. We talk most days—a quick call—but sitting quietly under a palm tree by his pool and beneath a canopy of stars, we can cut deeper.

"Best of times, worst of times," I say, explaining that things couldn't be going much better at work, or, with Cornelia—never more amazing than when she's challenged—or Walt, lunging forward, reaching for six-year-old glories. But we're not really sure what the future will hold for Owen.

"I see he's not speaking yet," Len opens.

Nope.

"Could it be a while?"

Yup.

"All these therapies, five or ten of them a week—at one hundred twenty dollars an hour. They covered by insurance?"

Nope.

Then we just sit there as a gentle breeze rustles the palm. I know he is doing some calculations. That's what he does for his clients, every day: life math. He's quite good at it—definitely got that from our mom.

After a minute of silence, I figure I'll sketch the size of the equation.

"Worst case, we'll have to support him for the next fifty years and thirty years after we're dead."

He's already there.

"That worst case or likely case?"

"Somewhere in between, but we're hopeful."

Hmmm. He's not one to discount hopeful. And he knows its uses, like the time in high school I convinced him to run for senior class president and he won.

"Hope's not nothing," he says, quietly, to his reflexively optimistic little brother. "Just tough to run the numbers on it, that's all."

And we both nod, get up, hug, and go off to sleep.

•   •   •

Two days later, we borrow one of their cars to drive the three hours to Orlando.

For the big day, Walt wears his Georgetown sweatshirt. He has a favorite babysitter who goes there, just down the street in the town where he now lives. Great basketball tradition—he knows all about that and can cite statistics. As a typical kid, at seven, his identity is becoming rooted to a place, his place, which he carries with him wherever he travels. This is the kind of awareness—of where one sits, or fits, in a widening world—that starts growing in most kids from around the time they're three.

It is hard to know whether any of these traditional steps are being crossed by Owen. His thoughts and feelings remain a mystery. We told his various therapists about what happened watching *The Little*

Mermaid. Cornelia and I could think of little else. It felt, in our video-inspired imaginations, like *Rain Man* had been replaced by *The Miracle Worker*, and that we had lived that iconic scene where Annie Sullivan breaks through to the young Helen Keller by signing w-a-t-e-r into the deaf and blind girl's one hand as water from a pump gushes across the other. We had to be Annie Sullivans, too, and felt we'd had a breakthrough on that rainy afternoon watching Ariel lose her voice. Owen reached out, if only for a moment, from his shut-in world. We spoke to our child.

The speech therapist tamped down our enthusiasm. Dr. Rosenblatt, too. He explained "echolalia" is a common feature in kids like Owen. It's something babies sometimes do between six and nine months, repeating consonants and vowels as they learn to turn a baby's babble into words. It's also something seen in the people with developmental disabilities who can't speak. Just like what the term suggests, they echo, usually the last word or two of a sentence: "You're a very smart and pretty girl," a mother might say to her daughter. "Pretty girl," the child will respond, an echo. Do those kids know what the words mean, we pressed Dr. Rosenblatt. "Usually not," he said. "They may want to make a connection, which is hopeful," he added.

"They just repeat the last sound," I croaked. He nodded. Why, I persisted, in a last stab, would he be rewinding that one part, for weeks, maybe longer, and choose that phrase—from so many in an eighty-three-minute movie—as the one he uttered? Dr. Rosenblatt shrugged. No way of knowing.

•   •   •

So, left groping in darkness, somewhere between Helen Keller and a pet store parrot, we now enter the gates of the Magic Kingdom.

It is remarkably unchanged from when Cornelia and I visited ten years ago, before we had kids, or from when I visited in 1971. It is *we* who have changed . . . now, as parents, seeing it all through our children's eyes, seeing what they see and feel. Walt grabs Owen's hand, and off they go, the two of us right behind them, down Main Street, U.S.A. There are attractions in Fantasyland—Mad Hatter's Tea Party, Snow White's Scary Adventures, Mr. Toad's Wild Ride—that echo movies they both love. Walt dives in full bore, laughing, joking, sitting with Owen on Peter Pan's Flight in the two-passenger flying schooner, the one just ahead of us, as it swirls and dips over landscapes and figures from Never Land—the "Lost Boys" frolicking in their lair, Wendy walking the plank, Peter Pan crossing swords with Captain Hook. They look like any other pair of brothers and—in the trick of this light—they are. We run to Disney-MGM Studios, in search of the Teenage Mutant Ninja Turtles. That day's park schedule says they're having an autograph session. The boys wait—the line is long—and get pictures with Donatello and Raphael, the characters they dressed up as for their last Halloween in Massachusetts. It's as if nothing has changed, as if the last year and a half was a bad dream.

And each time we feel that we catch ourselves. After the "juicer-vose" euphoria—and the cold water poured on us by doctors—we try to make sure we aren't just seeing what we want to see.

But by mid-afternoon it's clear that Owen isn't self-talking in the streams of gibberish, or flapping his hands as he usually does. Some, but not much. He seems calm and focused—following the group, making eye contact—and oddly settled, a slight smile, eyes alight, just as he is while watching the movies on our bed.

By day's end, we're feeling a bit of the same—settled, in a kind of walking repose that we've not felt since the days in Dedham. Owen seems at home here, as though his identity—or however much of it has formed—is somehow tied to this place.

On the way out of the Magic Kingdom, when Walt spots the Sword in the Stone near the carousel, we can't help indulging fantasy.

It is a fortuitous moment: A Disney actor dressed as Merlin appears near the sword periodically during the day. As the boys approach the sword, he's there, reciting dialogue—"Let the boy try"—and then, approaching the anvil, someone flips a hidden switch that loosens the sword. Walt pulls it out as Merlin cries, "You, my boy, are our king!"

Then both of them turn to Owen.

"You can do it, Owie," Walt whispers. "I know you can."

Owen looks evenly at his brother and Merlin, then steps to the anvil and lifts it true.

Did he understand what Walt was saying? Did he just imitate what he'd seen his brother do? *What the hell difference did it make!*

Today, in sunlight, he's the hero of his imagination.

chapter two

BUMPING INTO WALLS

Cornelia and I are changing. By March of 1995, our second spring of crisis in Washington, it's now something we can see in the mirror.

And not just in the bags under our eyes. We've become single-minded. She's now going on a year and a half of round-the-clock duty with carpools, therapists, school meetings, more therapists. At all hours of the day, she's executing a self-styled, round-the-clock version of Greenspan's Floortime: follow Owen around, try to pick up cues and dive into his world; show intense, upbeat interest. This sort of exertion demands focus and priorities. Niggling day-to-day concerns are sandwiched between frantic work with Owen and taking care of a growing Walt. Those "*What's new, how are the kids?*" phone calls that are the fabric of keeping up with old friends, or making new ones, have been jettisoned. Who has time for that? Some buddies from Boston wonder if we've entered the witness relocation program.

I'm changing, too, even if it's directed by subconscious drives I can't—or, at very least, won't—recognize.

A year before, in February 1994, to be exact—right after we met with the Ice Queen and first heard the dreaded word *autism*—I was chatting with my roommate from Columbia J-School, Tony Horwitz, who had just returned from Bosnia, where he'd written a powerful story for the *Journal* about the capacity of children to summon hope in war zones. As we talked, it dawned on me that to learn in some of the toughest "combat zones" of DC was a kind of feat, like one of those kids in Bosnia finding a calculus book on the street and learning calculus. Find a kid like that and we'd roll a red carpet from Harvard to the former Yugoslavia. But if it's an inner-city African American or Latino American kid—managing to learn while the bullets fly—we shrug. I sensed a gap, an unexamined one, and that's often the starting point of a story.

I looked for the worst high school in America and found a worthy nominee in Frank W. Ballou Senior High School in Southeast DC. So that was where I spent most of my time in those fear-filled days after Owen had vanished.

Cornelia gave me one of her favorite cassette tapes from college— John Prine—and driving from one side of town to the other, by the Capitol dome and down Martin Luther King Boulevard, I'd often play Prine's song "Hello In There," about reaching out to people who'd become invisible:

Please don't just pass 'em by and stare,
As if you didn't care,
Say, "Hello in there."

After a few weeks of watching kids pass in the hallways of Ballou—a school of virtually all African American students in a part of DC where 70 percent of the men between eighteen and thirty-six were somewhere in the criminal justice system, where four hundred students out of fourteen hundred were absent each day (but never the cops and security guards manning the building)—my eyes began to adjust. Did I consider these students, many of whom would end up in jail or worse, fundamentally different in some essential way from the kids in my suburban high school in Wilmington, Delaware, most of us bound for college? It's a stop-and-think question I wouldn't have asked—asked of myself—in my earlier days as a reporter, hustling forward, head down, working sources in day-to-day competitions to break the news or find that perfect anecdote to lead a story.

Looking at these discarded students, did some part of me see the way people stared at my son, seeing him flail and murmur just long enough to dismiss him? No doubt, though I wouldn't have said so at the time.

What I did do was spend days with the kids at Ballou, just listening to them—these delicately coiffed girls and baggy-panted boys, encased in their protective shells—as best I could. They were closed off to me, wary of the world I came from; we spoke different dialects, had few common references. But for every few words they'd utter, whatever the subject—a dispute in the halls, a new kind of Nike, the latest rap song—I'd follow *their* cue, wherever it led. Months along, they began to show me a few tiny glimpses of what was real in their lives.

One of the kids, a lonely, isolated honors student named Cedric Jennings, a geeky pariah in halls ruled by gang leaders, dreamed fervently of making it to the Ivy League. Though no one from his high school had made it to one of these esteemed schools in a decade, he was convinced his path to victory would be assured by acceptance into a highly selective MIT summer program for gifted minority students between their junior and senior years. He'd banked everything on a long-shot chance of getting in and could think of nothing else, even as everything around him collapsed—his dad in jail, his single mom struggling, drug dealers ruling every corner of his neighborhood, and even teachers saying, in his words, "You can't, you won't, why bother." He called them "dream busters."

Did I feel that everyone we talked to about Owen's prospects for an independent life was a dream buster?

Of course. Did I recognize it? Not in the least.

Not until I found myself in the empty *Wall Street Journal* office at three A.M. trying to bring to a close a five-thousand-word narrative about the struggle of Cedric and his classmates to summon hope when there was no reason to be hopeful. I'd arrived at my final notebook: about the night, after a long prayer meeting at church, when Cedric and his mother—a "church mom" who'd sacrificed everything for her son—passed the street-corner drug dealers, out in force at midnight, to grab the mail from the box in the foyer and ascend the crumbling steps to their apartment.

It was quiet in the deserted bureau. I don't know how long I sat, but at some point I wrote:

> *Under the* TV Guide *is a white envelope.*
>
> *Cedric grabs it. His hands begin to shake. "My heart is in my throat."*
>
> *It is from MIT.*
>
> *Fumbling, he rips it open.*
>
> *"Wait. Wait. 'We are pleased to inform you . . .' Oh, my God. Oh, my God." He begins jumping around the tiny kitchen. Ms. Jennings reaches out to touch him, to share this moment with him—but he spins out of her reach.*
>
> *"I can't believe it. I got in!" he cries out, holding the letter against his chest, his eyes shut tight. "This is it. My life is about to begin."*

I'm not much of a crier. I've cried just a handful of times in the twenty years since my father passed. But I wrote those sentences through tears.

I straggled home at four A.M. Cornelia had been awake for hours with Owen; just got him back to sleep. It'd been a tough few days of her trying to get through to him—to draw him out—and another fitful night.

I told her I'd finished the story, written the last line, and was over-come, sitting there at the desk. "I think I'm losing my mind, bawling my eyes out in the bureau in the middle of the night."

"No," she said, and, to my surprise, smiled.

"What?"

"It's a good thing. You're growing."

She lay down to catch a few hours' sleep before sunrise and I slipped into the boys' room.

It was dark and, sitting on the rug, I listened to them breathing heavily. All was well on the top bunk, with Walt; not so below. I began to think about how when your life's orderly and intact, it's so easy to write about things, to step back as the dispassionate observer, full of knowingness, that crafted omniscience. But once you've felt how complicated the world can be, how little you can control, that surety is harder to manage. I was a mess. My heart had never been much engaged in my work—too dangerous, a journalist is supposed to be "objective," whatever that means. Now my emotions were spilling out all over the place. But maybe that wasn't such a terrible thing; maybe that was what Cornelia was saying. All I knew was that in a few hours she'd be up, rising like she did every day, thinking this is it, this is the day when Owen's life is about to begin. Or begin again.

Every day since that night in the bureau—a year ago now—I wake up feeling that too: that today Owen's life will change. And at day's end, I realize it hasn't, that I know nothing worth anything.

• • •

Owen is starting to talk in the spring of 1995. It isn't much—a few words in succession. It's oddly arrhythmic, not like his voice once was. It actually sounds a little like Helen Keller, like someone trying to speak who cannot hear. Blunt sounds, spoken out of need. *Juice,* never left. But *Car. Mine. Hot. Cold.* And the words don't seem to be building into anything beyond a cluster of two or three.

The best word—the one of greatest utility—is *mine*. The key is to be quick. When he points to something, anything—a book, a video, a toy—and says "Mine," you move to grab it first. Hold it up and ask him what it's called. *Wait.* He doesn't get it unless he comes up with something. "A book. Owen, say '*book.*'"

Almost every evening, the teacher from Ivymount calls to go over, in detail, all they did during the day. Today, the trio—Owen; his nonspeaking peer, Julian; and the big-hearted Down syndrome boy, Eric—went to a concert in the gymnasium or outside to the soccer field, threw a ball or learned to hold a pencil.

Any of these things might provide a handle for some connection, at least in theory. But in the descriptions of how she guides the children, get them to sit, to look at her, to walk with the group, she is teaching Cornelia and me how to be with our son. In her tutorials, we're beginning to understand just how much has gone haywire. His auditory processing—the way we hear and understand speech—is barely functioning. Visual processing, too, is askew. He often turns his head and squints out of the corner of his eye, as though seeing you, straight on, is painful or overwhelming. These are all features of autism. As is getting up every night. His senses are untethered, floating each minute, hour after hour, on swift currents without a mooring or the anchor of sleep, when the body's sensory equipment rests and replenishes itself. Not for Owen. His last nap was in Dedham. Hasn't taken one since. He's sleeping about three hours a night, and maybe another hour or two after Cornelia or I rock him back to sleep. We've heard a new term, "regressive autism," for kids who appear normal, then experience a change—a regression—between eighteen and thirty-six months. Though we're still using PDD-NOS, this regressive autism seems to fit.

But when he's tired, wanting to fall back to sleep in the predawn hours, we hear a golden phrase—"hold you"—that takes us in the other direction, as he displays an urge for connection that autistic kids aren't supposed to have. He says it, and holds out his arms, as we sit in the glider that we saved from his nursery back in Dedham. It doesn't happen often, but a few times is enough.

A need expressed and met. Of course, it's the kind of thing a dog would say if it could talk, and variations of this desire to hold or hug is a favorite of chimps who've been taught to sign. But on this phrase, we hang the world and its many promises.

· · ·

As for the rest of life, it goes on. Family outings to the latest kids' movie, a Baltimore Orioles game, a trip to the Virginia mountains, and everything humanly possible for Walt. The prospect that because of this insanity Walt will be denied any of his due is unthinkable, even if mandated by laws of time and space. The only defense is a strong offense—to show we are like other families, only more so. Every practice—he is starting hockey—playdate, birthday party, neighborhood fair, museum visit, parent-teacher conference, and PTA meeting is in the nondiscretionary category. Everything has to be, and will be, done.

Of course, in malls, movie theaters, and restaurants with Owen, we're anything but typical. We draw stares. And sometimes it takes a while for folks to turn away. We've become experts on staring. With some disabled kids, it's clear that they're disabled—there's some sort of physical manifestation. Owen, like his classmate Julian, looks typical. In fact, they're both cute kids, with delicate features. So why is that curly-haired boy in the corner booth at the diner grunting, dropping silverware, shaking his head wildly, and spilling things? Clearly, he's a very badly behaved boy. Maybe abusive parents.

Booths, especially in diners, are preferable, so we can keep Owen on the inside, in the nook between the wall and the tabletop juke-box. That way, no one can see him all that well—we can reduce the number of onlookers.

Walt notices every eye in the room. You can see that, as his self-awareness grows, it makes him uncomfortable. How can it not? Cornelia and I force ourselves to act like nothing is happening, noth-ing different, or noticeable. *No, he's just talking to himself. Can we please have some extra napkins to clean this up? Thank you, and the check, please.*

We see Walt panning the room for stares. *We're just like everyone else, Walt.* That's our standard response. He looks at us like we've gone around the bend.

•   •   •

Cornelia is on the phone, sounding desperate to talk.

"What—is something wrong?"

"No," she says. "He's just doing it again—the movie talking."

So what, I wonder. He's been doing it since "juicervose."

"It's just echolalia. Parrot stuff. He's just repeating sounds."

I can hear her shaking her head on the phone line.

She explains in a measured way, like talking to a child, that the phrase of gibberish he's been repeating for the past month she's just deciphered. He's been watching *Beauty and the Beast* incessantly and he seems to be repeating something—"bootylyzwitten"—on a regu-lar basis. And he was just repeating it in the car. "You're not going believe it."

At this point, I am jumping though the phone. "What? What!"

"Beauty lies within."

I can't say anything for a minute.

"Are you there?"

"I'm here, I just can't believe it," I say, finally. "Of all the phrases, that one. That's what the movie's about—that's its theme. Could he actually be understanding what he's watching?"

I tell her I'll call tonight—definitely tonight!—but I have to run. I'm late for class.

It's the fall of 1995 and, on the surface, quite a bit has changed. Not that I've re-enrolled in college. I'm in Providence, Rhode Island, following Cedric through his formative freshman year at Brown University for a book. In the spring, the stories about him and other kids at his blighted high school won me the Pulitzer Prize. Those stories were, in essence, about beauty—as well as native intelligence and sensitivity—lying within, though these qualities are often hard to find and harder to measure, something we humans seem so anxious to do: to dole out credit and rewards. This was all on display in the portrait of Cedric and his peers at the gang-dominated high school. Readers were moved by the recognition of how hollow so many of our judgments are—something Cornelia and I began to slowly acknowledge around the time Eric, the Down syndrome kid, hugged us that day in Owen's classroom.

And now, in my hand, is a prize that, of course, has utterly the opposite effect in the reactions it draws. Like so many prizes, it's the ultimate shorthand for instant, tell-a-book-by-its-cover judgment. It's basically attached to your name—all people need to hear. These ironies are visible only to Cornelia and me, as are the ways our private struggle is now driving my professional life.

Owen, though, had a statement on the matter. Not long after I won the prize, he noticed it. A Pulitzer isn't like one of those peace medals, or the Nobels, with a golden disk hanging from a ribbon. It's quite small, a Tiffany & Co. crystal about the size of a plum with an engraving of Joseph Pulitzer's head next to your name. We put it on a waist-high table in the living room of the Georgetown house, next to some framed pictures. That'd be right in Owen's line of sight. It was only when he got close to the window that a shard of reflected sunlight coming off the crystal caught my eye. I was reading on the couch, which meant I could flip over its low back onto the floor and lunge. I caught his cocked hand as he was about to throw it through the window.

Cornelia and I had some good yuks at the irony—*Owen sees right through the bubble of reputation*—and then made sure to place it on a high mantel over the fireplace in our new house.

That new house is where Cornelia is calling from to tell me about bootylyzwitten. We used Random House's advance for the book as a down payment on a modest three-bedroom house in DC's northern-most corner near the Maryland line.

Of course, recognition of irony is no barrier to action. Prize in hand, we start to feel lucky again, for the first time in years, and empowered enough to shape the world into whatever we need it be, for Owen's sake. For every *why*, suddenly there seems to be a *why not*. Nothing dramatic. We just go a little crazy, in a very conventional way: we start to undervalue our fears and over-appreciate our hopes.

That means a change for Owen. A journey of hope has begun. Specifically, he's now spending half his days at Ivymount and half at a lovely little preschool in Cleveland Park with mostly typical kids from a privileged world. The school, called NCRC, was originally the National Child Research Center when it was founded by a Rockefeller grant in the 1920s as a place to study child development. The legacy of that, many decades later, is that they take a handful of special needs kids each year. It isn't easy to get in. But among an array of lawyers and lobbyists, think-tank chiefs and investment types, the family of a national affairs reporter for the *Journal*—who just won a Pulitzer for those stories about the hidden virtues of kids from the cross-town slums—is an indispensable addition. Yes, that's the way Washington works.

Cornelia is now racking up more miles than a long-haul trucker and is happy to do it, driving Owen north to Ivymount each morning, often volunteering at the school, grabbing coffee, or grocery shopping at a nearby mall—anything to kill a few hours—then handing him a bag lunch to eat in the car and racing down to NCRC, where he spends afternoons in the aptly named "Sunshine Room." There he's mixing with typical kids. The idea—loosely supported by our therapists—is that he'll model his behavior on those new peers and may form relationships that will stretch his capabilities, and rise to meet their challenge. To us, that all feels like sunshine.

Denial and hope, of course, are cousins. Bring them together, you've got illusion. There's no real social connection occurring at NCRC. At least, not for Owen. Cornelia and I, though, find plenty of it. *We make lots of friends.* Parents of typical kids, who are happy to welcome us into their orbit. Owen is now mixing in a group of children who are still at an age where their friends are often selected by the parents. With so few kids in each class, it all fits elegantly: a tight gang of two dozen parents and a dozen or so children, moving as one. Parties, barbecues, and then evenings when the parents all go out and have the kids all stay with a babysitter at someone's house. The best part: birthday parties. Everyone in the class is invited. It's beyond parental edict; it's a school rule!

Not that there's much interaction at those birthday parties. But everyone has a VCR and everyone has the Disney classics. So there is a bit of exchange, a hug or "hi" (one of Owen's new words) upon arrival; then they'll watch *Jungle Book* or *Snow White and the Seven Dwarfs* together, side by side, until the other kids drift away. Squint a bit, and it looks a lot like friendship.

•   •   •

As for Walt . . . *nothing to worry about.* He's like a junior adult at seven, able to handle anything that first grade can throw at him, and taking advantage of all Lafayette Elementary, our neighborhood public school in Northwest DC, has to offer.

Everyone crafts stories out of their experiences, a fundamental human impulse, and Cornelia and I have one for Walt.

It happened in the first month of first grade as Cornelia drove him to this new school. Daunting for any kid, right? Well, a few blocks away, Walt taps his mother on the arm and says, "Let me out—I can walk from here, mom." Cornelia's flummoxed. "Walt . . . they know you *have* parents. You're not some street urchin making your way in the world."

"I'll be fine. I know the way." And off he goes. Soon he starts biking the half mile or so to school, eliciting shock from a few of his classmates' parents—seasoned by years of milk carton photos to fear the worst.

We never fear for him. It seems like every step he takes toward autonomy is a worthy feat, deserving of affirmation, especially because he doesn't abandon his brother, something we really do fear.

Many years later, as he moved into adult life, Walt explained what was really going on. He was embarrassed by his brother. The looks, the questions, it was as though he was facing a wide world of prying eyes, too many to challenge, to face down. He told us he wanted to be dropped off because his brother was in the car. Walt knew that if Cornelia walked him in that first day, like the other moms, she'd have to bring Owen in with her. And God knows what might have happened.

In present tense, we're blind to this. We tell friends of the first day drop-off. Turn it into narrative. *That Walt. He is so independent.*

• • •

There are no stares in our basement. As Owen turns five in the spring of 1996, his life is, more and more, spent in front of a screen, with

Walt sometimes at his side. The Disney movies—we now had fifteen of them in our collection, and some shorts—rule the subterrain.

That's where the big TV is in the new house. It's a cave, dark and warm, with just a little natural light from the half windows near the ceiling. On the couch, we watch movies with Owen. Family members move in a rotation. Owen, after a heavily scheduled day of school and after-school therapies, settles down below. Corn might drop in to watch *Lady and the Tramp* with him. When he gets home on his bike in the late afternoon, Walt catches a viewing of *The Little Mermaid*. In the evenings, before Owen's off to bed, I squeeze in a little *Aladdin*.

Is this healthy? "Team Owen"—what we now call Owen's team of doctors and therapists—is uncertain. We tell them he's reciting long passages of movie dialogue in ten- or twenty-second bursts without, it seems, any discernible recognition of what he is saying, like someone who sings "Frère Jacques" for years and never notices—or, frankly, cares—that it's about someone named Brother John.

In school this recitation impulse is becoming a problem, something to be remedied. He's doing it when he is supposed to be quiet or listening to instructions or, most importantly, engaging in some sort of activity with other students. The doctors and now the teachers call it "self-talk" and formally define it as "perseverative behavior"—a feature of autism and pervasive developmental disorders defined in the medical literature as the "repetition of a particular response, such as a word, phrase, or gesture, despite the absence or cessation of a stimulus, usually caused by a brain injury or other organic disorder." Looking for ways to control it and reduce it, they recommend we limit the movies to an hour a day.

We say that's impossible. The movies run ninety minutes, and he gets very agitated if you cut it off before the end. After "juicer-vose" and "bootylyzwitten," we aren't about to turn away from the screen. Though his pronunciations are slurry, the cadence swift and arrhythmic, we are ever trolling the verbal stream for a familiar word. Or even a sound. Take "Seb." It's not a three-letter grouping you find much in common usage (sebaceous? seborrhea?). But it's got two strong consonants that stand tall in the flow of enunciation. Hear it, and we know he is reciting some passage that involves Sebastian, King Triton's crab sidekick from *The Little Mermaid*. And, of course, we dive in, with every reference from the movie we can summon. As we do, he looks at us, quizzically, often smiling. For a particularly good rendition of the crab—the voice actor, Samuel E. Wright, has a rich voice and uses a Caribbean accent—he might offer a "Sebastian is funny" before running off.

Toddlers engage in what's called "parallel play," where they play alongside another child but not *with* them. Developmentally, that stage tends to end between twelve and eighteen months. What's clear, is that in many areas Owen has regressed to a place before that. He is in parallel play in only the most general way; more like *proximity play*. The goal—everyone's goal—is eventually to get to the sunlight of interactive play—full of expressions, mirroring one another, quick responses that build a give and take, a kind of collaborative imaginativeness—that is such a powerful driver of growth and development in children. He was doing plenty of that in the last days in Dedham.

But you take what you can get. Side-by-side engagement is where we live each day. We draw warmth—and a sense of connection we desperately desire—from smiling with him at some parts of a Disney favorite, growing quiet at others. He definitely seems to be reacting to the movie in gesture, if not, of course, in word. There are times he laughs—like when Robin Williams, as the Genie in *Aladdin,* goes through lightning-fast transformations from Arnold Schwarzenegger to Jack Nicholson to William F. Buckley as he sings "Friend Like Me"—and we laugh uproariously in affirmation, even on the twentieth viewing. And then there are times when he seems to grow quiet, watching Mrs. Jumbo reach from the window of her prison car to wrap Dumbo in her trunk and rock him. Often he'll be sitting next to Cornelia or me and we'll pull him close.

• • •

But then we hear a phrase that troubles us: "Not happy." He's saying that a lot. And it's new. We investigate and find out it's the go-to phrase of an assistant teacher from his half days at Ivymount. Trying to control his behaviors, or redirect them, she's tells him she's "not happy."

It's Owen's main phrase—at home, in the car, at the mall—and it doesn't take us long to feel "not happy" with Ivymount. Owen seems slightly more able than some of the kids this year in his class, and his modest progress is enough to spur hope. By the fall of 1996, Ivymount—with the big-hearted Erics and a heavily structured "special needs" curriculum—is gone. It's a full day with the typical kids at NCRC.

Just before Thanksgiving in 1996, a Maryland psychiatrist, who's on a new National Institute of Mental Health committee to assess autism treatment, speaks at the school. It's been advertised. Interested NCRC parents from DC and Maryland crowd in, many seeking the next school for their own children. Before introducing the doctor, C. T. Gordon, NCRC's director asks Cornelia to speak about our family's experience on behalf of the other special-needs families.

"For all of us who have a special needs child, going places can be a difficult thing," Cornelia tells the audience. "There's the unpredictability of what our child may do in public. Worry about the reactions of other people and their siblings. And that's something that's with us all the time and weighs heavily. But being at NCRC is easy. It's a place that really cares about our kids, that's here to help our kids, and everyone on the staff makes us feel welcome and at home, not different."

Afterward, she and Dr. Gordon talk. He also has an autistic son, a year older than Owen, with no speech. Dr. Gordon will soon join Team Owen.

It's a glorious night, a moment when we feel settled. But it's also late fall, when the parents are beginning to angle toward the big prize: entry of their young pride-and-joys into one of Washington's storied private schools, like Sidwell Friends, where the Clintons and Gores sent their kids, or St. Albans, the private academy for future leaders. NCRC is a feeder school for both, and for Washington's other exclusive schools. There's much talk at the punch-and-cookie reception about who's applying where.

How about Owen?

"He's doing great," Cornelia says, with a frozen smile. That's all. They're planning for the future. We live in the present. Hold onto it for dear life.

The next afternoon, I'm back at the school, wearing a red-and-yellow-striped stovepipe hat. As in *The Cat in the Hat*. It's something I did from time to time over the past year: come around to lead the kids in some high-energy games, making it a little show.

I'd known some of them for over a year, and many of their parents. As I look across the smiling kids, I think what I think on every one of these visits: who, in this group, might break from the pack to play with Owen—curious about what was behind the distant smile and soft patter of recited dialogue. Maybe it will help that he's the son of the clown, especially if I can draw the kids, in unison, into shared, raucous activity. Like always, I'm trying to create a circle of *normal*, an irresistible, swirling place—that Owen might inconspicuously slip into. Inside, maybe he'll find a friend.

After an hour of running, juggling, and flipping kids up on my shoulder, I crawl into the foyer of our house, dripping in sweat.

"How'd it go, Mr. Clown Face?" Cornelia has made a late lunch for us.

"Great joy, had by all; Owen, too."

"Any of the other kids engage with him?"

"No, not today."

We'd talked late into the previous night about the reception: Corn's speech, the nice reception, meeting a doctor with an autistic son. Now, at lunch, we talk about how all the kids are angling toward their next steps. "After this spring, I don't imagine he'll see many of them again," I say. "They'll be moving on, moving up, that'll be that."

This school has been a brief fantasy. Here, on any given day, he moves among typical kids, like one of them. It's an illusion, now slamming into a brick wall of reality.

What will be his next step? At that moment we felt Ivymount wouldn't work; it'd be a step backward. In the coming months, we look at a few schools that aren't right for him. DC has terrible choices in the public system. There are no other options.

Save one.

•　•　•

"Shining city on a hill" was the Ronald Reagan phrase that so swiftly washed away the earnest, problem-solver glumness of Jimmy Carter, ushering in a new era of willed optimism, a time of experimentation in the uses of that magic word: *confidence.*

When there's cultural change, often institutions arise that embody that shift, suffused with the rhythms of the period. One such institution sat resplendent, atop a crest of hill overlooking the upper Potomac: the Lab School of Washington.

Redemptive narratives are always appealing and the story of the school and its founder was a snapping good one. It starts with the brassy daughter of a New York department store magnate who found herself in the late 1960s trapped in a proper life of official Washington as the wife of a socially ambitious State Department official. All seemed intact until it became clear her child was born with special needs. Sally Smith made him the focus of her life. She was soon divorced and was tutoring her son, Gary, with a few other special needs children in her home. She had skills—having studied dance with Martha Graham as a Bennington College undergrad and received a master's in psychology from New York University. Now she had a mission, especially after DC recommended her son be placed with kids who were either emotionally disturbed or retarded. She said he wasn't either—that he seemed alert, even bright in a few areas, but didn't learn the way most other kids learned.

There was no school for him. So she built one, and they came: lots of kids with no place else to go.

The school was immediately overwhelmed by demand and moved from building to building across the decade. Smith wrote extensively from her post as an American University professor about learning disabilities, especially the most common one, dyslexia, and how the learning-disabled (LD) population—already estimated at 3 percent of children—was growing fast. She attempted, in a best-selling book, to kill off the stigmas around LD, to show that LD kids would often compensate for problems with reading or language by becoming visual learners or developing artistic skills. It was a framework that, twenty years hence, would be applied to a vast and growing population of kids with autistic spectrum disorders.

But LD came first. And Smith's big break, in 1984, was a major reason why. She'd moved into a new building, a stone castle overlooking the Potomac in desperate need of renovation. She decided to try a fund-raising gala and sat down with a parent of one of her students: the *People* magazine bureau chief for Washington. Through a few stories in the magazine—where actors or artists would talk about "problems in school"—and lots of phone work, the duo lured an astonishing quintet to DC to receive awards as what they called *Learning Disabled Achievers*.

That fall a thousand Washingtonians in gowns and tuxedos gathered on a vacant floor of the newly built Hecht's Department Store in downtown DC—a vast room outfitted for a formal gala, with House of Representatives Speaker Thomas "Tip" O'Neill stepping to the podium as master of ceremonies. Sally Smith, though, carried the night, introducing each guest with a "This is your life" flourish. Her twist was to turn it into a brutal litany, drawn from her interviews with each guest, that went something like this: "You [fill in celebrated name] were called stupid, someone who'd never amount to anything. . . . You were held back in third grade because you couldn't read. . . . You felt ashamed of what you'd received on a test and hid the paper. . . . But one teacher took you aside and said, 'Let me help.' . . ." Then, none other than Cher, Tom Cruise, Bruce Jenner, and the artist Robert Rauschenberg stepped up to receive engraved crystal bowls and speak, voices cracking, of long hiding their disability. Rock Hudson had just died, after revealing he had AIDS. The ugliness of shame and secrecy was on everyone's mind—forces to be vanquished. As the awardees spoke, the crowd, including a healthy number of congressmen and cabinet secretaries, stood and cheered themselves hoarse. The Lab School gala, plastered all across the next morning's *Washington Post* style section, raised $386,000 that night.

Soon, the castle on the hill was receiving more publicity, brick by brick, than almost any school in the country. PBS did specials, and Smith's model using the arts as a gateway to educate kids with dyslexia or ADHD soon became widely adopted. Rauschenberg came every year to the school to train and celebrate art teachers who used creativity to unleash the talents of "untraditional learners."

More celebrities came to be honored, a glittering roster every year, and the replacement of "learning disability" with "learning difference"—a swap encouraged by advocacy groups that generally drew raised eyebrows about the hollowness of politically correct speech—soon had an affirming army of forthright LD achievers.

Many parents began to see their children with new eyes. Learning difference? Seemed to make sense. A traditional learning pathway is blocked; compensatory skills develop to find another way.

The practical effect of this? More parents and developmental pediatricians were willing to embrace the LD diagnosis, which often seemed to bump up alongside a smaller but growing number of diagnoses for kids on the autism spectrum. They all shared a legal right under 1975's Individuals with Disabilities Education Act and related legislation for publicly funded placement in the "least restrictive environment," or, in English, a school tailored to the child's needs.

What, in fact, were coalescing were two vast communities of special needs: LD and autistic spectrum disorders. A quarter century after that glittering night in DC, geneticists would begin to discover that a wide and growing array of disorders, including OCD, bipolar disorder, and schizophrenia, may be genetic cousins to the LD or autism. All of them emanate from the same self-regulatory functions of the brain. No one is clear why the incidence seems to be rising in this family of disorders. Link them all together, like so many buoys attached to a shared anchor, and, by 2012, they affected almost 20 percent of the population.

But Sally Smith and LD were the first over the wall. After that gala in 1984, lines began forming outside the Lab School and other schools like it. And soon it seemed to stretch to the horizon.

• • •

Of the learning disabled students at the Lab School in 1997, about a quarter of the younger students had autistic-like behaviors and profiles. There is nothing we won't do to get Owen in. Smith understood that many of the kids applying would be difficult to test, especially the spectrum kids. To be considered, she demanded something— anything—to show innate ability or aptitude.

Dr. Bill Stixrud, our testing guru, is a specialist in measuring aptitude, even when it is deeply submerged. One of the country's leading neuro-psychological testers, his challenge isn't simply to measure Owen's underlying intelligence—but to discover it. Owen seems more attentive. He'll often look at you now. He'll sometimes smile when you do. What Alan Rosenblatt saw under the chair that day—where Owen was playful—had grown and flourished. But testing whether he has sufficient aptitude to get into Lab: where to begin? He'll soon turn six and barely speaks. He isn't much on following directions, either; crucial in test taking of all kinds. Tests Stixrud administered last year placed his capacities at between 1 and 3 percent for kids his age; his estimated IQ at 75, the threshold for retardation.

Those test scores were so dismal it isn't even worth sending them in.

Tests in the early months of the year were so dismal it wasn't even worth sending in the scores.

In late February, a few days before the March 1 application deadline, the phone rings in the kitchen. It's Stixrud with an idea, a last stab. There was a test they used in the 1950s for deaf children—the Leiter Test of Nonverbal Intelligence—a big clunky thing, with blocks and other manipulatives for kids who couldn't read or hear directions.

But where to find one? We all put our heads together. He has names of old psychologists in the area, mostly retired. Maybe one has a Leiter Test in a closet. We begin calling. Dozens of calls. The next day, a retired psychologist living in one of the apartment buildings on Connecticut Avenue, not far from our house, says she might have one in a closet.

Cornelia races over and soon she and Owen are in Stixrud's office in Silver Spring, Maryland, as Bill intently reads the directions. Having never done one like this before, he'll have to administer the test, analyze the results, and get them to the Lab School by the next day, the application deadline.

He asks Cornelia to sit behind Owen so she won't distract him. But she can see Bill's face as he and Owen, crowded around one of those Formica-topped kid-sized tables, start to handle the "manipulatives."

Cornelia is also conducting an experiment: how long can a person sit in a plastic, third-grader's chair without breathing? Or blinking? She watches for tiny changes of expression as Bill takes one set of blocks after another from a large burlap bag. They're like early versions of the Rubik's Cube. He's poker-faced—part of the test-giver's art—as Owen tries to figure out what is being asked of him, and then execute it. With Owen's jumbled auditory processing, Bill might as well be speaking Japanese.

As for Cornelia's data on cessation of breathing, she goes eight minutes. That's how long it is before she sees Owen's little shoulders shift as he leans forward, suddenly attentive. He sees a pattern—how the blocks, scattered across the table, are supposed to fit—and begins assembling them with swift precision. Stixrud pulls another cluster from the bag—one Owen solves with spins and clicks in an instant. It is only then that Stixrud finally lifts his eyes, offering one of those slow, purposeful nods—the universal gesture for "It's going to be okay."

The final experiment, then, for Cornelia, is how to let months of tense, volatile emotions lodged in every nerve, every hidden ganglia, flood through the tear ducts without making a sound.

That coming fall, six-and-a-half-year-old Owen Suskind enters the Lab School of Washington, which can be his home for the next eleven years. They can find his strengths and widen them into a gateway of learning, the school's mission for students with special needs from kindergarten through high school.

chapter three

IN CHARACTER

Pattern recognition takes a bit of distance. Patterns are easily hidden in the noise of life, of preference and prejudice. Love tends to get in the way.

Which means parents are lousy at it, something statisticians, doctors, and toy-company marketers know. Every little child, after all, is unique, a snowflake. And, if that's the case, the eye will wander toward what affirms that distinctiveness, especially when it sheds a warm light on how well the youngsters selected their parents.

For Walt, we're looking for that golden combo: growing capacities to meet the wide world, look it in the eye, make it bend to his will . . . and someday use that acquired strength on behalf of his little brother. That's one reason why we celebrate his unflinching autonomy.

An inconvenient fact, that he sometimes gets emotional on his birthdays, is thrown into a drawer marked either "family trait" (I'm that way, too) or "exception that proves the rule" (it only happens one day out of 365). He's tough, resilient, and resourceful. Anything outside that is an aberration.

It's Walt's ninth birthday, September 1997. Owen is six and a half. And, it so happens, after roughhousing with buddies in the backyard at the end of his party and bidding them farewell, Walt gets a little weepy.

After he calms down, wipes tears, and resumes roughhousing with one straggler—a neighborhood boy who could walk home—Corn and I return to the kitchen to clean up the party. Owen walks in from the backyard, right behind us.

He looks intently at us, one, then the other. He seems to have something to say.

"Walter doesn't want to grow up," he says, evenly, "like Mowgli or Peter Pan."

We both nod, dumbly, looking down at him. He nods back, and then vanishes into some private reverie.

It's like a thunderbolt just passed through the kitchen.

A full sentence, and not just an "I want this" or "Give me that." No, a complex sentence, the likes of which he'd not uttered in four years, since the last days in Dedham. Actually, never. This is something else, entirely.

We don't say anything at first, and then don't stop talking for the next four hours, peeling apart, layer by layer, what just happened.

Beyond the language, it's interpretive thinking that he's not supposed to be able to do: that someone crying on their birthday may not want to grow up. Not only would such an insight be improbable for a typical six year old; it was an elegant connection that Cornelia and I had overlooked.

It's like Owen had let us in, just for an instant, to glimpse a mysterious grid growing inside him, a matrix on which he affixed items he saw each day that we might not even notice.

And then he carefully aligned to another one, standing parallel: the world of Disney.

After dinner is over and both boys retreat upstairs to their attic lair, Cornelia starts to think about what to do now.

I'm thinking parallel planes. She's thinking about loneliness. That he's in there: "How on earth," she says almost to herself, "do you get back in there?"

I feel she's asking me. I've been lecturing reporters for years on this point: that there's always a way in. If you can't get someone to open up, it's your fault,

Walt saunters by toward the basement. That means Owen's in the attic room, alone.

I tiptoe up the carpeted stairs. Owen's sitting on his bed, flipping through a Disney book—he can't read, of course, but likes to look at the pictures. The mission is to reach around the banister, into his closet, and grab his Iago puppet. The parrot from *Aladdin* is one of his favorites. He's been doing lots of Iago echolalia, easy to identify because the character is voiced by Gilbert Gottfried, who talks like a busted Cuisinart. Once Iago's in hand, I gently pull the bedspread from the foot of his bed—just a few feet from the top step—and slide under it. And I do it all without having him look up. It takes four minutes for Iago and me to make it safely under the bedspread.

Now crawl, snail-slow, along the side of the bed to its midpoint. *Fine.*

I freeze here for a minute, trying to figure my opening line; four or five sentences dance about, auditioning.

Then, a thought: *be Iago*. What would Iago say?

I push the puppet up through the crease in the bedspread.

"So, Owen, how ya' doin'?" I say, doing my best Gilbert Gottfried. "I mean, how does it feel to be you!?"

Through the crease, I can see him turn toward Iago. It's like he was bumping into an old friend.

"I'm not happy. I don't have friends. I can't understand what people say."

I have not heard this voice, natural and easy, with the traditional rhythm of common speech, since he was two.

I'm talking to my son for the first time in five years. Or Iago is.

Stay in character.

"So, Owen, when did *yooooou* and I become such good friends?"

"When I started watching *Aladdin* all the time. You made me laugh so much. You're so funny."

My mind is racing—find a snatch of dialogue—anything. One scene I've seen him watch and rewind is when Iago tells the villainous vizier Jafar how he should become sultan.

Back as Iago: "Funny? Okay, Owen, like when I say . . . um . . . So, so, you marry the princess and you become the chump husband."

Owen makes a gravelly sound, like someone trying to clear his throat or find a lower tone: "I *loooove* the way your fowl little mind works."

It's a Jafar line, the next line from the movie, in Jafar's voice—a bit higher-pitched, of course, but all there: the faintly British accent, the sinister tone.

I'm an evil parrot talking to a Disney villain, and he's talking back.

Then, I hear a laugh, a joyful little laugh, like I have not heard in many years.

• • •

After dinner on a weeknight in late September, Cornelia and I lead the kids down to the basement.

It's a week after the Iago breakthrough, and we've been thinking of little else. Tonight, we decide to try an experiment.

Owen usually picks the animated movie whenever we gather in front of the twenty-six-inch Magnavox. On this night, we pick it for him: *The Jungle Book*. It's a movie both boys have long loved and one Cornelia and I remember from our childhood: Disney's 1967 rendition of British Nobel laureate Rudyard Kipling's tales of Mowgli, a boy raised by wolves in the jungles of India, schooled by Baloo, the obstreperous bear, and Bagheera, the protective black panther. In the film, largely drawn from the second of Kipling's stories, "Kaa's Hunting," written in 1893, Mowgli ultimately triumphs over his fear, embodied by the great tiger Shere Khan, and then is returned, somewhat reluctantly, by Baloo, to the Man-village, where he can grow to manhood among his own kind. The movie, like Kipling's saga, is full of moral tales about the survival of individuals and communities, the nature of interdependency.

We watch the movie until, a few minutes along, we get to its signature song. "The Bare Necessities" is a talking song, with the melody broken up by dialogue—not all that common—and it starts with a line of dialogue. We freeze the screen and turn down the sound as everyone gets up and mills about near the couch. In my best attempt at the voice and inflection of Phil Harris, who voices the bear, I hit play and then say: "'Look, now it's like this, little britches. All you've got to do is . . .'"

Then we all sing, trying to get the words right, following along with the low volume of the set:

Look for the bare necessities
The simple bare necessities . . .
When you look under the rocks and plants
And take a glance at the fancy ants, and maybe try a few.

Baloo lifts the edge of a large rock in the movie; in our basement I lift the edge of a couch cushion.

Just as Baloo looks at Mowgli, I look at Owen; he looks squarely back at me—then it happens. Right on cue, he says, "'You eat ants?'" That's Mowgli's line—he speaks it as Mowgli, almost like a tape recording—then sticks his head under the raised cushion, as though he's scooping up ants.

I'm poised with Baloo's next line: "'Ha-ha, you better believe it! And you're gonna love the way they tickle.'"

Then Cornelia, as Bagheera, the wary panther, cries, "'Mowgli, look out!'"

Owen jumps back as I drop the cushion, just like Mowgli does with the falling rock.

We'd slipped into roles that actually fit quite well—something we recognized a bit later—with me in the rambunctious, impulsive character, Cornelia, ever watchful and protective.

A few minutes later, when King Louie, the crazy orangutan—voiced by jazz trumpeter/singer Louis Prima—sings to Mowgli about becoming a man, Walt's ready: "'Teach me the secret of man's red fire,'" he says, pulling on his ear, waiting for the whispered secret from the boy. Owen recoils—just like Mowgli does in the movie—and says, "'I don't know how to make fire.'" Cornelia catches my eye; I shake my head—both of us feeling the same unmoored sensation. The inflection, ease of speech, is something he can't otherwise muster. But it's in context, as are his reactions.

It's almost like there's no autism. He's not playing the roles as well as we are; he's playing them *better* than we are. Mimicry is one thing. This isn't that. The movements, the tone, the emotions, seem utterly authentic, like method acting.

So begins the basement sessions. For Walt, with his nimble memory, this is a cinch. Though his tastes have evolved to action movies, these Disney classics were once his métier. Cornelia, with terrific retrieval skills, is right behind him. My contribution is imitations, and my recall seems to improve when I slip into character.

Owen, though, leads. His memory is flawless, but of a different cast. At three, his comprehension of spoken words collapsed. That's clear from every test and, later, his own recollections. Listening to him now, it seems that as he watched each ninety-minute Disney movie, again and again, he was collecting and logging sounds and rhythms, multi-track—each one like pi, stretching to thousands of digits. Speech, of course, has its own subtle musicality; most of us, focusing on the words and their meanings, don't hear it. But that's all he heard for years—words as intonation and cadence, their meanings inscrutable. It was like someone memorizing an Akira Kurosawa movie without knowing Japanese. Then it seems he was slowly learning Japanese—or, rather, spoken English—by using the exaggerated facial expressions of the animated characters, the situations they were in, the way they interacted, to help define all those mysterious sounds. That's what we start to assume; after all, that's the way babies learn to speak. But this is slightly different, because of the way he committed these vast swaths of source material, dozens of Disney movies, to memory. These are stored sounds we can now help contextualize, with jumping, twirling, sweating, joyous expression—as we just managed with *The Jungle Book*. We, after all, are three-dimensional, we have heartbeats. We can touch him, and he can touch us back. Strictly speaking, we're interactive. In the parallel worlds—real and Disney—we're crossing over.

During daylight, we go about our lives. Walt rides his bike to school each morning, back home each afternoon. Cornelia manages the house, the bills, the overloaded schedules of both kids. With my book about Cedric and his peer almost finished, I begin editing and writing again for the *Wall Street Journal*, putting on my suit and subwaying downtown to the bureau.

No one knows we're all living double lives. At night, we become animated characters.

•　•　•

It turns into the most extraordinary six months, as in so many *extras* to ordinary that it's hard to keep track. Cornelia and I begin to watch the movies in an utterly new way. Up to now, we were looking for something—anything—that caught his interest and diving in, trying to manage an interaction. Now it's reversed—the other end of the telescope. We have fifteen or so Disney videos in the house. Almost any scene we pick, he wants to roleplay. And he can manage it with ease. He's clearly memorized them all.

We start watching the movies with appraising eyes. *What scenes should we pick for the next basement session?* And the one after that? Line up our collection—from *Pinocchio* and *Dumbo* in the 40s to *The Lion King* in the 90s—and the menu is vast.

We role-play selections from nearly every one—scenes of joy or challenge or pathos—through the winter and into spring.

That's when Disney Club starts spilling out of the basement. It's happening in the kitchen, the backyard, the screened-in porch.

It's even happening in the car! We start to regularly converse in Disney dialogue. Grab a line—throw it out there. You had to feel it to do it right, because the tonality was almost as important as the words. Really, you needed both, and if you could summon the rhythm of the line, its cadence, the accent, all the better.

Because Owen will match you. He fires back the next line, gleefully. Lights up like a firefly, at the ready.

Baloo and Mowgli and the rock? Sure, that's rich terrain. But there are plenty of characters to choose from, countless scenes—one for every occasion, feeling, and moment. When Owen is being challenged, something he's avoiding, running from—like not wanting to swim, or try riding a bike—you might stick with *The Jungle Book*, and go with Shere Khan, the tiger, voiced in that lowest register of George Sanders. There's a brief and pointed exchange about fear, when he asks Mowgli: "Could it be possible that you don't know who I am?"

That's the opening line. Whatever he's doing, Owen will snap around . . . as Mowgli: "'I know you, all right. You're Shere Khan.'" It's flawless, but there's more: Owen's posture, as he steps forward, shoulders back, is just like Mowgli's in the movie, like a boy trying to summon courage.

"'Precisely,'" I retort in Sanders' formal accent, checking my nails, which is what Shere Khan does at that moment: "'Then you should also know that everyone runs from Shere Khan.'"

"'You don't scare me. I won't run from anyone.'"

"'Ahhh. You have spirit for one so small.'"

Of course, that last line is the destination, the inspiring kicker to the exchange. Hearing it, Owen smiles. I smile back, knowingly, conspiratorially, and then he'll often do something he's fearful of. That's the most amazing part. It works.

Often the exchanges are just for fun. Walt will say, "'You'd make one great bear,'" in Baloo's voice, and Owen will knock him down, sit on his stomach, and cry out, "'Oh, papa bear!'"

At bedtime, Cornelia talks about Dumbo sleeping in his tree. She just has to throw out one line, like Timothy Q. Mouse saying, "'Come on, Dumbo, you can do it,'" and Owen slips into context, integrates the tree reference, and hurries off to bed. At breakfast, the time to walk our dog, Annie, it's all about *One Hundred and One Dalmatians*.

Though all of our words are scripted by others, we are literally communicating through these words and the stories they tell.

. . .

In April 1998, the book about Cedric, his family, and the two sets of kids he connects—one from blighted Southeast DC and the other from the freshman class at Brown University—is published. Called *A Hope in the Unseen*, the book is a weave of stories of Cedric, his mother, and thirteen other supporting characters, written in present tense and devoid of traditional explanatory passages—a journalistic standard I'd long practiced—telling readers what's important, what's not, and how they should view the characters. The narrative threads twist along; readers could decide for themselves what they thought. The idea was that stories are like Rorschachs—people see all sorts of things in them, including themselves.

This is the way it is in our house, after all. What Owen sees in, say, *Beauty and the Beast*, might be different from what we see. But we share the story, itself; one of the few things we do share.

If it only were that easy elsewhere. There is little he was sharing with teachers or other students at Lab School.

The first year has been a struggle. Though both the LD kids and autistic spectrum kids wrestle—as Smith often says—with a "disorder of the way the brain organizes itself and its inputs" in regard to words, the struggle for dyslexics—the school's predominant LD issue—is largely with the reading of words. Autism, as a pervasive developmental disorder, is well, more pervasive, especially in the way it disrupts the auditory processing of speech. For spectrum kids, basic instructions like "now let's collect our markers," "time to line up for recess," or "everyone find a partner" often pass swiftly, like chocolates on the conveyor belt in that famous scene with Lucille Ball. You've got to box them in the proper part of the brain so they're understood and the appropriate action is fired—*begin collecting markers!* When these processes are on a delay switch, the chocolates don't hit their boxes, new ones on the belt pass through unprocessed and you end up like Lucy, with a mouthful of chocolates and boxes everywhere. And the chocolates keep coming! That's when the teacher says, "Owen, Owen?!" He's not the only one, but the stress builds.

And it does through Owen's first year, until we get a call in late May that there's a problem. He's throwing poop.

This is unacceptable, the head of the lower school tells us the next day in a meeting. Yes, we know. But why is he doing it—*we need to get to the "why."* He's been potty trained for two years. For some reason he either isn't asking to be excused to go to the boy's bathroom or is so stressed, or distracted, that the issue catches him by surprise. He has always been clean conscious, not comfortable being messy, like some boys are. He has to rid himself of the accident. Hence, finding an inconspicuous corner and, well, throwing.

They say we need to do something. We say we will. And then the school year ends.

Which is why we're sitting on the couch with him one evening in early September 1998, a few weeks into his second year at the school. We're terrified of flying poop. One or two incidents to start this year, and he'll be out.

But we have a hook. Each year, the classes shape their curriculum and activities around an idea—a brainstorm by Smith to help them integrate knowledge around an interest or affinity—and this year Owen's class is called "Cave Club," where there will be some talk of dinosaurs.

And he likes the Land Before Time movies, an animated series started by Steven Spielberg. So we try to build on that, saying that Lit-tlefoot—the main character—always had time to go to the bathroom. He would tell the other dinosaurs to wait, that he'd only be a minute, and still everyone made it to the Great Valley. We work this for a bit.

"Do you understand about the poop problem at school, how that won't work in Cave Club?" Cornelia asks. He nods.

We haven't had another moment like that night with Iago—a year ago, now—where I address him as a character and he responds in his own voice. Maybe the key to that moment was the element of surprise: of the character addressing him directly as Owen. After a few moments, Owen did begin to respond as Jafar. Character to character seems more comfortable to him, as does discussing some rudimentary meanings of various scenes to help shape his behavior.

By mid-October, we're feeling guardedly optimistic—no more poop incidents—but still trouble in class. He's talking under his breath, often in the voices of his characters, when he should be lis-tening or participating. On a particular day near Halloween, we get a report he's been reprimanded for this, and had a "time-out."

I see him sitting, glumly, on the rug in his room and think of *The Sword in the Stone*, just about the richest terrain of any of the movies. Like *The Jungle Book, Aladdin,* and *The Lion King,* there's a male hero—a bit more to work with. But the affectionate guidance Merlin offers the orphaned Arthur is right out of any parenting playbook. There's a particularly good scene in the movie where Arthur is reprimanded by the feudal lord he works for and loses out on a trip to London.

I duck my head in the door. "'I know that trip to London meant a great deal to you,'" I say in the gentle, reedy tone of Karl Swenson, the actor, long dead, who voiced Merlin. It's easy—basic British.

Owen looks up and smiles. "'Oh, it's not your fault. I shouldn't have popped off. Now I'm really done for,'" he says as Arthur.

And off we go:

"'No, you're in a great spot, boy. You can't go down. You can only go up from here.'"

"'I'd like to know how.'"

"'Use your head. An education, lad.'"

"'What good will that do?'"

"'Get it first. Then, who knows? Are you willing to try?'"

"'Well . . . what have I got to lose?'"

"'That's the spirit! We'll start tomorrow. We'll show 'em. Won't we, boy?'"

"'We sure will.'"

Owen and I have never had a conversation like this. But as Merlin and Arthur we do. It has a knowing, sentient quality. The grammar is perfect, as is the word choice. Is this just a more complex, interactive version of echolalia, or are we really talking? Can't say for sure where to draw that line.

But I'm certain about one thing: the warmth passing between the characters in the movie—one Owen has watched a hundred times—now passes between us. I can feel it.

• • •

Walt's team has just batted and now he's putting on his catcher's gear, getting ready to warm up a new pitcher. It's springtime, 1999.

Cornelia hops off the lower bleacher to check on Owen, running to and fro in a playground area next to the field. She was constantly shifting her gaze between the two boys. A few minutes before, she'd caught a glimpse of a man—a father from the opposing team—looking at him, clearly wondering what was up. She tried to ignore him—she wanted to see Walt bat, to focus on that. But now the guy's staring again.

"Hey, honey, what are you playing?" she calls to Owen, as she approaches the sandbox and swing set. He ignores her until she gently takes his hands and, squatting, looks at him intently. Do it right, he can look back with equal intensity.

"Gargoyles."

She knows that means *The Hunchback of Notre Dame*, the Disney movie he is enamored of that spring. "Which one?"

"Victor."

"Which part?"

"When they dance with Quasimodo."

There were two other gargoyles: Hugo (to complete the homage to the writer of the famous novel) and Laverne.

"Can I do Laverne?" she asks.

"No, I'm okay."

"All right, I'm going back to Walt's game. I'll be right over there."

Owen looks over toward the bleachers, nods, then spins back into a song and dance routine about an outcast in fifteenth-century Paris.

At this point, the value of the Disney role-playing—now eighteen months along since that night with Iago—is indisputable. It's a hidden kingdom, and it's important to tread through it carefully. We're interested in his world, but not in a clumsy and disruptive way—stumbling in and knocking over furniture. We're curious and respectful. When we ask him questions, about what characters do and feel, it prompts him to talk. The result is that his pragmatic speech is improving, along with islands of more complex expression.

Owen, running about, reciting scenes in a public park, is as oblivious to what he looks like as he's always been. It's our view that's changed—our view of him. There was reason to his rhyme.

Cornelia walks across the grass on her way back to the bleachers. But not our bleachers. She was walks directly toward the gawker, who turns as she approaches, like someone spinning away from a blast.

"Can I help you with something?!" she says, hands on her hips, glaring.

"Huh. What?"

"It's impolite to stare."

"I wasn't, I mean I'm not . . . umm . . . staring."

"He's different, okay. And that's the way he plays. Do you always stare at special-needs kids?"

He pauses and starts to mumble something but she doesn't listen. She's already turned on her heel. It was the first time she ever confronted anyone and she's shaking from the exchange.

•   •   •

Animated movies, especially the Disney ones, tend to finish with a reprise of the theme song in some pop version—sung by a star vocalist, like Michael Bolton or Elton John—that plays while the credits run. That's when, after some umpteenth viewing, Cornelia or I tend to hustle out of the basement for all the things that'd been left waiting for the past ninety minutes: a simmering pot for pasta, a story in need of editing, calls to friends, relatives, news sources, housework of every possible variety, grocery shopping, a dog to feed, walk, bathe, unmade beds, untended gardens, or just a few minutes in the sunlight above ground. For Walt, usually homework. Owen invariably stays behind. We figure it's for the music. He seems to like the reprise and always wants to stay to the bitter end. The movie isn't complete for him until it fades to black. Anxious to get on with neglected tasks, no one did the math: the credits take between two and four minutes, but he's down there for a half hour.

It isn't until the spring of 1999 that we notice this after burn and double back to see he was rewinding that final song, halfway back, all the way, a third of the way. Doing it a few times over. Like so much else, why he did it was a mystery. Maybe he just loved the theme songs.

We don't think of the credits because, well, he doesn't read. Not really. And not for lack of trying. Just turned eight, he knows the alphabet, the sounds of consonants and vowels, and is trudging through very basic phonetics—dog, cat, run—with a once-a-week after-school educational tutor. Lab School marshals a host of techniques for students with reading problems, which was the one thing both the LD kids, many of whom were dyslexic, and the autistic or developmentally delayed kids all shared.

But then his tutor says something must be working. His decoding of words, creeping at a snail's pace for two years, is picking up speed and precision. She wonders if they're trying something new at Lab.

So we checked. No, it isn't the school.

Disney Club seems to have added a class to its curriculum: MOVIE CREDIT READING AND COMPREHENSION.

It's actually independent study—Owen is self-directed, which we are fast realizing, seems . . . to be the only way he can learn. The basic model of early education—sit, listen, memorize, discuss, then measure progress (a test)—isn't really working. Of those five steps, four are nonstarters for him. And memorization can't be willed; it only works if he's interested.

But he has become intensely interested in who is behind these screens of color and motion that give him such joy, such sustenance.

We're not sure when the light went on. Only that it did. A third plane, a grid, joined the first two—the real world and parallel Disney world. Both are connected by a third grid: all the people—artists, voice actors, script consultants, directors, character animators, and on and on—who craft the shifting landscape where Owen walks in his imagination for so many of his waking hours. It isn't searching for God. But it's close. He's seeking out the creators.

Play, stop, rewind, play, stop, rewind, frame by frame. The methodology is logical and deliberate. He doesn't seem to want to do it while we are in the room, so we start eavesdropping from the kitchen, just up the stairs. Here's what we hear one night that winter: First he decodes the name of the character. Pick one. Urrrr . . . Urrsss . . . Ursssaaa . . . Urrrssooo. Considering it's *The Little Mermaid*, he can, and does, finish up by quickly deducing "Ursula." That's a warm-up for the tougher, fresher terrain of the actor who voices the sea witch. He hits play for a minute, then stop, to get it frozen just right on the screen: P-p-p . . . P-paaaa . . .

After a few minutes of struggle, he pulls it all together: Pat Carroll. We hear him say the name softly, almost reverently, repeating it a few times. And then other words, like *assistant* and *associate*, *lighting*, *director*, and *producer*. He seemed happy and focused, scrolling frames, calm and intensely engaged, with so many movies to choose from. Our only job is not to disturb him.

• • •

Walt is with Owen on a Saturday in early June 1999. They're milling about, fingering books at the DC Public Library about a mile from our house. Or they were a minute ago, when I last looked.

I hear a man raise his voice—a constrained attempt at volume—and turn in time to see a scene unfolding. Actually, the first thing I see is how wide Walt's eyes are.

The *sotto voce* shouter is the librarian, who is speed walking over from the checkout desk: "What are you doing?!"

I have a good span of carpeting to cross from Contemporary History to get to them, about five seconds in a slow trot, and I watch the librarian, a youngish, bespectacled man, looking—in urgent need of explanation—at Walt, then at something low, which is out of my line of sight, then he looks back at Walt, whose eyes grow even wider. As I get there, Walt turns and runs out of the library.

I see what they're looking at: Owen's butt and kicking feet, sticking out from a low shelf. He's parted the books and wedged nearly his whole body in the dark space between the bookcases.

I know immediately it's *The Pagemaster*, a 20ᵗʰ Century Fox movie Owen's been fixated on. Along with Disney favorites, he's folded in a few movies—including this one and *Space Jam*—that mirror the growing oddity of his life and that of the whole family: combinations of animation and live action. First released in 1994, *The Pagemaster* was all but designed for him and his fast-shifting reality. Its main character, a cautious boy named Richard Tyler—played by Macaulay Culkin—gets trapped in a library on a stormy night, only to meet a mythical character played by Christopher Lloyd. That'd be the Pagemaster, a wizardly type who shepherds the boy into the stacks and a world—hidden between the bookshelves—where the great stories, like *Dr. Jekyll and Mr. Hyde* and *Moby Dick*, come to life. The boy's guides are three talking books, each representing genres—fantasy, adventure, and horror—who lead him on a journey to face his fears.

The movie is one of the reasons we're at the library today. Looking for an activity for both boys on a Saturday afternoon, Owen jumped at the suggestion of a visit to the library.

This is the flip side of our role-playing. It has no natural boundaries. The world now is Owen's stage. I pull him from between the shelves and sheepishly apologize to the stunned librarian. "It's just this movie he's really into about a library . . . I'm sure you'd love it."

Outside, I track down Walt. He's sitting on a bench, shaking his head.

"Dad, does he have to be this way?" he says, in a kind of plea.

I'm not sure what to say. I talk a bit about this being the way Owen was born. "He didn't do anything to be like this, and I'm sure if he could choose, he'd choose not to. But he has no choice, and we don't either. We just have to be there for him."

Walt knows all this, but it doesn't help. He's really upset. This has clearly been building for a while. "He has no idea how you're supposed to behave. None!"

I agree with him. We both know he's right. I just sit with him for a moment, while he begins to calm down. He was angry when Owen and I got outside. Owen begins to dance nearby on a patch of grass; I put my arm around his older brother's shoulder. "You know him better than anyone, Walt. It's just the way he is. I know it's hard, but we have to find a way to embrace him, to celebrate him, just like people embrace you. He's lucky to have you as a brother."

As we drive off a few minutes later, I feel dots connecting around the words "supposed to."

That phrase Walt just used, I'm using a lot lately. Since *A Hope in the Unseen* came out a year ago, I've been giving speeches where people invariably ask how Cedric defied both the low expectations and destructive codes of behavior that so defined his school and neighborhood. There are various reasons, having to do with his upbringing, his mother, his faith, and the way his pariah's status divorced him from social norms. But he's a rarity. Recent research on something called the "stereotype threats and boosts" shows the astonishing power of expectations carried in cultural stereotypes—African Americans are athletic and spiritual; Asian Americans are math whizzes—in determining how a hundred babies, all identical in basic human capacities, end up looking so different as adults. From the earliest age, these expectations shape how others see us, how we see ourselves, and the capabilities we develop as we're encouraged, or discouraged, by the eyes of others.

These "supposed tos" arise, of course, from the fundamental human capacity to swiftly size up the surrounding context and our place within it.

It's the quality that most distinguishes Walt from Owen.

It's hard-wired and instinctual in Walt, as it is in most people, and already well along in shaping his behavior and identity.

Owen's specialists say his inability to do this is his most basic, and defining, disability. In autism circles, it's called "context blindness."

He has no sense of the "supposed tos" because he can't read all those looks, expressions of favor or disfavor, the ripple in the crowd, borne within each passing moment that builds into a life. That means he doesn't know what you're supposed to do in a library—as opposed to a playground—or what movies most eight-year-olds are watching. The questions researchers are busy asking are whether this deficit is a matter of will or capability; can it be developed in a person; and if so, how? But day-to-day facts are clear: like a growing number of autistic spectrum kids and adults, Owen is driven, shaped, and guided by what bubbles up, often quite mysteriously, from within. There are plenty of self-directed urges in everyone. It's just that our impulse instantly slams against our lightning-fast assessment of *context*. The atmospheric zone created by that collision is behavior.

Walt's upset because he has endured many moments like we just did in the library and suspects we will have many more, and he's probably right. From an eleven-year-old's first-person perspective, that means he'll have to go through his whole life being embarrassed or he'll have to stay away from his brother, at least in public. A tough set of choices.

Owen, meanwhile, wonders why Walt is so upset.

• • •

A month later, in the summer of 1999, we step into an alternative reality—sometimes called the "Happiest Place on Earth."

On this, our third trip to Walt Disney World, Owen is nine. He can do more, and say more. Much more.

Context blind? Suddenly we see him mastering a context that's invisible to us.

And to the Mad Hatter.

That's who we see on our first morning at what's called a character breakfast, where a conventional hotel breakfast is interrupted by Disney characters. As we eat pancakes, suddenly Alice appears, and behind her, a crazy little man with a tall green hat.

Owen rises from the table matter-of-factly and approaches him, the rest of us scrambling behind.

"Excuse me," he says, as the Mad Hatter turns. "Do you know Ed Wynn?" That would be the former vaudevillian who voiced the Mad Hatter in the Disney movie.

"Of course, he's a good friend of mine," the Mad Hatter responds, in a stock response of the characters, who, after all, must always remain in character. Owen looks at him intently, trying to detect an inference from behind the fake nose and pancake makeup. None visible. He presses on.

Owen: "So you know Verna Felton—the voice of the Queen of Hearts?"

Mad Hatter (befuddled): No response.

Owen (equally befuddled): "She was also Winifred in *The Jungle Book*, the Fairy Godmother in *Cinderella*, Aunt Sarah in *Lady and the Tramp*, one of the three fairies in *Sleeping Beauty*, and one of the four elephants in *Dumbo*—the mean one!"

Mad Hatter: "Verna who?"

Then off he rushes, like someone late for a very important date.

Owen, that is.

We're delighted—scratch that, ecstatic—to have him lead. So much to do in three days at Walt Disney World, so many attractions, so many characters yet to question. Of course, almost none of them talk. Only the ones who are human, in actor's makeup, like Alice or the Mad Hatter or Ariel can respond. But in those brief conversations—or through what Owen asks the nonspeaking animated characters walking to and fro—we catch a glimpse of an Atlantis he's building under the sea. He's not only learning to phoneticize words by reading the credits. He's remembering the names, cataloguing them—those are five movies for Verna Felton—and creating a cross-referenced index in his head. When he meets characters, there is so very much to discuss.

During its first fifty years, the Disney studios relied on a roster of actors—some famous, some less so—that it mixed and matched to voice the animated characters that were drawn, laboriously, only after the voice tracks were laid down. These voice actors move behind the scenes in little clusters. Verna Felton, for instance, matches up in three major movies with Sterling Holloway— he's Kaa the snake in *The Jungle Book*, the Cheshire Cat in *Alice in Wonderland*, and the stork who delivers the big-eared baby in *Dumbo*. Winnie the Pooh—famously voiced by Holloway—is asked about all of this by Owen later that day in Fantasyland. Pooh nods and shrugs, and Owen embraces him. It's strange for Cornelia and me to watch: after years of one-way conversations with Owen, now he's having one with Pooh. Pooh seems to understand and Owen acknowledges it with a hug. How many times did we do that with Owen? And, standing there, our eyes begin to adjust, to see what he sees. These characters are part of a family. His family. He's grown up with them, relied on them, learned from them. This is his chance to tease out their relationships to one another, discover what binds them to one another.

When he sees Goofy, whom he's been looking for and was worried he wouldn't see, Owen runs toward the giant dog, or horse, or whatever Goofy is, and throws his arms around him. They just hug for a moment, until I can get Owen to spin around, still in Goofy's embrace, for a picture.

It's enlivening and humbling. He is expressive and affectionate with these characters in ways he rarely is with us, or anyone else.

Cornelia and I talk about this in the café at the Wilderness Lodge that night. Is it okay for him to have such a strong emotional bond with them? Is there a danger here? Are there views and truths he was ingesting that were all but invisible to our adult eyes?

Where do you begin? It's a whole, self-sustaining artificial world. She mentions what we saw late that afternoon: a crowd gathered around the lagoon near Tom Sawyer Island, looking down at something in the water. *What could it be?* We crowded in and finally caught a glimpse. It was a small alligator, maybe two feet long. Gawkers were debating whether it was animatronic or real; no consensus was reached.

I went with real: "And it's been the only real thing we've seen here in three days." "Well, there's this beer," Cornelia quips, as we lift our mugs and toast whatever Disney executive decided the Whispering Canyon Cafe should serve alcohol.

These emotions Owen has can't be equivalent to "real emotions with actual people," I say, staying with it. "He has to know, deep down, that these characters—that they're not real."

She shrugs. "Look, kids believe in Santa Claus long after they suspect there may be some logistical issues. Belief and nonbelief can hang together for quite a while. Mysteries of faith and all that."

The question, she says, is more how it makes him feel and how he behaves. After spending every day with him, for years, what she sees is how calm, self-possessed, and sure of himself he seems here. And he clearly isn't doing nearly as much "silly," the self-stimulatory behavior, like self-talking or flapping his hands, that more and more we are recognizing is prompted by situations whose complexities he has trouble understanding. "Context blindness" causes stress. When challenged, he retreats inward.

But here, everything is inverted. He knows the context, can size it up swiftly and move easily within it, just like most folks do each day, with unconscious ease. Sure, he's still having to talk, walk, interact, and make choices, like in the real world. But now those split-second decisions—what Disney-themed ice cream to order, whether to ride Peter Pan's Flight again—rests on a firm, brick-and-mortar landscape drawn from movies he can recite; movies that seem to be shaping his identity—just as that wider world was shaping Walt's. Whatever he's feeling for the characters, we both agree that, here, he's more attentive, affectionate, and available *to us* . . . even if, after seventy-two hours neck deep in Disney artifice, we can't wait to get back to the real world.

Owen could stay here forever. He's comfortable at home and he's comfortable here.

Two places.

•   •   •

He's angling to add a third place—school—to that list.

We all are. By the start of his third year at the Lab School in the fall of 1999, we see his skills improving—his rudimentary reading, his new ability to do simple math—but it's uneven and unsteady, as is the building of social connections with potential friends.

It's a struggle for him to keep up, mostly—the school warns us, darkly—because his mind so often races through the parallel universe of movies.

This hyper focus is part of the struggle with his PDD-NOS. We aren't using the word *autism*, at least not in public, where we feel it still carries so many *Rain Man* stigmas. His presentation, as Rosenblatt rightly said, was not neatly aligned with more severely or classically autistic kids, who seem more shut off to the world. Owen, from that first day, beckoning Rosenblatt from under the chair, had the capacity—and, importantly, the periodic desire—to engage. But we now began to see that these labels have always been more strategic, socially and legally, than functional. The reality of "autistic-like behaviors"—where the kids are "self-directed toward narrow interests"—is what we live with. We begin to see the slip-sliding qualities of a spectrum, a concept many medical professionals have by now embraced: on one side, we notice kids like Owen, who more readily attend to their school work and manage more flexibility in moving to unfamiliar topics and new experiences. They are often socially obtuse but are building social skills through experience because they are better able to listen to the teachers, pick up cues from peers, stick with the group.

On the other side, we notice kids like Owen who are more "involved," according to the nonjudgmental term of art, like the son of Owen's psychiatrist, Dr. C. T. Gordon.

Gordon, who now sees Owen once a week, is one of a growing array of doctors who've found a specialty after discovering that their child was autistic. With the seeming growth in incidence of autism, there are now doctor-fathers and doctor-mothers across the medical landscape, rising—in part, from their relentless, night-and-day urgency to help a son or daughter—into leading roles in research and national debates. Gordon founded an organization that examines new treatments, claims of causation, and the latest scientific discoveries, and publishes those assessments in a journal of growing import. His son, Zack, has no speech—like many more involved autistic kids—and relies on a small device, a keyboard with a screen, on which, by age seven, he can type one hundred words a minute. His passion, though, is exactly like Owen's: the Disney classics. He's organized his viewings in vast, complex rotations and rituals, and derives inchoate joy from each session. Gordon's view—like that of most professionals—is that this passion should be used as a tool, a reward, to encourage Zack to complete educational tasks and personal care goals he was otherwise resistant to undertake. Of course "Finish your homework before watching TV" is a common refrain in every household. But a typical child—the term of art is "neurotypical"—is able to discover and nourish interests much more broadly, more liberally, whether managing to find something provocative in that night's homework, or seeking the joy, and affirmation, of bringing home the "A" on a test. With the autistic kids, their interest, say, in the desired video is deep and maybe unquenchable; their interest in so much else, often very faint. Left to their own devices, the thinking goes, they would slip into their chosen area, to the exclusion of all else. For some kids, their affinity is for train schedules; for others it's maps. Or, in the case of Owen and Zack—and we're certain, many others—it's Disney movies.

Don't cut it off, Gordon suggests. Control it. Use videos as a reward, to be viewed at a designated time if certain things are done. And *no rewinding*, which Gordon feels just deepens the perseveration, like a wheel in a ditch. That's what he did with Zack. Scheduled viewings and no rewind button: the videos were important, largely as a motivational tool.

We're already placing some controls on viewing. Now we add to them. We set up a point system at school, a behavioral technique, where he can pick up points for appropriate behavior—listening to the teacher, attending to his work. Enough points meant a video that night. Some nights, there are not enough points. Sorry. No video.

There are modest improvements in his behavior at school— nothing dramatic—but after two successive days of no-video edicts, Cornelia is awakened in the middle of the night.

She jostles me out of a deep sleep. "I definitely heard something downstairs." I check the clock. It's three A.M. Five minutes later, base-ball bat in hand, I meet Owen in the basement. He'd settled in for a movie marathon.

He's profuse in his apologies. He says he won't do it again. But, a few days later, we see clues in the morning. He's just gotten better at covering his tracks.

Soon, the house slips into low-grade guerilla war—a hearts and minds struggle that draws from us decidedly mixed feelings. It's like we're cutting off his supply lines. School is hard and stressful. His release, his refuge, is being cut off.

Cornelia calls me one morning as she's driving him to school. Owen is snoring away. What's the point of bringing him to school, she asks. We need to bring in heavy weapons. After work, I stop by the hardware store.

That night, we all gather in the basement to discuss the new house rules. I've padlocked the cabinet that holds the big TV. I hold the key, like a federal marshal.

"Mom and I will hold this one key. There will be no other."

Disney is now a controlled substance.

chapter four

MUSICAL CHAIRS

The concept is a massive redirect.

With TV now limited inside the house, with us trying to help Owen control his passions and impulses, we need to channel the animated river toward school. Lab speaks endlessly about its arts-based learning. Let's see if they can harness Owen's self-directed learning, just as we've been doing in the basement and, now, everywhere. All we do is act out scenes; drama is one of Lab School's specialties.

Of course, the self-directed part makes it all a bit more complicated. We have to be guided by whatever Owen is *into*. As the fall of 1999 turns to winter of 2000, he isn't into just any Disney movie. He's deeply besotted with *Song of the South*.

It was trouble when it was released in 1946. And that was before the civil rights movement.

After its debut, *Time* magazine wrote that the movie's rendition of race relations in the years just following the Civil War was "bound to land its maker in hot water." It did. Activists picketed movie theaters with signs saying it was "an Insult to Negro people." No doubt it was to some. It also won the Academy Award for Best Original Song for "Zip-A-Dee-Doo-Dah."

Oh, America.

Owen loves the song. It plays continuously inside Splash Mountain at Walt Disney World, his first high-intensity ride with a long rollercoaster-style drop at the end. Fear and joy fused together, and everything was "satisfactual." He's now starting to use the computer, and finds a clip of Uncle Remus singing the song. It's among the first attempts at live action blended with animation—with the bluebirds flying around the smiling Remus. That combo—a live-action actor with animated characters swirling around his head—is pretty much Owen's life, his particular *context*.

Our seeing things through the lens of context is the great breakthrough of this time: seeing that, yes, he is disastrously context blind about the noisy, shifting, dodge-and-fake world of fast-fire human interaction, and understanding—as he becomes more active—what it really means to live a decontextualized life. Among the many things you are oblivious to are advertisements during commercial breaks, in magazines, on billboards, in shopping mall toy stores, and what they are all saying you just *can't live without*. The constant buzzing bombardment—resulting in incessant "Please, please buy this for me," or, for that matter, a consumer culture based on ever-escalating wants becoming needs—simply bounce off of him.

But, in his chosen area, he's context-deep. All he wants comes from that deep well. And the video of *Song of the South* tops this year's wish list for Hanukkah and Christmas.

Soon, "Santa" is locked in eBay hell.

The movie has, of course, not worn well. Recognizing this, the company never released it on video in the United States.

But, in this early chapter of connectivity called the World Wide Web, it can be found. It's had limited release in some other countries, like Japan and the U.K., which is where we find a copy to bid on. We really didn't want to know who's on the other side of the transaction. All we know is that someone in England made a hundred dollars and we, soon, are looking at a box with Uncle Remus and those bluebirds smiling at us.

It's unplayable. The United Kingdom, we discover, uses a different video format from the United States. It needs to be converted. I'm doing some work as a guest correspondent on ABC's *Nightline*, with Ted Koppel, and know video editors at the network. Even they couldn't manage it, but they know of a video production house that can. And only four hundred dollars!

So, as the new year approaches, we settle into the basement to begin to watch a five-hundred-dollar video. The kindly Uncle Remus is basically set up—with possibly horrific consequences in the Reconstructionist South—by some vindictive white kids. At that point, I'm regularly appearing on panels and doing speeches as a white guy who "gets race." But that's aboveground. Inside the house, we're living inside a collection of Disney movies. In this case, one selected by an eight-year-old who is oblivious—often blissfully—to history, culture, social codes, and accepted customs outside his wonderful—and safe—world of Disney films. Even as a sixth grader, Walt knows more than enough to be mortified. Basically, he watches the movie shaking his head and saying, "Oh, my God." When the movie ends, we try to explain to Owen why some people don't like this movie. It's hard to know where to start. "Remember when Jafar, as the Genie, put Aladdin in chains . . ." After a few minutes, he says, "Can we sing now?"

So we join hands—Cornelia, Walt, and I, shrugging in resignation—for a rousing chorus of "Zip-A-Dee-Doo-Dah."

• • •

His fixation on the film is a tough turn for our massive-redirect strategy, but we get some lucky breaks: his teacher, Jennifer, had been his assistant teacher for the past two years and bonded with him, often putting Owen on her lap to calm his self-stimming; and the Br'er Rabbit tales have a long history among folk traditions of Africans that predates Disney.

It's just enough wiggle room. Jennifer takes charge, calling us often for strategies on how to manage Owen and pull this off. By the spring of 2000, there are regular practices of the play and props being created in art class. With Jennifer's guidance, Owen is the casting director, placing kids in various roles—Br'er Bear or Br'er Fox—that seem to fit with their looks or personality. Owen, knowing the long rendition of dialogue of Br'er Rabbit's battle with the tar baby, is the lead.

On a mid-April Tuesday, kids, parents, and teachers gather inside the Lab School's black box theater, modeled faithfully on the experimental theaters of New York. No one in the room knows what an edgy experiment it is for Cornelia and me: our double lives are becoming one. Disney Club is going public.

Owen doesn't disappoint. He's immediately in character. Of course, he's in character all the time. That means knowing his lines is not a problem, talking to the pot of tar—"What's the matter with you? I said, 'Howdy!'"—as he gets one arm stuck, then the other, then his legs, and finally his head, talking all the while and drawing laughs and nods from the audience. "How often has he practiced that?" a mom next to Cornelia whispers to her. "If only you knew . . ." she whispers to herself. It's exactly the way it is in the movie, every movement and syllable.

It's strange to watch him do this in public. It's his first performance—if you can really call it that. Not that he's particularly attentive to the audience. Most kids are looking for their parents— one eye on the crowd, and its reaction, as they go through their lines. He's not. But he's mindful of the other kids, and we know it's because they're also doing dialogue that mostly comports with the movie. When they stray from it, so does he.

Mostly it holds together, with the other actors playing their roles, if more interpretively and not quite as precisely. What we've been doing in the basement he's now doing with other kids. This, after all, is the dream. We feel a wild aspirational uplift, and at the same time recognize how difficult it was to construct: this was months in the making.

But it's a victory won. At the end, they all bow together, hands joined, as the applause washes over them. Owen is not the straggler, struggling to keep up, not this time. And—as other parents applaud as lustily for their kids as we do for him—Cornelia and I realize that is all we really want: for him just to be in the mix.

The show is followed by a reception for the visiting parents, and we mingle, warmed in the glow of this victory, this momentary easing of our concerns. The parents are all very nice. But after three years at this school, we aren't really friendly with many of them—a result so different from the many friendships we've so readily forged with the parents of Walt's friends and the so-called "neurotypical" kids at Owen's previous school, even though those children were not nearly as inclined to be a friend to Owen—a genuine friend—as were his current classmates.

●　　●　　●

As the years pass, we hold tightly, fiercely even, to carefully vetted locations and inhabitants on the continent of normal. We stick by old friends and bond with new ones, who are what might be called "context-astute." They tend toward the eclectic and searching, questioning types, rather than the dug-in and reflexively certain. And if they don't "get Owen," if they are unsettled or impatient or dismissive of him, it was like a trapdoor. They are gone.

But for the core group—a dozen or so families who were in the club—it is the opposite. Their familiarity with Owen, his habits, his rhythms, have grown across years. The fact that many of them were from Boston and know him from before the sudden change at two and a half places them in a mindset we still secretly embrace: of the old Owen, being trapped in some sort of neurological prison, someday to emerge. The attentiveness, both of these parents and their children, allows our quartet to move among them with ease and comfort. Walt has created lasting bonds with the other kids, we with the parents, and Owen takes on a role—much like he has within Cornelia's extended family and mine—as the one kid in the mix whose demonstrable differences prompt a kind of generalized search for the special, the particular, the unique. Other people's children, who stand by him and nose around for a way to look inside and then draw him out, are embraced as heroes. They usually know the path inside was Disney. And Owen loves their entreaties, even if it was sometimes difficult to express his excitement.

Which was precisely the dilemma: the children with those heightened interpretive skills will eventually need a tenor of reciprocity that Owen has trouble providing if they are ever to develop a bond of true, mutual friendship.

On a fall day in 2000, four families of our oldest friends meet at a working farm in Rochester, Vermont.

This is the eighth year we've been meeting here at Liberty Hill Farm for a long weekend of hikes and hayrides, brilliant home cooking, and shared appreciation that none of us have to work anywhere near as hard as Bob, the dairy farmer, or his wife, Beth.

And an appreciation of *story*. It's not just that we all tell stories of what was going on in our lives. We've created a game. Tonight, like every night at the farm, twelve eager kids, including our two, gather in an upstairs bedroom. It's about time for lights out. And everyone, by now, knows the drill. I go around the room as each child names a favorite character from any book or movie or TV show, and each does, with Owen offering a Disney character, as usual: Sebastian from *The Little Mermaid*. I invent a story, getting Owen's Disney character in at the start—to keep his attention. The other kids, with the traditional capacities for anticipation and focus, listen intently, waiting for their character to appear . . . "and then Sebastian and Madeleine met the Tin Man!" The story builds, as the characters undulate along, a growing band, cresting toward a finale, which tonight, as usual, involves one invented character, a baby with an exploding diaper being toted along by the band. With kids this age, potty humor always works.

Each character, of course, is the avatar for its child/patron. I mix them, just as I hope the kids will mix, with Owen's character—his avatar—always right in the thick of it. The characters couldn't be much more different—a crab, a little French girl, a woodsman of rusted tin. But they stumble forward, feeling their way, relying on each other, moving as one.

That's the story I want to tell. The one I want to be true.

• • •

Sally Smith is also telling a story she wants to be true.

I'm there to help her.

She'd pulled Cornelia and me onto the gala committee in our first days at the school. As journalists, we were good at getting phone numbers and breaking through the protective webs around the powerful or celebrated. With Cornelia's plate full, this was more my job. Smith and I bonded. We had many meetings each year about the gala, which became a passion—some might say, an obsession—for Sally.

We swapped lists of possible learning-disabled achievers—a mention in a news story about difficulties in school, a tip from someone who knew someone—and I'd often make the call. In 1998, I worked the phones to get Rene Russo, who couldn't make the gala. We defaulted to Vince Vaughn, then an up-and-coming star.

On the day of the gala, we'd usually have the honorees visit the school and then attend a luncheon with big contributors, which is where, over the years, I saw a subtle tension in this equation of perception and reality as they gazed across classrooms with students who bore little resemblance to what they were like as children.

At the luncheon atop the Mayflower Hotel, Vince Vaughn asked me about my son. I just said it outright—"He's autistic." Vaughn, a very tall and gentle guy who had mild LD issues, looked at me quizzically. "Are there a lot of autistic kids at the school?" he asked.

Of course, there weren't, and there were fewer each year. Which may be why I'd just said *autistic*—one of the first times I did. The game of labels—PDD-NOS, classic autism, Asperger's—was one we'd grown tired of playing.

The great gala—a signature night in the nation's capital—has worked all too well. The school is being overrun with LD kids from moneyed Washington families or folks who moved to DC for Lab. Clear away the clouds of dyslexia or ADD, and many are off to good colleges; outcomes that easily advertise the school's effectiveness, even if it is largely due to the much shorter distance for the children to travel.

As I'm working on the gala honoring James Carville and Kelly McGillis in 2000 Cornelia is feeling a creep of despair. The springtime victory of Br'er Rabbit isn't continuing into the fall. Owen is making progress—more than we could have imagined—but the other kids are moving faster. The brightest spot is his art. They let the kids draw whatever they chose and he is beginning to draw characters, including his Disney favorites, with a kind of joyful exuberance. But that's as far as self-directed passions are expressed at school. The production of the play was a special event; energies that are hard to integrate into the daily curriculum.

Disney is still a controlled substance, the lock in place, and he's doing less self-talking at school. But with the school not channeling his budding creative urges, Cornelia steps in.

She takes him aside after dinner—a time we often go to the basement for some Disney role-playing. "Owen," she says, taking his hands and crouching so they were eye to eye. "We're going to act out a movie, one of your favorites, with all the Kennedy cousins this coming Thanksgiving—and you're going to be the producer, the director, and the star."

Owen lights up. He knows exactly what all those jobs are. And he immediately makes his selection, one of his favorite movies of that period: *James and the Giant Peach*, a Disney production of the Roald Dahl classic that mixed live action with Claymation, a technique using intricate clay figures. Move them a smidge, photograph, move another smidge, photograph again. This "stop-action" method has been going on for a while—that's the way they did *King Kong* in the 1930s, with an eighteen-inch-tall puppet—but with the latest bonanza of animated movies, stop-action—easier, in a way, than drawing countless frames of animation—was taken up a notch.

And Disney's *James and the Giant Peach*, like Dahl's book, is a beefy fable, with all the big issues—fear, loss, abandonment, redemption, maturation—and a strong array of evocative characters, led by the orphaned James, whose parents are dead. He is left with a pair of vicious aunts—Sponge and Spiker—conjured by Dahl in a nightmarish reach toward Dickens. Magic intervenes, making a peach tree in their yard grow a single, monstrous fruit. James crawls inside the great, moist vessel as it drifts off to sea and finds inside an array of talking, human-sized insects. James starts out withdrawn, battered, put-upon, but makes discoveries through his new firends—about himself and the wider world—as the peach makes it way to America, the place James dreams about.

Of course, we want Owen to be the star, to be James. We egg him on, Walt included: "Owen, you're the only one who knows all the songs and dialogue!"

Owen will have none of it. "Brian is James; he's the right one." Brian, the son of Cornelia's older brother Deane and his wife, Kathleen, is a year younger than Walt but having a tough go of it. Some trouble in school. Some discipline problems at home. And playing football with the cousins—games led by Walt—Brian was regularly battered. After a bit, we accede. Owen is the casting director. It's his choice.

Cornelia had long been wanting to have a colonial Thanksgiving—to have the extended Kennedy clan come to Williamsburg in a kind of reunion and retreat. This is the year, with the play as the weekend's capstone.

In a large, carpeted social room at the Williamsburg Inn, the family gathers on Thanksgiving Day—in all twenty-seven people with the eight siblings, including Cornelia, their kids, aunts, uncles, and her parents. Owen and Cornelia have made simple costumes, a telling prop or two for each—a hat, a cane, a vest—that identifies each character, and the kids receive some rudimentary scripts to play out scenes.

And then, the metaphorical lights come up. Acting as the narrator/stage manager, I start by introducing each of our players, beckoning them to come forward from the wings, a nearby hallway, to introduce themselves.

Matt—Owen's confident and smart first cousin, a few months older than Walt—steps up first, cast as the tough-talking Centipede, who, under duress, eventually shows his soft underbelly. With a cap and cigar, Matt describes the character in a few, blunt twelve-year-old utterances and gives way to Walt, who steps up and introduces himself as the Grasshopper, a worldly arthropod who plays the violin but, with his powerful legs, can also pack a wallop. And onward, until all nine characters—boys and girls—have come forward, save one. "Finally, our producer and director is also an actor, playing the Earthworm," I say with flourish, as Owen comes forward, wearing the rounded glasses of the meekest of the characters, who serves as the story's improbable protagonist. In the movie and book, the Earthworm is reluctantly used as bait to draw hungry seagulls, who are then webbed by Miss Spider into a flying force that lifts the peach to safety, bound for America.

Owen looks out at the familiar faces, the aunts, uncles, grand-parents, from one face to the next, each looking back with some version of an encouraging smile, knowing and nudging, gentle and ready. In some ways, they're all here for Owen, something the older kids sense, and even some of the younger ones—down to his four-year-old cousin, Grace, playing Miss Spider. She sees that Owen is standing closer to the audience than the others, only a few feet away, having missed the X taped to the rug. But she doesn't say any-thing, knows better, though she's seen—like everyone—Owen being helped, corrected, guided in doing some of the simplest things.

Because that's what happens when no one tells you about the moment the "special" kid arrives. How a whole extended family, top to bottom, gets changed by someone who stops the constant drum-beat of me and mine, who's up, who's down, the irresistible drama of bloodlines, birth orders, and familial politics. Why? Because the ways he's different compels a minute-to-minute search, humanizing and heart-filling, for all the ways he's not different. It's us at our best.

And now he stands before the group, to address them all, really, for the first time. There's silence, but he's looking down, or some-where inside—the invisible places where he so often lives—to find something, to be the giver.

"The Earthworm," he says, quiet but steady, "is scared sometimes and confused. And he's jerlous . . . jelerous . . ." There's a word he's seeing in his mind and trying to decode, something he must have read, or heard, but never said, and not one of the twenty onlookers, crowded close, can seem to finish it for him; until, after a second of silence, his aunt Marita—who's especially close and often able to coax things from him—says, "Jealous?"

Owen looks up and nods, the thread restored. "He's jealous of the Grasshopper and the Centipede and characters who can do things that he can't. And that's why I'm the Earthworm."

It's good now that he misses cues so he doesn't see how the eyes of all the grownups are shining with tears.

And the play commences, suddenly everyone in their roles, deep in them, led by Owen—both himself, in the lead, telling them lines they've missed; and as the straggling, terrified Earthworm—the two now joined in the fable of journey, adventure, facing fears.

Until a discovery, well along, that they've missed a song. Yes, right. Cornelia hustles, passes out the song sheets—mostly for the parents, the kids know this one—of the movie's theme, all in song.

Take a little time,
Just look at where we are.
We've come very, very far, together.
And if I might say so,
And if I might say so, too,
We wouldn't have got anywhere if it weren't for you, boy.

The singing is strong, the song sheets allowing the parents to dive in, as Owen, knowing these lyrics and feeling them in ways that remain mysterious, dances in song—arms akimbo, reaching, swinging—at the very center of a crazy celebration that he's unleashed. And this, with that last lyric—"if it weren't for you, boy"—seems to cue the Grasshopper and the Centipede, who can do so very much, to lift the Earthworm onto their shoulders as all the kids crowd close, wanting to touch him. Voices rise with him—everyone singing out emotions, hoarded across years, finally freed—suffusing the room with light.

> *Love is the sweetest thing.*
> *Love never comes just when you think it will.*
> *Love is the way we feel for you.*
> *We're family, we're family, we're family,*
> *All of us and you!*

And this is how, on Thanksgiving of 2000, the plot of *James and the Giant Peach* shifts to make an earthworm the hero. No offense to Dahl, or to James. It is a family using a story to get what it needs. We live, after all, in a society that celebrates the winner; lifting one above all others. We know what that looks like. Though Owen plays a supporting role, we make him a hero of the traditional caste—lifted, triumphantly. He is uncomfortable; this is not his way.

But we are bigger than he is.

• • •

On 9/11, Cornelia tries to pry the lock off the television to turn on CNN.

In her panic, with the Pentagon in flames, four miles from Walt at Sidwell Friends and just one mile, across the Potomac, from the Lab School, she can't remember where she'd hidden the key the day before—a day that suddenly seemed like an eternity past.

I'm far off, on a reporting assignment. She's on her game. And after grabbing both kids from school, she has a neighbor take a bolt cutter to the lock. There'd never again be a lock on the television. That era is over.

Other eras were ending, as well.

By Thanksgiving, I'm sitting in Sally Smith's office.

She says it just isn't working out for Owen at Lab. I make my case. He's making progress in his own fashion, improving by the day. I mention how the club for older kids in the elementary program—Greek Gods—is a cinch for him, building upon an interest he developed by memorizing *Hercules*, Disney's 1997 feature.

"He's turning these movies into tools that, more and more, he's using to make sense of the wider world," I tell her.

She looks at me sympathetically but doesn't budge. "Many of these kids are just too hard to teach. Their affinities are too narrow. There aren't enough handles to grab and use—at least not in a classroom setting." She pauses. "Look, not picking up social cues is just too great a burden. They can't engage with teachers or peers with enough ease, enough capacity, to push themselves forward."

I tell her I'm not going to argue with her. She runs the school. She decides what kind of students it should serve. Of course, we both know everything: that the gala, first created to bring much-needed funding to the Lab School, is now shaping it. The students are looking more and more like younger versions of the celebrated awardees, and less like the son she originally started the school for.

We talk briefly about this year's learning-disabled achievers: David Boies, the super lawyer whose dyslexia forced him to build the extraordinary verbal memory he used to overwhelm opponents in court; and John Chambers, the CEO of Cisco Systems.

Two of society's titanic winners. "And learning that they had some struggles early," I say, trying to not sound bitter, "will change views far and wide about the potential of people with learning differences."

"Something like that," she says. "Killing off those negative expectations isn't nothing. It matters."

It's time to go. She says she hopes we can remain friends and that I'll continue to help with the gala. I rise from my chair. "You started this school so your son, who'd been discarded, would have a place to go," I say, putting on my coat. Gary, now well into adulthood, has significant challenges, much like Owen. "Do you think he'd be accepted here today?"

Those are fighting words. I can't help it—I am thinking how difficult this is going to be for Owen. To her credit, Sally doesn't rise to battle.

"Look, I'm sorry," she says, quietly. "Times change. We're serving a need and serving it well. Just not anymore for someone like Owen."

They plan a small graduation ceremony for early June 2002. Owen's fifth-grade class will be moving up to the middle school.

Save one.

There are few options. We call Ivymount and tell them he's been "counseled out." They're sympathetic. It's like a game of musical chairs, with the autistic-spectrum kids not able to hear when the music stops. The assistant director says his old school will gladly take him back.

We tell Owen in early May, a month ahead. We go out to dinner and say he'll be going back to Ivymount. He's made a few friends at Lab. They do things together, are starting to form little rituals. Quite a lot about friendship, after all, is ritual. He feels like he belongs there. "It'll be great, Owie," Walt says, putting his arm around Owen's shoulder. "I'm sure you'll see some of your old friends at Ivymount will still be there."

Owen gets this look where he raises his eyebrows and presses his face into the widest of smiles. He calls it his "happy face." He does it when he's worried he might cry.

On the day of the ceremony, the kids give Owen cards they've made for him, wishing him well. He's been with them for five years. They drew pictures of Mickey Mouse, of the Simpsons, which Owen got into at Walt's behest. Elizabeth, one of several girls adopted from Russia with developmental delays, wrote, "I am your friend Owen. I will miss you so much. I like helping you to be quiet when we are told to be quiet. I think it is nice you like *James and the Giant Peach*. I also love Disney movies and characters too!" Another friend, Sebastian, drew a picture of Mickey next to Homer Simpson and wrote, "I will miss you and so will Homer." Most said they hope he'll make new friends and the card they signed, all together, wishes him "100 years of Walt Magic in Disney World."

They all hug him good-bye. Neela Seldin, director of the lower school, hands him a certificate that "acknowledges that Owen Suskind has successfully completed the Elementary Program." They put a gold seal on it, to make it look like a diploma.

Owen isn't fooled. He doesn't say anything or make a sound in the car on the way home. He just looks out the window. All through the "ceremony" sitting on the grass behind the school, Cornelia tried to hold it together. She wasn't going to let them see her cry. She feels a combination of anger and devastation—not only for Owen, who is being thrown out of a place he loves—a place she has worked so hard to keep him in—but for all the other spectrum kids she feels have been treated unfairly by a school that had committed to educate them.

At home, Cornelia tells him she has an afternoon of activities planned—a trip to the video store, the bookstore, some ice cream, and then pizza for dinner. All of his favorite stops.

Owen thinks for a minute and then shakes his head. He'd rather not. "I think I'd like to just go to the basement and watch my movies. That will make me feel better."

chapter five

THE PROTEKTER OF SIDEKICKS

Something's going on in the basement.

We can't be sure what.

It's a new basement in a new house, just two doors down the street. The house is a little bigger—it has a backyard with a writer's studio—but everything else is the same. Owen finds comfort in ritual, in sameness, and we're careful to find just the right places in his new cave for all the key items—the sofa, the TV, and the two small bookcases for his library of videos, all in their original clamshell cases, tightly tucked, spines out, arranged in a system understood by Owen alone.

On a mid-June day he's settled in, sitting on the basement's soft wall-to-wall carpeting—freshly laid just before the move—taking one video off the shelf to study it, front and back, return it, and then take out another.

I watch from the bottom of the stairs. Since the ouster from Lab School a few weeks ago, I'm doing a lot of this. So is Cornelia. We know it was a blow, but there's no way to really discuss it with him. His speech is still mostly needs-based, except when something bubbles up from within, something deeper. But that's rare, and you never know when it might come.

So I study his moves and float assumptions. A VHS cover for

a Disney movie is usually a drawing of all the main characters in a montage, which, for him, must feel like looking at a family picture, an array of loved ones. That's clearly the way he's looking at each cover—handling it deftly and so gently, cherishing it, looking from one animated face to the next. Does he love them? What, then, would be the nature of this love?

He's logging more time with them than with us these days and more time in the basement, here, than in the old house—which is saying a lot—sorting and watching his videos, trolling online with a new computer we bought for the kids, going about his business, quiet and purposeful, like he's working on some kind of project.

He developed a new habit of announcing his descent: "I'll be in the basement if you need me." He says this with a more traditional cadence and ease than almost anything else he's ever said. It's like someone else's voice, an octave lower than the atonal alto that usually propels his speech. Cornelia and I are convinced that he heard either Walt or me say this, and he locked on it, like some line of Disney dialogue he'd speak in the voice of Merlin or Jafar. However he got there, though, it's a leap: a sentence that stretches beyond the first-person singular of what he wants to a directive, helping *us* know what to think: "*Mom, Dad. Please don't bother me unless it's important.*"

And down he goes. It's clear his chronological age may mean less than we once figured, or sometimes hope, but in a pinch we rely on it—saying to each other that he's eleven, an age when kids start to need their space.

That lasts a few weeks, until Cornelia is struck with a spasm of separation anxiety—*What's he doing down there?*—along with a more generalized anxiety about online chat rooms and the like. I go down that night to check the computer's history. All his URLs are Disney sites, the Internet Movie Database, or eBay, which he likes to troll in search of discontinued videos, original posters issued at a movie's debut, or figurines from Disney movies, which were the prize, for decades, inside McDonald's "Happy Meal" bags. The only predators I detect are Shere Khan and Scar.

We try to keep the surveillance light—just us, being attentive, all smiles. The yield is modest—there's no easy way in—and he doesn't seem to want us prying. In the last days at Lab, when he sensed pending disaster, he mustered every ounce of energy to try to rein in the self-talking, self-stimulatory reverie. He would snap to attention, arms at his side, eyes wide, chin out, like a Marine Corps grunt, whenever a teacher approached, and say, "No silly!" It was like holding back a raging river. After a minute or two, it would crest its banks. But at this point, it had become a matter of back and forth: a minute thinking about, say, how all the Disney villains have some red in their costumes; a minute listening to what the teacher was saying about the Gettysburg Address. At least he could turn it off.

Which is what he is often doing now as *we approach*.

It means, for the first time, he's developing the ability to hide in plain sight. To pick his moment, dive into his secret world, resurface to do what's asked of him, then dive deep again.

This growing capacity to control the thoughts and pictures popping into his head is something we want to help with and expand. At the same time, it makes us crazier; proof, it seems, of some pain he's hiding, rather than simply his natural reaction against a parental stop and frisk.

And getting at what he's feeling—sharing with him, comforting him—trumps all else. So we resolve, hereby, to be better about gathering clues, to be better organized, write down observations, tips, anything suspicious, and exchange reports each night.

Spies in our own home.

• • •

A Disney movie called *Lilo & Stitch* is released on June 21. Owen, now Internet enhanced, had been anxiously waiting for the release date and also knew that there'd be trouble. Usually, on a Disney debut day, we end up in one of his favorite Washington-area theaters, first in line.

Not this time. By mid-June, we're already in New Hampshire for a summertime ritual that seems open ended, like it might be repeated in coming years, with Walt away all summer at a nearby camp and us in a house on a lake. *Hope in the Unseen* was selected as required freshman reading two years before at Dartmouth College and they asked me to sign on as a visiting scholar in the summers. I'd left the *Wall Street Journal* to write books full time and, with Dartmouth providing us a lake house for the summer, we'd officially begun the self-scheduled life.

All the better to match Owen's increasingly self-directed life. Which means, on a late June evening, we drive an hour and a half to a drive-in in Fairlee, Vermont. That morning, Owen saw *Lilo & Stitch* pictured in the movie section of the local newspaper—the only area showing.

At dusk, we turn onto the main street of the one-street town, which seems happily locked in a time warp: a wood-framed ice cream stand, a white clapboard town hall, a general store, a diner, all capped by one of only two drive-in motels left in America. This was a 1950s invention, driven by the primal need—deep in the species— to watch first-run movies from a bed. The beds were in a stretch of hotel rooms with picture windows facing the big screen, with those hanging car window speakers now sitting on the night table. Such bold innovations have been long ago overtaken by the VCR, HBO, DVDs, and pay-per-view, but this drive-in holds on—the motel rooms now mostly empty—in Fairlee, which, like other tiny towns, had grown accustomed to watching movies from a grassy parking lot of pickups.

It's jammed on a muggy night for this Disney offering about an alien—an intelligent, destructive, dog-like critter—who crash-lands in Hawaii and is adopted by Lilo, a friendless, orphaned little girl (Disney, like Dickens, is very big on orphans). She loses her adopted extraterrestrial, Stitch, chaos ensues, villains are revealed then defeated, and in the end she gains him back.

A key line in the movie relies on the word, *'ohana*. In Hawaiian, it means family, but it has broader cultural connotations, referring to any relatives bound by blood or by choice. In the movie, Lilo— trying to make Stitch understand their growing bond—says to the alien, " *'Ohana* means family. Family means no one is left behind."

This line leaves no discernible impression on either Cornelia or me, eating popcorn in the front seat. The movie's fine, if predictable, and we're already over-loaded with dialogue from a dozen Disney classics—a mountain of memorization.

Eight months later, when the video is released the first weekend in February 2003, Owen makes sure we are the first ones in line to make the purchase. Soon, it's a favorite in the basement, running nonstop.

He's now more than halfway through his first year back at Ivymount and not being challenged, either academically or socially, where so many of the kids have trouble forming connections. Cornelia's response is to crank up his programming. She starts piano lessons with an Ivymount teacher who specializes in teaching special needs kids. There are still the rounds of therapist visits and any after-school activity we can find. Not many playdates, though.

Owen doesn't seem to mind. All he wants are pads and pencils. Markers, too.

He'd started drawing three years before at Lab—one of his few strong suits there was art class.

But this is different. He goes through a pad in a few days and wants another. "Where's the other pad, Owie?" Cornelia asks. He looks blankly at her. Okay, back to the CVS. A few more days, he needs another one. I look around for what are now two missing pads. They're nowhere. Could he have hidden them?

Cornelia's acting director of our intelligence service. She's with him most of every day, and at night she reports her findings. He's distracted. He's watching lots of videos. The school reports that he's doing lots of "silly." I listen, more analyst than agent.

"Boy, he's really gotten into drawing," I say to her on a sunny Saturday, as midday approaches.

"Wonder what's up with that," she says with a shrug, before slipping out with Walt for an afternoon of errands.

After Owen and I have lunch, he's seized by an urge and leaves the kitchen table for his room. A moment later, he's back, padding across the ceramic Mexican tile on his way to the basement—pad, pencils, and one of his large animation books in hand.

I wait a minute before I tiptoe behind him, stopping at the bottom of the stairs. He's over on the rug, kneeling but hunched forward, flipping furiously through the book; as I edge closer, I see it's a book with artwork from *How To Draw Disney's The Little Mermaid*. My fear he'll spot me begins to fade; he's so engaged I probably could knock over a vase and he wouldn't turn.

Standing silently over him, I can see he's stopping at pictures of Sebastian, the wise crab, who watches over the heroine, Ariel. There are lots of Sebastians—twenty or so, one with Ariel, one alone, pencil sketches when the animators were developing the character, full-color renderings of key scenes from the movie. Which is where he stops, late in the book: at a slide of Sebastian with a fearful look—mouth open, eyes wide—on his little crab face.

The sketchbook flies open, the black pencil in hand. He looks from the picture to his pad: picture, pad, picture, pad. And then the tightly gripped pencil begins to move, a lead-lined crawl. Most kids, most anyone, would begin with the face—the first spot we all tend to look—but he starts on the edge, with the crab tentacle, then claw, which take shape in a single line. I think of those old-style drafting machines, with two pencils poised above two pads, the pencils connected to a mechanical apparatus, a crosshatch, so that moving one would create the same motion, the same precise line, with the other. At the end, you'd have two identical drawings, side by side.

It's happening below me: his eyes following one line, the Disney artist's line, as a foot away his hand repeats it.

But here's the crazy part: every part of him starts moving except that rock-steady hand. His whole body begins twisting and flinching—moving as much as you can move while kneeling, with his free arm bending in the angle of Sebastian's left claw. Five minutes later, when he gets to the face, I look up and see a reflection of Owen's face, me behind him, in the darkened screen of the TV, just in front of us. The look on the crab's face in the book is replicated in my son's reflection on the TV where, of course, we've watched this scene—of Sebastian watching Ariel lose her voice—so many times.

And then it's over, like a passing storm. He drops the pencil, rears back, turns his head, and out of the corner of his eye starts squinting down at an almost precise replica of what is in the book.

It freaks me out.

He can't write his name legibly. But here is a fairly sound rendering of a Disney character that might have easily appeared in any one of twenty animation books in his room.

I'm about to say something—I have to speak, looking down at his creation—but his motion preempts me, leaping up and bounding off. Doesn't even look my way, and then vanishes up the stairs, most likely to play out some *Mermaid* scene.

I'm left standing over the sketchbook. I squat down and begin flipping. It's one character after another—the Mad Hatter next to Rafiki, and then Lumiere, the candelabrum from *Beauty and the Beast*, and, on the next page, Jiminy Cricket. The expressions are all so vivid, mostly fearful. Dozens of them, page after page.

I hear a noise and snap around. Annie, our black lab. "Just me, girl, spying on your brother."

I settle in cross-legged on the carpet to examine the pages. What do the drawings mean? Are the faces of these characters a reflection of hidden, repressed feelings? Does he race through the books looking for an expression that matches the way he feels and then literally draws that emotion to the surface?

Could be a half hour I'm sitting, maybe longer. I'm inside him, or so I imagine, running my fingers along the slight indentations of carbon—a smiling mouth of Baloo, a weeping Dwarf, a soaring crow from *Dumbo*—to try to touch him, his tears and smiles and moments of sudden flight. This is the crushing pain of autism. Of not being able to know your own child, to share love and laughter with him, to comfort him, to answer his questions. Cornelia spends time in here, in his head—this child she carried—whispering to him. Now I'm in here, too.

Time passes, pages turn. And then I see writing. Next to the last page of the sketchbook, there's something. It's his usual scrawl, the letters barely legible: "I Am The Protekter Of Sidekicks."

I flip to the last page. In the chicken scratch of a kindergartner is a single sentence.

"No Sidekick Gets Left Behind."

• • •

That night, Cornelia sits up in bed, pillows propped, waiting.

"How was your day with Owie?"

I tell her it was good and fascinating, all quite nonchalant, and hand her the sketchbook.

"You found one—where was he hiding them?" she asks, opening the first page to a drawing of Timothy Q. Mouse from *Dumbo*, and gasps. "My God, look at this?!" She flips two more pages, eyes widening. "An animator—he can be an animator!" I'd been thinking that all day, of course, even after seeing that his technique—drawing the figures freehand while looking at the book—isn't exactly the animator's freehand invention. Close enough. We didn't need much to leap back into fantasies of conquest; that a remade and triumphant Owen would emerge—*Hey, guys, how've you been, sorry I've been away*—making everything right.

Then she did what I did: gaze intently, page by page, at the characters' faces, each so expressive. "Lots of fear and surprise," she says after a few minutes, still flushed with excitement. Until she comes to the last two pages.

She reads them, looks up, and lets out a long, even breath: "The Earthworm."

I exhale, too, like I've been punched in the gut. "Right. Sounds like all this has been brewing, from somewhere deep down, for some time."

Not that we didn't think of the Earthworm now and again, and how Owen spoke, two Thanksgivings ago, about being jealous of the Caterpillar and the Centipede and "other characters who can do things I can't." That, of course, would include James, the hero. We wanted him to be James—the star—and he said, no, he was the Earthworm, the very least of the supporting characters—the *sidekicks*, we see now, in his choice of parlance—and also the one who is "scared and sometimes confused." And it wasn't just us wanting him to be the hero—even the kids lifted him on their shoulders for the final curtain.

We lay there for a few minutes, side by side, racing back, silently, across the years as they suddenly come into a new, sharpened focus. It's as though a one-way conversation—a monologue has just become dialogue. He's responding to us, and the wider world he is now beginning to see.

Other kids are racing forward, with their dreams of heroism. He's caught in the starting blocks, a sidekick. And he becomes a protector of the sidekicks, the supporting cast, demanding that none of them be left behind. That's all. Not asking for the world, here—just don't leave us behind.

"And you and I lifted him to the famous Lab School," I say. "Only to have him lose a brutal game of musical chairs—musical chairs where he couldn't even hear the music, much less hear it stop."

"He can hear it now," she says.

. . .

We need the right moment to respond. Every second we're with Owen in the coming days, Cornelia and I look for our opening—a moment when he's alone, or settled, or upbeat, or a bit more talkative than usual.

Meanwhile, I search the Internet for sourcing. If he's cribbed the line from something he'd seen, a movie, or some online video, we could use that as a conversation starter. Nothing comes up. Just the last half of that line about 'ohana from *Lilo & Stitch*. A typical kid might be able to explain the origin of those lines, how he thought of something or what was going on in his head. Impossible with Owen, as it was impossible to know which came first—the "sidekick" part or the "left behind" part. The former is an identity; the latter, a circumstance. Together, both form something larger.

Then, the stars align. He's watching *Beauty and the Beast* and wants us all to join him. Soon, we're together in the basement, watching the familiar opening, where the handsome prince spurns an old, ugly woman on a forbidding night, only to have her transform into a beautiful enchantress, who turns him into a hideous beast; a spell that can be broken only if he can "learn to love another and earn her love in return." We've heard these words dozens of times, but now they sound different—everything seems to—since reading those last two lines in his sketchbook. Is the Beast a sidekick? The movie, after all, is really about Belle; she's the heroine. Owen jumps up at key moments, moving in sync with the movie—like it's his mirror—then sits back down in the sofa; then, up again. Walt takes off to do his homework. The movie crests forward to its final battle and happy ending. As the credits roll, we do a few voices—I say, "*Sacre bleu*, invaders!" as Lumiere (Jerry Orbach, doing a stagey French accent). Cornelia throws in a Mrs. Potts (Angela Lansbury, upper-crust British) line, "He's finally learning how to love." Owen rises to each with a burst of follow-up lines. We respond, in character. Nothing special. Just your average American family speaking in Disney dialogue.

Both characters, though, are vividly drawn in his sketchbook.

"They're a great pair of . . . sidekicks," Cornelia says.

We've never used the word with him in conversation.

Owen snaps to. "I love Mrs. Potts and Lumiere."

Tell us about them, I ask.

"They're sidekicks," he says.

"What does that mean?" Cornelia follows. Owen looks at her blankly.

"What is a sidekick?" she says, trimming it down.

"A sidekick helps the hero fulfill his destiny," he chirps. Rolls right off his tongue.

Neither of us says anything for a minute. My mind begins to race, wondering if he heard that line before, maybe in one of those "making of" videos, with the writers and directors talking about the goings-on behind the scenes, or if he heard someone say it. I shake it off—*what difference does it make*. It's a classical, elegant definition.

Cornelia isn't similarly distracted.

"Do you feel like a sidekick, Owie?" she asks him softly. Their eyes are aligned, just the two of them now, looking into each other, until he suddenly breaks into "happy face"—that big plastered-on smile, lips tight across his little teeth.

"I am one!" he says. His voice is high and cheery, no sign of a quaver. "I am a sidekick." The words come out flat, without affectation. But he compensates, giving them expression by nodding after each third word.

"And no . . . sidekick . . . gets left . . . behind."

• • •

The radio is on nonstop in the kitchen. The Iraq War started last week on March 20. Reporters are embedded with the troops. There's blanket coverage.

I listen as I slip by the counter, foraging for pretzels, nuts—anything—as dusk arrives. A week before, we listened to George W. Bush address the nation telling Iraq to accede to U.S. demands in forty-eight hours or be invaded. Now, troops are fighting their way to Baghdad.

I'm working on a book these days about the conduct and character of the Bush administration, and especially how, after 9/11, they brilliantly and brazenly sized up the prevailing context of fear—and used it—to achieve their ideological goals. My main source is the recently fired Treasury Secretary Paul O'Neill, who just gave me 19,000 internal documents. They show, among other things, that the stated predicate for war—the fear of Saddam Hussein having weapons of mass destruction—may not, in fact, have been the cause for last week's invasion.

Neck deep in documents all day in my backyard office, I'm starving. Cornelia shoos me away. "Don't eat junk. We have a big dinner tonight." She doesn't need to tell me. Earthy smells of corned beef and cabbage fill the kitchen.

It's the latest St. Patrick's Day dinner in America. Walt was away on a trip to Puerto Rico with his classmates from Sidwell Friends, where he's now in eighth grade. They built houses in poor neighborhoods, and then got to spend a day on the beach. In our house, that meant the annual tradition of a big St. Patty's day feast was bumped from March 17 to tonight, March 24. Insofar as the leader of a Jewish household remains an un-reconstituted Irish Catholic, all traditions that Cornelia's loved from her childhood are celebrated, with gusto. She isn't about to pass on this one.

It's nearly seven o'clock when the kids grab their usual chairs and I fiddle with the radio. At school, Walt's beginning to wade into more sophisticated, open-ended discussions about war and peace across modern American history. He also knows what I'm up to, with all those documents. Owen has just watched *The Lion King*, for the umpteenth time. The movie's scene, with hyenas goose-stepping like Nazi storm troopers, pops into my head.

I brush it away and look up to realize we've assumed an oddly formal, almost reverential posture, sitting at an elegantly set table, listening to NPR's reports about allied planes attacking Saddam's Republican Guard positions near Baghdad while the U.S. Army has driven to within fifty miles of the Iraqi capital.

Cornelia asks me to please turn off the radio. I jump up—yes, of course.

I turn off the radio as Cornelia and I bring out the big serving dishes of corned beef in its cabbage stew and homemade Irish soda bread.

She suggests we say grace. Walt has been saying grace each summer night at his camp, which has Episcopal roots, and Cornelia has been thinking it'd be a nice tradition to start, another one she was raised with.

We go around the table, each of us offering a bit of something—all now having joined hands—until we come round to Owen.

"Would you like to say something, honey?"

He looks at Cornelia quizzically, confused it seems about the concept. "It's just talking to God," she says. "That's all."

Owen nods once. He understands.

"Dear God," he says after a moment. "Let people around the world tonight find peace and honor, freedom, and choice." He stops, looks at each of us. "And may we at this table always be a part of one another."

Walt looks at me, startled. "Are you giving him this stuff?" He can see otherwise from my hanging jaw. Cornelia's cheeks are already wet.

I know Walt so well—we can exchange looks that house volumes of shared understanding, common reference; his little brother, still, barely talking at all. And then a window opens.

We begin to eat and I think . . . *of Billy Felch?*

I haven't thought once of this man for ten years. Suddenly, I feel like he's sitting at the table with us. Our only model for an autistic man had been the dreaded Raymond Babbitt. Until this moment, that is, when Dustin Hoffman gets bumped by someone I actually know. I wrote about him for the front page of the *Wall Street Journal* the year Owen was born, and *I had no idea he was autistic.* Clearly, he was.

What originally drew me to Felch was a tip from a student in a journalism night class I was teaching at Harvard: she knew a "perpetual mourner" in Seabrook, New Hampshire, not far from Boston. I'd always been fascinated by someone who mourned perpetually, probably because, around the time my father died, I saw *Harold and Maude* in which Ruth Gordon goes to strangers' funerals as a way to stay in touch with the ephemera of life. What I found in Seabrook couldn't have been further from all that: a portly, middle-aged man who fixed lawnmower engines from a garage behind his house on the edge of town. Billy first became known to the local clergy when, as an eleven-year-old boy, he arrived at the funeral service of an elderly friend and pounded out "Old Iron Cross" on the organ by ear. He played it every Sunday at church after that and, as a teenager, started to show up at funerals on his motorcycle to direct traffic and assist in any way possible, which is what he'd been doing for the three decades since. I just thought he was a good-natured oddball, who seemed to remember everyone's birthday and relentlessly delivered candy to kids at the local hospital. As I was standing with him at his garage, trying futilely to make both eye contact and conversation, he looked over my shoulder at the tail end of a passing car. "Not from here," he said, under his breath. I asked how he knew. "Not a license plate from our town." I wrote all that up through my lens, my life context, as an eccentric man who kept tabs on the comings and goings, life and death, of a small town.

But none of that spurred the recollection, as Owen finished his prayer. It was something that never appeared in the article: an incident where Billy received a call in the dead of winter from the wife of a Seabrook pastor who'd retired and moved to western Massachusetts. She told Billy that her husband was dying and needed to see him, immediately, and Billy drove that motorcycle three hours in a blizzard to rush to his bedside. The old pastor said he couldn't die unless Billy told God that he was a good man, who'd lived a good life, a life of kindness. Which Billy did, praying, as he held the hand of his old friend, ushering him out of this hard world.

I originally wrote about the dying pastor in three or four paragraphs to end the story. The *Journal*'s page one editor said it was too schmaltzy.

Schmaltz. For the unaware, it generally means overly sentimental, with the best working definition, for a writer at least, coming from J. D. Salinger, who says, sentimentality—"the great enemy of writing"—means giving your characters "more love than God gives them." It's not just that, though, at least for nonfiction. It's giving them more love than society gives them, because maybe to do so upends the order of things; namely, our surety in the ways we measure human value and some of us see ourselves, quite comfortably, as better than others. I agreed with my editor. That thing about Billy and the pastor was schmaltzy. So I cut it.

Now, looking back, I wish I hadn't. But that still leaves the matter of what exactly happened that night at dinner. The last thing I'd ever want to do is sentimentalize my own son. I tossed in bed that night trying to settle what I saw that was indisputable and fact based. On a night when the nation, and much of the world, is gripped with tension—an anxiety we're sure Owen could feel, even if he didn't understand all its particulars—we asked him to say a little something. Maybe what's missing in him, the reasonable doubts and common hesitations, allows him to look upward, unfettered, in a way that focuses some invisible capacities. After all, it's a big deal to talk to God, if you believe he can actually hear you. All of this I think about, walking the floors as dawn approaches, wondering how it's possible, after all of our efforts, that just about the most cogent and heartfelt thing my son has ever uttered was to a deity I didn't much believe in.

• • •

Cornelia and I have not slept well for years. And we're still not, but the quality of the insomnia has changed. It's more like the way we didn't sleep after the kids were born, when the newness of it all, of a new life, screaming its presence, revealing itself, made us press ourselves and each other to stay awake.

Owen is making some kind of move, here, with the sidekicks. The lines keep running through my head. I think about them when I wake in the morning. Cornelia and I talk about them that night.

There's no doubt, now, that he sees what we see: that kids of all stripes—typical kids, his old classmates at Lab School, are moving on, while he's left behind. He chooses the Earthworm as his character and then the sidekicks emerge, sketch by sketch, in the difficult months after he's ejected from Lab. His response is to embrace it, the pain of it, and be a protector of the discarded. Of course, that was my job, mine and Cornelia's, to protect him against judgment and loss, to ease him forward into a warm bath of a life, as independent as possible, on terms we would do our best to set. That was bound to fail at some point. I suppose we knew that. What choice, though, did we have, walking around as he does, without the protective skin of social instinct or acuity, his heart so utterly and perilously exposed.

Exposed, yes, but beating in ways we suddenly can see. He starts giving sidekick identities to his classmates at Ivymount, so many of whom are so heavily burdened—some with physical infirmities and plenty of autistic kids with little speech. But they have qualities that he's identifying—this one was loyal, that one gentle, another one silly in some lighthearted way that makes Owen laugh. Instantaneously, he races across the pantheon of sidekicks and, for each of them, finds a match.

The heroes in many fables tend to be flat, constructed with a sort of solid, accessible simplicity that allows readers or viewers to hop aboard to travel the hero's journey. As well, it's often the supporting players in these fables who are more varied and vivid. Even in the earliest Disney movies, the first sidekicks—Goofy, Pluto, and then Donald—often carried confusions, frailties, foolishness, pride, vanity, and hard-won, often reluctantly learned, insights. The spectrum of complex human emotions is housed with the sidekicks.

There are hundreds of them in Disney. Every hero has sidekicks, usually several of them. Some are goofy, or dim-witted; some comical, some resourceful. There are protective ones, loving ones, wise ones.

Owen has become an aficionado. We can barely keep up. In the carpeted cavern downstairs, he seems to be developing a vocabulary, using the sidekicks, through which he can organize his emotions.

Including, what he feels for us. On Cornelia's birthday in late February, he draws her a picture of Big Mama—the owl from *The Fox and the Hound*, who takes in the orphaned red fox, Tod—because, Owen tells her, handing her his card, "She is the gentlest and most caring of all the lady sidekicks."

For Father's Day in June, he gives me a drawing of Merlin, next to which he wrote, "You are the best Dad I could ever have. Thank you for being so guideful." I tell him I love it, of course, and that I'm honored to be among the wisest sidekicks, Merlin. But "guideful" is not really a word. What does it mean?

"A sidekick who is a loving and a careful guide." He doesn't care if it's not a word. In his language, it now is.

In September, on the day of Walt's fifteenth birthday, he draws Aladdin and writes, "To the greatest brother I ever had." By now, sketchbooks are piled high—hundreds of drawings—but this is the only hero he's drawn, this one picture. He so often watches his brother, intently, from the corner of his eye: Walt with his gang of friends, moving in and out of the house; in his football uniform, muddy, after a game on Sidwell's junior high team; talking on the phone to what might be a girl.

A few days after his birthday, Walt takes a break from homework to catch a little *Dumbo* in the basement, wanting Owen to fast-forward until the end when the little elephant, learning to spread those giant ears like wings, soars across the big top, firing peanuts at the cruel elephants, proud and vain, who'd ostracized him. Walt always liked this part. "Certainly gives it back to those nasty elephants in the end, huh, Owie?" And Owen laughs—"Yeah, Walter, Dumbo flies."

"Those elephants really deserve it, don't they?"

"I don't know—do they?"

In many ways, the only other boy Owen really knows, and knows well, is his brother. He's his only model.

And Walt is drawn as the hero. Owen, who wields the pencil, has told us—in no uncertain terms—that he, himself, lives among the sidekicks.

•   •   •

Cornelia slips into Owen's bedroom and retrieves his backpack, turning the knob before she gently closes the door so as not to wake him. Walt's already crashed. It's autumn 2003, football season, and with afternoon practice, he's exhausted following a long night of homework. She's spending a lot of time alone, with me all but living in the converted garage behind the house—and distracted when I'm not—with thousands of internal government documents swimming in my head. I have to work like a madman, especially with a book deadline looming.

Sitting on the stairs, she pulls Owen's binder from the backpack and opens to the color-coded insert for math. It's simple addition, two plus two—math that he did three years ago at Lab. She flips to reading. Same thing. The most basic stuff—the cat runs, the dog sits. God knows, he worked hard, back when, to master this level of material and move beyond it. Going backward—which is what he's doing—is a sin. She thinks about Sally Smith and what she'd say to her if they met on the street. If only.

In a compartment next to the dispiriting academic binder is a modest and cherished counterpoint—his piano book. He's begun taking lessons once a week from Ivymount's sixty-something music teacher, Ruthlee, at her home. He's making steady progress and, in a way, so are we. About a dozen children and adults with special needs crowded into her basement a few times a year for recitals— we've just been to our first—and we left the room subtly altered. The students are about one-third Down syndrome, two-thirds spectrum, with a few other disabilities mixed in. Many managed extraordinarily well. Watching a forty-year-old woman with Down syndrome—a twenty-five-year student of Adler—tap out notes, after what you know are countless hours of toil, was a soul-shaping experience, capped by the moment the student stood unevenly and bowed, as everyone applauded themselves raw, led by her mother, just about Ruthlee's age.

Maybe this doesn't draw such powerful emotions from everyone. But it does for Cornelia and me. And it's not because we pity her, or her mother, who must remain in a mother's role for her long life. We know better—bonds of love are not to be pitied. It has to do with how each perfectly arrayed note once scribbled by Mozart, Beethoven, Chopin—or infectious pop song celebrating love, hummed by all—is offered, faithfully, unflinchingly, by someone who must live so much of their life defined by some visible and enveloping imperfection. We all work so hard to present ourselves as perfect, win laurels, and rise above those who cannot. It is our nature but one we might rise above. Or so it felt as twelve or thirteen such performances—including Owen playing a piece and usually belting out one of his Disney anthems—were haltingly mustered, with each performer feeling, as the applause washed across them, like a creature of indisputable perfection. At some point, I whispered to Cornelia, "If there's a God, he's in this room."

In the half-light, Cornelia flips through the piano book of songs he's learned to play, a feat she never could have imagined years back. In her head, she can almost hear him tapping out these songs. This rises. His academic work falls. *Aren't music and math handled by the same part of the brain?* It makes no sense. She shoves all the books back into his pack.

• • •

The next afternoon, a Wednesday in late September she pulls into the parking lot of an office tucked behind a commercial strip in Kensington, Maryland, just north of DC. Owen gets tutored once a week here by an educational specialist, Suzie Blattner, who has been working with him since he was three.

Cornelia and Suzie are in a sisterly relationship, eight years along. She's seen every stage, every twist, looking at what's being assigned in school—what's in his backpack—and walking Owen through it, turning the written equations or mysterious words into something visual, or vivid; the symbolic and theoretical made real. As important as anything is knowing how to keep him focused, on task. "Look at me, Owen—look in my eyes." Suzie has said that a thousand times.

At this week's session, Cornelia gives Owen a few extra minutes in the waiting room; tells him she'll be right back.

"Suzie, we're going backward," she says a moment later, dropping low into a kid-sized chair. Suzie sits down across from her as they slide worksheets across a table built for kindergartners. Suzie knows he's lost ground and figured Cornelia would eventually be here, ready again to sound the battle cry.

"Why did we fight so hard to get him into Lab and to keep him there," Cornelia says, "just to have him lose it all now?" Suzie knows Cornelia was battered by the ouster from Lab and thankful Ivymount took him back. But a year has passed. It's time.

"I can only be with him an hour or two a week, maybe add another session," Suzie says, pushing aside the worksheets. She says it's not that they don't focus on academics where he is. It's just at a lower level. Their emphasis, for obvious reasons, is tilted more toward building up the basics of social interaction.

Both already know this, and they sit quietly. In the typical world, parents grow close to, say, a pediatrician they see once every six months. Cornelia has been seeing Suzie once a week since Clinton's first term. At this point, the two of them can communicate quite ably without words.

Cornelia rises to go fetch Owen. "A lot more could be done for Owen, too—on the *'social piece.'*"

Social interaction is not usually viewed as a *piece* of anything. Everything sits within it. Typical people interact as a matter of desire and inclination. They're shy or gregarious, some love solitude or can't bear it. They engage, or don't, as they wish or are able to.

That's a difficult nature/nurture line to draw for anyone. But for Cornelia the turf between will and capability, between the learned and the innate, is quicksand. Owen's sensory equipment may be so out of sync that he can't interact even if he wanted to. And that disability may so strongly diminish the joy of human interaction that he has little will or desire to reach out and build those capacities. If, in fact, they can be built. And around you go—trying anything.

Which is why Cornelia crosses the hall from Suzie's office to reschedule an appointment with Christine Sproat, Owen's longtime occupational therapist who deals with the complex issues of sensory processing—namely, the way your body and brain organizes input through the various senses. New ways to study this quietly took hold in the 1970s but received a boost in the mid-1990s with the growing notoriety of Temple Grandin, the autistic author. Grandin, born in 1947 and diagnosed with autism in the early 1950s, developed in her teen years something she called a "squeeze machine"—a sort of heavily padded coffin with levers to apply pressure. The simultaneous pressure on all parts of her body made her feel settled and organized, as though her disconnected senses were pulled into integration, allowing her to more successfully go about her day. In best-selling books, Grandin's acute descriptions of the hypersensitivities she's long lived with—as well as techniques, like the machine, that have helped her navigate daily life—changed the landscape. People could now understand what autistics couldn't generally describe: *what it feels like.* Beyond the value of public understanding, it helped create many offices like the one in which Cornelia is now standing. It's filled with strange swings, fabric-covered boards, balls to throw or roll on, beams to walk across.

Christine Sproat, an energetic young occupational therapist, says she had a cancellation and can fit Owen in after he's finished getting tutored by Suzie. There's nothing new about OT, which broadens out physical therapy to focus on specific goals and include interactions with the surrounding environment. The recent growth comes from what parents and therapists noticed about autistic kids: that they were more socially available and interactive after they were squeezed, like Grandin and her machine, or spun, like a whirligig. Even after many studies, it's not all that clear why this seems to be effective—just as it's not completely clear, neurologically, why people feel certain ways after strenuous exercise—or why it seems to build underlying capacities for the senses to better integrate.

But we do it because it works. And after Suzie, Cornelia watches Owen go through his exercises, working hard on the equipment, and laughing with the ebullient Christine—like he should be with a gang of buddies—and thinks: "This kid needs some friends."

• • •

"We can get a turnout for birthday parties, because they're an event—someone's birthday—and clubs at school have weekly meetings," Cornelia says, leaning against the kitchen counter. "So what if we merge them?"

She's keeping me up. It's usually the other way around.

"Can we talk about this tomorrow?"

"Look, I have to get on this—this could change things."

"It could," I murmur. "It could. "She's attacking the "social piece" head-on. Her concept is a weekly event, a social, something a few of the boys in Owen's class would have on their schedules for every Thursday night, say, or Saturday afternoon. They'll go bowling or catch a movie and pizza. The activities could change, the kids could decide, all together, and the parents would rotate as chaperones. If it was just four kids or five, it would be a once-a-month commitment for a parent. A group makes it special and with more kids there will be more avenues for interaction, opportunities to connect. With the holiday season upon us, there's so much to do. the *Washington Post* is full of great activities.

The next morning, she's revved and ready, working the class phone list, calling the moms.

A week later she's sitting in the kitchen, wondering if her cell phone would break if she threw it. Must have been a dozen calls, at this point. It sure was a good idea. Everyone acknowledged that. Their kid will be so happy. *Let me get back to you.* And most of them did, laying out a few problems. Cornelia was sympathetic. They had lives like ours, with many of the moms and dads both working outside the home, and facing a full complement of stressors. Call by call, the brittleness of family life, with kids needing support—and the parents, too—became a theme. Every family was locked in a set of crafted rituals that they dare not break: when one parent drops a son off at therapy; when the other picks him up; a day reserved for a special family activity, an afternoon when he's always tired, especially with some medication they're just trying.

By this morning, she's cut her hopes and losses, figuring if she could start with just Owen and one other kid, maybe it would grow. Social connections are about finding one's level, a level of comfort or kinship, whether it's the jocks finding their table, and the nerds finding theirs at a typical school, or kids in Owen's realm who often will pair up with kids who match their capacity to engage. As his social skills were growing at Lab, he found some of that, building friendships with kids of similar, if slightly stronger, capabilities. He was rising to meet them. This is harder to find at Ivymount, a lifeboat to kids with a wide array of disabilities, many of them quite severe. But there's one mom left to call, of a kid—Phillip—who Owen seems to like. He's also one of the more able and interactive kids in the mix. This could be his match.

The mom has been away on business but is now back and taking the day off—and is in good spirits when Cornelia calls.

They seem to hit it off, which is encouraging, even if not all that surprising. After all, Cornelia cut her teeth on the mean streets of Fairfield, Connecticut, where Catholic dads—many of them commuting to Wall Street—filled large houses with broods of Matthews, Marks, Johns, and Marys; homes with eight, ten, or thirteen children, who ran freely, house to house, kitchen to kitchen, and then out across driveways and sidewalks to the trusty woods. It was a kid's world. You learned how to get along.

And Cornelia did. She could tell a ribald story—voted Best Sense of Humor in her senior class, her social skills were admired and her manner—gentle, steady, and attentive—had built friendships to last up and down the East Coast.

But you live through your kids; a circumstance, here, that created acute distress for a woman who could always find a friend. Now she couldn't beg, borrow, or steal one for her son.

She and this very nice mother, Helen, have been talking, all warm and willing, for fifteen minutes. Every subject is crossed, both telling their stories like seasoned pros—upbringing, college, husband, work, kids, and then the special-needs battles both families face. Their life is very much like ours, Cornelia thinks. Like Owen, Phillip has also mixed a bit into the mainstream and has one brother, too, a year younger. Helen says they wrestle with the same issues we do, of trying to find ways for the little brother to include Phillip, whenever possible, in groups of typical kids.

Cornelia lays out her original idea, runs through how it's been a difficult week, and then drops her last card. Actually, throws it down with a laugh: "At this point, if someone just invited Owen over, I'd be happy."

Helen pauses. "The problem is that the only night's that possible, with our crazy schedule, is Friday."

Cornelia cuts in, excitedly. "No, Friday's a great night for Owen."

Helen seems to regroup as Cornelia tries to close it. "You know, Helen, he's always talking about Phillip." Okay, he did one time, but close enough.

"No, and Phillip always talks about Owen. But as I was saying," Helen continues, "Friday evening we always have a pizza party with Phillip, his little brother, and his brother's friends."

The line goes quiet for a few seconds. Cornelia's on her knees, but she will not beg or speak the words forming in her tightening gut: *"Would it kill you just to have him come over and eat pizza, just to sit with Phillip and his precious little brother, with his precious little oh-so-normal friends, and just be? He's gentle as can be, he really is, he wouldn't hurt anyone. And we'll reciprocate, tenfold. For God's sake, he just wants to have a friend."*

But, of course, she doesn't say that—no one would.

And Helen shuts the door: "So that's the problem, Cornelia. That one night is already taken."

Cornelia's not sure she can speak. But she does.

"Right, Helen. I understand."

chapter six

A JOURNEY SONG

On an early March evening in 2004 I slip down into the basement and settle on the couch. I've started to spend more time down here with Owen, just the two of us, watching movies, talking about his sidekicks. It's not so much for him.

I'm feeling some acute stress and this helps. Specifically, I'm under investigation by the U.S. government for supposedly making off with an unspecified number of classified documents among those nineteen thousand.

It's been going on for nearly two months since Paul O'Neill and I were on *60 Minutes* in early January, two days before *The Price of Loyalty* was published. On the show, they flashed the cover sheet from a classified packet from January 2001, the first National Security Council meeting of the Bush presidency. I didn't have that document or any classified documents—they were all cleaned off the discs I received from O'Neill. But the cover sheets weren't, and I used this cover sheet to discover that from his first weeks in office, long before 9/11, Bush was intent on finding any rationale to complete his father's unfinished business and overthrow Hussein, including capturing Iraq's oil fields. I told Leslie Stahl to make sure the broadcast noted I didn't have the underlying classified packet. They didn't. And the next morning an official from the U.S. Treasury Department called our house. He asked Cornelia if she was my wife (after some hesitation she acknowledged matrimony) and then told her that agents would be coming over to seize documents believed to be in my writer's studio in the backyard.

The ten seconds it took him to explain all this was plenty of time for her to summon her "How dare you?" impulse—finely tuned from years with Owen—telling him that her husband was protected by the First Amendment and that "no one will be coming to my house to seize anything." But if he left his phone number, she'd be happy to find me and have me call him back.

She did find me—in mid-interview for a taped segment on NPR—and we talked for a few minutes about lawyers I might call. I did, and several five-hundred-dollar-an-hour Washington lawyers called the Treasury Department back by the end of business that January day, starting a legal battle that's still raging by early March, when Owen and I settle in for a screening.

"Hey, buddy."

"Hey, Dad."

"Whatchya watching?"

"*The Lion King*—I love this movie."

"And you know what it's based on?" I ask.

"Hamlet!"

We've often talked of this movie's roots and he likes getting that answer right. I think it's because knowing what's behind a movie that means so much to him is satisfying, in the same way he relishes trolling through the deep data of film credits—about the careers of James Earl Jones (the lion king, Mufasa) or Jeremy Irons (his villainous and fratricidal brother, Scar). Knowing this is Shakespeare with lions gets behind the wall of flickering light, where the makers of this thing he loves are hiding, winking at him.

Or maybe it's just to please me. I like Owen to summon this Hamlet reference when friends—both Walt's and ours—come by.

He often has, almost always at my bidding. I want people to see him as smarter, and more able, than they might otherwise. I figure they'll treat him then with more care, or interest, or respect, and that he'll respond to that. It's about binding him to what pretty much everyone in America north of early childhood is supposed to know. Because connecting him to all that, strand by strand, is my definition of self-awareness, and those who are not self-aware are swiftly identified and preyed upon.

So when Owen, now splayed across the black leather chair, asks me, "Is George Bush angry at you?" I'm perversely delighted he knows what's happening in the world and how it's impacting our household. After interviews with media across the globe, I'm forced to answer him plainly, in a way that doesn't induce concern. I say I'm just doing my job and the president is doing his—a simple, frank response that's better than almost anything I'd said in all those interviews. He asks, "Are we okay?" I say we are. And he turns back to the movie. He believes Cornelia and me when we tell him things. Doesn't poke around for subtext, agenda, or hidden meanings.

So I don't either, a moment later, as we watch that marching hyena scene. Did Owen ask me that question about Bush, knowing this scene was coming? Can't really say. His prayer a few nights after the Iraq invasion helped shed any remaining doubts that he absolutely breathes in ambient tension, from inside the house or beyond it. He can't process much of the spoken word that's offered face-to-face—too stimulating in some way, his therapists say—but have Cornelia whisper something to me with the slightest emotional tone, and, from even two floors away, we'll hear a polite but urgent: "Everything okay?" "Yes, Owie!" Cornelia will shout back. "Dad and I are just having a discussion."

On the screen, Simba—exiled after his father's murder—is having a heart-to-heart with the meerkat, Timon, and the warthog, Pumbaa

(Rosencrantz and Guildenstern), who help him forget his troubles. Owen laughs, singing the African-themed song, "*Hakuna matata . . . it's our problem-free philosophy, hakuna matata.*" I'm there, singing beside him. And when Owen dances before the screen, I do that, as well. He's forgetting his troubles down here. I am, too, by entering the context where he lives—a river of symbols that flow in this half-light, far beneath the noisy surface-world of passing events and impressions.

Drawing him to that surface, connecting him to the wider world of conventional knowledge may be futile. There's a hook for Hamlet that spurs his interest. That's a gift. Try asking him who invented the light bulb or why it rains or when the Civil War was fought (right century gets you credit) or what seven times three is, and you'll often get a blank stare. Some of this type of general knowledge was beginning to stick in the last days at Lab, when he was prompted to know things of no particular interest to stay in the mix with new friends, but that—along with his skills in writing and math—have since slipped.

I want to fix that, fix him, but lately Cornelia is saying, maybe we have to think more about just enjoying him for who he is and not trying to improve or repair him every minute of every day.

It's a difficult impulse for me to control. I want to fix everything, make it just so, make it right. But singing "Hakuna Matata" with him eases me and my corrective impulses. The movie comes around to the scene where Mufasa's ghost comes to Simba, now maturing into young adulthood, and beckons him to fulfill his destiny. We watch it, silently, the ghost of a dead father hovering over a teenager, telling him who he is meant to be.

"I had another dream about Big Walter," Owen says quietly, referring to my father, who, of course, he's never met. His eyes stay on the screen.

There had already been a first dream, a few weeks earlier, which he'd told me about when we were flipping through some animation books in his room. He just blurted it out: "Big Walter visited me in my dream." It took me a second to get my bearings. I don't dream about my father and have often wondered why. I just asked Owen what my dad looked like in his dream; he said, like the picture of him (full-bodied, smiling, just before the cancer hit at forty-five) that hangs on the wall in the den. That was it, all he said.

This time, I don't respond, wanting to figure out some perfect thing to say that'll encourage him to tell me more. So we just watch as Simba fulfills his destiny. His sidekicks—the protective hornbill, Zazu, the wise old baboon, Rafiki—make it possible. They usher him forward. Owen drinks it in, gets up, and stretches, requited, now, in this underground universe, his safe place of family and fable.

"You said Big Walter was in another dream," I mention casually. "So what happened?"

Owen hadn't sensed I was waiting to hear more. He just got involved in the movie.

"Well, he was an old man this time with gray hair. He had lived his whole life. He was gentle and kind, and we talked and played. And he told me he loved me."

•   •   •

The crowd gathers on a splendid spring afternoon—April 17, 2004—in a modernist synagogue, all blond wood, soaring asymmetrical ceilings and skylights, built for sunny days.

It will be one for Owen—got to be. Though we, like the two hundred or so well-wishers now settling into their seats, are not sure what to expect.

Almost anything could happen. Which is why many kids like Owen don't go through anything like the formal bar mitzvah ceremony, a ritual that rests on study and performance and meeting expectations of what a thirteen-year-old boy can—and now must—do to be accepted as an adult in a Jewish community.

Being blissfully and sometimes disastrously self-directed, either Owen feels it or it doesn't happen. He could easily decide to say a prayer, nod in affirmation, and walk off the stage.

We've spent six months trying to ensure otherwise. It has been an almost frenzied struggle for the entire family, from the moment—the previous fall—when I asked Owen if he wanted to have a bar mitzvah like Walt's, or something simpler. He said, "Like Walter did it. Now it's my turn."

Between those two sentences stretched an uncharted landscape and a set of deep chasms. Bridges needed to be built. Strong ones. Bar mitzvahs actually do justice to that well-worn phrase "rite of passage." They're every bit as fraught as weddings, but with unpredictable adolescents, who generally need a lot of urging.

For Owen, we naturally start with the movies. Were there movies with Jewish themes that could provide handles, anything to work with, to draw him in?

We went with one indisputable favorite: *An American Tail*, a 1986 Universal animated film about mice from Russia, with thick accents, who come to America because "the streets are paved with cheese." It's Jews as mice, led by one of Owen's most beloved characters, Fievel, the young mouse who is separated from his family and wanders through the gritty circus of 1890s New York. He has lots of sidekicks helping him fulfill his destiny, most of them among a set of Jews/mice that pretty much match—mouse for Jew—my ancestors who came through Ellis Island. After several viewings, this offered a strong opening hand: "The Jews, Owen, have always been history's sidekicks." That, he definitely got!

As for the portion of the Torah that bar and bat mitzvah boys and girls read in mid-April, we got a lucky break: a passage from Leviticus where Moses receives the Ten Commandments. There, too, was a convenient animated movie: *The Prince of Egypt*, the 1998 DreamWorks rendition of the Exodus story. It was a movie he'd seen and didn't like, because, he said, "There were no sidekicks for comic relief." But we forced mandatory viewings—our version of Hebrew school—and eventually talked through the commandments and issues of right and wrong. He took to this, to a structure of dos and don'ts. This is common among spectrum kids. They like a rule, which, by its nature, narrows the many options of unpredictable behavior. We read through the English translations of the Ten Commandments and other rules listed in his passage from Leviticus. He nodded along. Some seemed to strike him, especially the ones that prohibit preying on the weak.

But then he went about on his own business, writing up a speech—each bar mitzvah boy or girl has to give one, based on what they read in Hebrew from the Torah. He wrote down rules that he felt were important to him in colored markers on a few pages of his sketchbook. We told him to do what he does in prayers before dinner—now, just to write it down—and that we'd have to hear it at least a week before the big day. He'd been offering prayers at the dinner table a few nights a week for almost a year, ever since the Iraq prayer. We knew he had it in him, but only if we got out of his way and he really felt like he was talking to God.

But the central task—applying study skills that most kids pick up in school to learn to read from the Torah—was simply untenable. He was never going to read Hebrew. My skills peaked precisely thirty-four years prior at my bar mitzvah and had diminished steadily since. We needed a tutor; one with the patience of, well, a saint. What we found was a gray-haired, Justice Department lifer, a lawyer/prosecutor exuding a quiet, no-nonsense firmness that would've impressed Eliot Ness. Miriam, who went by Mim, was also the granddaughter of the founder of Reconstructionist Judaism, our fast-growing slice of the faith that weaves traditional worship with a progressive sensibility, embraces mixed marriages (like ours), and advances its founding credo of making religion more relevant to daily life. As for a personal credo, Mim tapped an even deeper well: in the 1920s, her mother was the very first girl in the United States to have a *bat* mitzvah. *Ever.* This left her sixty-something daughter, who'd volunteered with special needs kids, with a powerful affinity for boosting someone many folks would not consider suitable for participation in such a rigorous, ancient ceremony; a purpose and patience that guided her, hour after hour, as she sat—reciting Hebrew and discussing it, in a way Owen could understand.

All of this is pretext, a behind-the-curtain drama that is invisible to the expectant, mixed religion crowd now settled into the sanctuary of Adat Shalom in Bethesda: a gathering of Suskinds from New York and Florida, Kennedys from Connecticut, and a far-flung array of friends from Boston to Washington, many of Owen's teachers and therapists, along with a few classmates and their parents. Just about everyone he knows in his life and a few folks from the congregation, who came around out of curiosity. This was the temple's first-ever *mincha* service, what the ultra-orthodox, who pray all day, call their afternoon worship. For us, it was a way of meeting a basic requirement: that the bar mitzvah take place in an official capacity before the community into which a boy or girl is now to be accepted as an adult—without the prospect of things going haywire in front of the temple's whole congregation.

But the goal for all these elaborate plans is stark in its simplicity: for Owen to have his "turn," as much like Walt—and every other Jewish kid—as is humanly possible.

And this subtle pressure and hope, to make it happen for this kid, ripples through everyone involved in the emotive choreography of a Torah service. One after another, people get summoned to the stage, called the *bima*—with the Hebrew word *"ya'ah'mode,"* for "rise up"—to usher Owen forward through the service. The procession starts with Cornelia's parents, who, together, read a Sanskrit prayer in English. Cornelia's father, John, a man with a famously narrow emotive range, caps it with a surprise flourish. "Owen, may you always walk in sunshine. May you never want for more. May Irish angels rest their wings right beside your door," he recites, his voice cracking with emotion on the last word.

Cornelia squeezes my hand. "Oh, boy," she whispers, "here we go."

Sitting beside her in the front row, I feel the pull of a current, a deep mysterious thing that runs on its own twisting path from the *James and the Giant Peach* play, where the kids lifted Owen on their shoulders, to a warm sensation of this whole room now here to lift him. As people are called forth for the many ritual roles—opening the ark where the Torah is held, removing it, carrying it around the room, removing the heavy velvet and silver ornamentation so it can be unscrolled, and then reading short passages, preceded and followed by short prayers—you can see them whispering to Owen, there in their midst—"This way, Owie" or "Walk beside me, buddy"—as they nudge him along, lifting him.

Or maybe he's lifting us. Lines are blurred. As Cornelia and I are called to the *bima* to present him with his prayer shawl, or *tallit*, we're all smiles and a little unsteady. This moment, when the parents say something to the child, is a moment of oddly public intimacies, where you encourage and praise your child, express love, and reach for some religious verity . . . with a roomful of eavesdroppers. It's spiritually voyeuristic—with the sorts of things you may never have said to your kids turned into oratory.

Cornelia tells the story of Walt's friend who once called Owen a "magic boy," and she now tells him it's true, "because you get so much joy out of life and see the wonderful things so many of us miss." She's speaking about his goodness, for sure, but also hinting about how that makes him vulnerable. "My prayer for you Owen," she says, "is that you always see life with your heart and that you trust in all the people here today who hold you in their hearts with such love, and you continue to teach others with all the gifts God has given you." To the trained ear, it's a plea that this boy, with gentle gifts, will need help and protection and caring, up ahead, in a long life, which is, hereby, the obligation of everyone in this room—a verbal contract affirmed, Cornelia fervently hopes, with silent nods, row to row.

Throughout her speech, Owen is looking all over—the skylights, the thick rug under his best shoes—and barely at Cornelia or me. It's gaze aversion. It's his way. I pull him gently toward us, holding both his hands, slipping a "Hey, buddy" in between her lines to compel his attention.

And it's no different for my turn, as I tell a crafted story about Owen to Owen, with witnesses, that I hope will subtly alter everyone's view of him and his of himself. I'm trying to bind it—just as Cornelia has done—into a contract with everyone in the room to hedge against my own fears. I cite a nascent shift we'd seen in the preceding months where he decided to start calling us Mom and Dad, not Mommy and Daddy, and mentioned, once in passing, that he was giving some of his Disney movies "a rest" in favor of a growing passion for the live-action Batman films, where Tim Burton, he said, "turned Gotham into a dark, gloomy character." We figured, with the bar mitzvah coming he was taking cues from Walt and, in some subconscious calculus, I wanted to lock that in, to encourage his reach for the socially acceptable and age-appropriate. This was both for Owen and for everyone in the room who might help along this adolescent maturation. So, after framing this little story as part of "becoming a man," I recite Owen's own words from a month before back to him: "Owen, you told me 'It's time for me to leave the Disney villains behind and move past little kid things. That it's time for Batman, for a little darkness and complexity.'" Of course, this draws laughs.

And even bigger ones, when Owen responds—"And Sponge-Bob!"—basically killing the whole gambit.

"But, Owen, *some* darkness and complexity?"

"And SpongeBob!" he exclaims again (more laughs), and—leaving it there—I push to close it with a grasp at something spiritual, talking about his special quality of talking to God, of feeling his presence. "And as you grow and explore and reach for the stars, keep talking to God. And, while you're at it, tell him thanks from us, for bringing you into our lives."

Then we're done speaking on his behalf. Cornelia says love him the way he is, or else; I say help him change, so he can make his own way in an unforgiving world—a pair of political/emotional statements of parent to child, read from typed pages shaking lightly in our hands.

We step down, as he puts the prayer shawl over his shoulders and steps to the podium; the Torah, unscrolled, awaits. This we watch from our seats—nothing we can do now; just him up there, with the imperious Mim, his tutor, on one side, and Rachel Hersh—the temple's Judy Collins-like cantor leading the service on the other.

But he seems calm and starts looking with intent curiosity at the sea of eyes. He's never had so many people look at him. He appears free of fear and the performance anxiety that usually accompanies knowing what people think and caring so deeply about it. And he's got an asset here: the memory that allowed him to store and encode a few dozen hours of Disney films, though—at the start—he couldn't understand the English any better than he now doesn't understand Hebrew. He doesn't memorize anything he doesn't care about. But Mim whispers the first word of his Torah portion, and it's clear he cares, chanting line after line of Hebrew, looking out at the crowd, Mim by his side, silently reading each word in the old scroll—something she often does in services, as the no-nonsense guardian of the sacred book—her lips moving gently. After a few minutes, he's

finished with this long and startling recitation. She nods. *Perfect.*
And after he recites the closing prayer, perfect again, she smiles and
holds out her hand. He palms it, a gentle high five, and she gets out
the word *"ya'ah'mode"* trying to call forward those to now redress the
Torah—before her voice falters and sudden tears blind her. Seeing
this woman cry kills me, and Cornelia, too, in some echo, I suppose,
of a thousand years of girls who were told they didn't belong up here,
either. And Mim—genuinely surprised, like someone caught in a
spring shower—wipes her eyes and slips off the bima.

And all this was before he got to the English.

We knew what was coming—we'd heard the speech. It was like
a four-paragraph-long grace before dinner, exercising this invisible
prayer muscle of his. It makes no sense, really. Ask him to write
about what he's read in a third-grade textbook or heard a teacher
say, repeatedly, and you get two thin sentences, with simple verbs
and misspellings. Ask him to dig deep inside for something to say
to God, in front of all the people he knows, and it flows like music.

And we know everyone in the room is about to witness this
contradiction—just as we know the way many of them look at the
"left behind" as Owen would say. The way we used to.

He says that his Torah portion contains many commandments
about ethics, "about right and wrong," including "one of the most
important rules in this chapter: that you should not put a stumbling
block in front of a blind person. This means you should never trick
someone or be unkind to them. A blind person has a handicap and
God tells us that we should never take advantage of another person's
weakness."

As he talks, he rhythmically punches the end of each sentence—
something we told him makes for good public speaking—and he
says that his passage tells us to "love thy neighbor as thyself" and that
neighbor doesn't just mean the person living next door but "all the
people we know and meet in our life."

He pauses. Adjusts the pages. Then, up comes his index finger. It's not clear if it's accusatory or just keeping time, like a metronome. "Sometimes it's hard for people to love their neighbors as themselves," he says, pointing matter-of-factly to the crowd. "People can be angry or jealous or mean or hateful or rude or scared and that can keep them from treating their neighbor with love and understanding." He flips a page. "Sometimes people are scared of people who are not like them. They can be mean and ignore them sometimes." His voice goes soft as he says this last sentence, like he's talking to himself, in an empty room, and then he looks up, almost surprised to see the full house. "That would make you scared or sad if someone treated you that way, wouldn't it?"

Now he's talking right to them, everyone at once, his index finger pointing out each word.

"I feel like I'm a special person because God made me special." He nods. His lips purse. "God gave me strength and courage and a big heart."

He looks out for a long minute. We see his eyes moving across the faces, studying some as they grimace with suppressed emotion, others as they speak with their nods. He's clearly trying to connect, to all of them at once. Then he turns back to the speech for a line that we know he feels most strongly.

"God wants us to treat everyone in our life like they're special, too."

• • •

If you ask people years later what they remember from the speech, their memories tend to stop with that line.

The few who recall that Owen went on to talk about his dinnertime prayers and how he "prayed that God would take care of Granny and Lizzy and make them all better"—tend to be in the

Kennedy family, who had been struggling with their matriarch's lung cancer for the past year, and the cancer that Cornelia's sister, Lizzy, was battling at the time of the bar mitzvah.

A handful who remember he ended his speech with "My prayers always start with the word *hope*—I like the word *hope*," tend to be from my side, who know that the word *hatikva* means *hope* in Hebrew. That's the song—the Israeli national anthem—he then played on the piano to finish the service, looking up from the sheet music and across the eyes of the guests, like he did when he recited Hebrew.

Memory is like that. A hook—some powerful association or moment of changed perspective—that helps keep it locked in tight, fresh for retrieval, years hence.

Which is why no one in attendance that day will forget the way one very unique young man told them how all of us should be treated, in the eyes of God, as though we are special.

At a reception after the service, Paul O'Neill and Cedric Jennings ask pointed questions about Owen and what autistic kids are capable of. I tell them a bit about the sidekicks and heroes. O'Neill laughs—"I suppose I was a sidekick to President Bush, but I'm not sure if he was hero or villain." The church-bred Cedric wonders if Owen would ever consider becoming a preacher.

My mother, Shirl, a former concert pianist and schoolteacher—whose second husband also died of cancer, just a few years after my father—has long felt that a dark cloud was following her. She couldn't help but see Owen's struggle as part of that, of that cloud settling over us now, and struggled to see him as anything other than damaged and diminished. After the service, she seems strangely unmoored, joyous. Something about Owen defining "special," then playing a song called "Hope," while looking directly at her, helped her see him anew. "He was really something up there," she whispers, taking me aside as the crowd moves toward the temple's reception hall. She looks intently into my eyes, as though searching for cues. "Really, Ronald, I wouldn't have believed it." She doesn't talk to me this way—ever.

A bit later, my oldest friend from childhood, also takes me aside. "Is Shirl okay? She's not her usual self, you know, missing stuff." He was right, the first to notice the early stages of Alzheimer's.

Later, visiting her in an assisted-living apartment, I would think often of that moment, and how her hard judgments—born, like any, from formative experiences and selected memory—may have been loosened by the illness, freeing her, in a way, to see with new eyes.

That, after all, was what had been happening naturally and forcefully, day by day, year to year, inside our home: the judgments Cornelia and I once housed—widely accepted suppositions about those with so-called "intellectual disabilities"—were being dislodged, often against our will, and replaced with a much deeper understanding.

Now it's happening as a group affair. The lightness we've sometimes felt, the lifting of burdens—like on the night with Iago, or the discovery of Owen's sketchbook—now seems to warm the temple's banquet hall, detectable in the glistening eyes of friends, the rosiness in their cheeks, the way they hug Owen.

And, to our surprise, in the way he hugs them back.

• • •

Walt wakes up on Saturday morning, the first week of May, with a plan.

Cornelia and I are away for a few days in Utah—I'm giving a speech and we are celebrating our seventeenth anniversary. As a full-blooded ninth grader, in the springtime of his young life, it's a golden weekend.

And—as we find out some time later—he's committed to make the most of it. He's really stretching his legs these days. Works hard at school—Sidwell's an intense place—but he's got his guys, his gang. His friends are hugely important to him; they're his brethren. He loves his real brother, but that's not always easy. It's hard to connect with him. Walt hoped it might get easier when he and Owen got older, but it really hasn't. We tell him just about everything concerning Owen, and he's forthcoming about lots of things; more than most kids tell their parents, but there's plenty that goes on that we're sure we miss. We go to everything all the other parents do—the school assemblies, PTA nights, the football games. Cornelia even runs quite a bit of it, a display that we're like everyone else, only more so. But we're so busy with Owen, Walt can slip away sometimes. He's always been an independent guy. He can take care of things.

Eugenia, the Ecuadorian cleaning lady who is staying with them for the weekend, is up early. Breakfast is ready when Walt and Owen get downstairs to the kitchen.

Walt's got it all planned, a grand scheme. They'll get Nathan, a good kid, Owen's age, who lives next door, and they'll all go see a movie. Eugenia can drive. Nathan—the child of our first friends from the Georgetown days—is really the only typical kid in DC that Owen's friendly with, as much as Owen can be a friend. By virtue of this, Nathan is welcomed into our house like a reigning hero and he actually has a lot in common with Walt—good guy, pretty good athlete, funny, people like him. And he's really nice to Owen.

In Walt's plan, that's what this day is about: *being really nice to Owen.* The key, as usual, will be a movie, and Owen is very much into the new one from Disney—*Home on the Range.* The thing I said at the bar mitzvah, about Owen giving up Disney for Batman and more of the teenage stuff: wishful thinking. There are some exceptions, which is good, but Disney still rules. Owen's already seen this one three times, and something about it really speaks to him. Singing the songs all the time. Crazy about it.

As they down bowls of cereal, Walt explains what's up to Owen—"How would you like to see *Home on the Range* with me and Nathan?" Owen is over the moon. "Yes, Walter!"

Eugenia drives them that afternoon, and it's a lot of fun having Nathan along. Fun for Owen, too. The movie's okay—not one of Disney's best. They're all enjoyable enough, though. It's not like it's a struggle to watch. And Owen, of course, loves them, which is a great thing. It gives you a way to talk to him, hang with him, just like normal brothers. It just has to be about Disney.

After they get home and Owen goes to the basement, Walt follows him down.

The whole day was really planned for this moment.

"Was that fun, Ow?"

"It was great. I love that movie!"

"Me, too. Listen, I need your help with something."

Owen gets a look of anticipation, then puzzlement. Walt never asks Owen for help. Ever. Why would he?

"You see, I might be having some friends over tonight, and I don't want Mom and Dad to find out, you know, when they come home."

Owen nods slowly. "What should I do?"

"Not tell them," Walt says. "We okay with that? You're not lying to them. There's just no reason they need to know."

Owen stands perfectly still for a few seconds and then nods. He gets it.

"Thanks, buddy. I really appreciate that."

$$\bullet \quad \bullet \quad \bullet$$

Walt can manage things. That's his specialty. And he's managing just fine at the beginning of the party. He told Eugenia he was having some friends over and everyone was told to go right to the basement.

Owen is mostly staying up in our room on the third floor, where Walt's set him up with pizza and his movies. And no one needs to go upstairs; the basement can hold plenty of people. Or so Walt figures, until about ten o'clock, when the seniors from the football team stop by—someone texted a guy who knew Walt—then a lot of their friends come, and people flood out into the backyard, rotating in and out to cool off because the basement's jammed, with people crushed into the den and the laundry room, with the Ping-Pong table, under which are a bunch of boxes of leftover liquor from the bar mitzvah. We overbought, so there's quite a bit of it—vodka and gin, mostly. And, boy, does it go fast with eighty kids, maybe ninety now. Everything goes fast, it seems, until Walt and his two best buddies are shampooing the rug at three in the morning. Scrubbing, laughing. Not even all that drunk. What an amazing night.

Walt feels fine the next day, though he slept maybe an hour, and he's ready—as charming as a guy can be—when he chats with Eugenia, who slept on the living room couch.

"You had many friends over, yes?" she asks.

"I invited a few and more came than I thought."

She looks at him. "You were a good boy, Walter?" she says.

"*Más o menos,*" he says, with a shrug and smile. "What can I say, Eugenia. I have a lot of friends."

When we come home that Sunday evening, Walt makes sure he greets us, all smiles. Eugenia slips out quickly, offering a sheepish smile and little else. Walt doesn't make eye contact with her, but he watches her go. He owes her, big.

A few days pass, and he's home free. It's amazing what a party like this will do to the social standing of a ninth grader. Seniors are coming up to him in the hall: "Hey . . . great party." He just nods. *Right. No problem.* Things were fine before, but they just got that much better.

Then, sitting on his bed on Tuesday night, instant messaging a buddy about the party, it dawns on him. *He's going to need to replace all that vodka and gin.* We're definitely not drinkers. We might not notice it's gone for a couple of weeks, maybe longer. Stuff sits under that Ping-Pong table collecting dust—Christmas ornaments, boxes of books, photo albums—for years, sometimes.

But the chill—somehow not even thinking about replacing that liquor—makes him flinch. He's not in the clear. Not yet. He's not sure how much Owen saw, but he definitely could see everyone in the backyard from our bedroom window. He gets up and saunters into Owen's room. "Hey, buddy."

Owen's at his desk flipping through an animation book. He looks up.

Walt's cheery—"Everything good!?"

Owen looks back. "Yes."

And they just look at each other. "Okay, just checking." In a second Walt's back on his bed, door shut, thinking hard, with quite a bit at stake, about how Owen's mind really works. At least, compared to a normal kid, how he doesn't seem to catalog things to report to parents, something kids start to do pretty young, when they're describing how they feel and watch their parents' expressions change. Then, a little later, it's grows into *How was school today?* and *What did you do at your friend's house?* And after a while you start to figure what they'd be interested in hearing about and what—especially when you get to be a teenager—you actually want to tell them.

None of that, really, goes on with Owen, Walt figures, except when he reports back about, maybe, a Disney movie he's seen—what happened with the characters—and we're all over that, like some kind of big celebration. Other than that, Owen really doesn't seem to consider what the *parental units* will want to hear, including that there were eighty kids in the basement and all over the backyard a few days ago.

Just as long as we don't get suspicious and ask him, Walt's good.

Because the little guy can't lie. Walt thinks about this and how truly weird it is, just like Jim Carrey in that movie *Liar Liar,* where he gets hit with a spell and everything he says is true. It's kind of beautiful in its way—and why that bar mitzvah speech just crushed everyone. Not being able to lie, just like in that movie, it'd be a nightmare. But Walt thought all that through, too. That's why he was very clear when he talked to Owen after they saw *Home on the Range.* Mom and Dad didn't need to know about the party. That's all. It wasn't a lie.

On Saturday, I notice that my bike is not in the backyard shed and ask, "Walt, where's my bike?"

Walt who's stepping out of the kitchen into the backyard, stops to think, but only for a second. He explains that one of his buddies came over and borrowed it. I tell him he better go get it back. "No problem, Dad. I'll call him right now."

But then I find the bike a few houses away in some bushes.

Walt overhears this news from his bedroom—I tell Cornelia in the front hall, just within earshot. His mind is racing. *Got to get to Owen.* But to tell him what? The last thing he wants to do is talk to Owen about the party from seven days ago, to try to reinforce his edict of silence. It's not like Owen forgot about the party. He remembers what he wore ten years ago on a Tuesday.

The clock ticks, fear burns, and Walt starts thinking about how nice it would be to have a brother who was on his team, his partner. Some brothers fight, he's seen that, but they're still pretty much on the same side—the kid team versus the parent team. That goes deep, never changes really, and they watch each other's backs. He loves Owen. He'd literally kill someone if they messed with the little guy. But it'd be sweet to have just a regular brother right now. And he feels shitty for thinking it.

Then his brain freezes. "Owen, can you come and talk to me and Mom in the den?" It's me calling Owen up from the basement.

Walt ever so gently slips out of his bedroom to the top step and sits, quiet as a mouse. He can hear everything in the den, just one floor down and around the bend. I talk to Owen like I'm working a source. "Hey, buddy, sit down, I have to ask you something."

Walt listens with all his might. There's a pause.

"Did Walt have a party here Saturday night?"

Nothing.

"Owie," Mom says. "You can tell us the truth."

Nothing.

Walt pumps his fist. But he's not breathing. He's talking, telepathically, to Owen: *That's my bro. Hold out, Owie.*

There's a long pause. It may be over. Owen may be free.

No, no. "Okay, Owen, forget about a party. We don't care about that," I say.

Walt's trying to figure the next move: *Where the hell is Dad going with this?*

"So here's my question: were there any girls in the house Saturday night?"

It's silent again. Walt cranks up the brother-in-arms telepathy: *Don't fall for it, Owen. Party and girls are the same thing. Party equals girls. He's trying to trick you.*

"Yes," Owen says, his voice tentative. Walt knows there's a look with that voice, where Owen looks for cues—probably looking at my face.

"That's great, Owen," I say, all cheery. "Lots of girls?"

"Yes! Lots of them!"

"Roughly, how many?"

"Forty-one."

•   •   •

Cornelia notices the white bloom of a dogwood—a nice addition, she thinks, to the sorry patch of grass between the sidewalk and the street.

Her car idles by the curb. She thought this morning's appointment was at nine-thirty—it's at ten—so she has half an hour to kill before meeting a couple of members of Team Owen at an office in downtown Silver Spring.

Just as well. She doesn't know what she's going to say anyway. On her calendar, today's appointment is marked "progress report," but there's no real progress to report.

She sits in her car and thinks about how she's come to hate this time of the year. Everyone else is finishing a school year, looking forward to the summer, and next year, maybe, tearing open some thick envelope of acceptance, planning the glorious *up ahead*, with all the damn cherry blossoms blooming everywhere you look. For the Suskinds, it's a time of crisis, every year, of whether Owen's in the wrong school or if it's the right school and he's about to be thrown out of it.

The school where he spends his days is not serving his needs. There seem to be no others in the area that would. We've looked at so many now, as far afield as Baltimore and Annapolis. She's here to discuss school options with Suzie Blattner—who not only tutors kids like Owen, but is also an educational consultant—and Bill Stixrud, Owen's longtime testing specialist. She flips through his most recent neuropsychological assessment—a comprehensive report she's been using in this latest round of school visits. He's slipping in all subjects and in overall cognitive attainment. A lot of the schools demand some effort at measuring IQ, though they know it's problematic with autistic kids. He's hovering right near 75, the threshold for retarded. His peaks—visual aptitude, word analogies, which are up in the 90th percentile—are called splinter skills. There should be a law against tagging these kids with IQ scores, which get them chucked into the discard bin for the rest of their lives. She starts to stew on it. What's the IQ score for that bar mitzvah speech? Or inventing a language out of thirty hours of memorized Disney movies? *What's the score for that?*

She slips the twenty-two pages of charts and figures, raw numbers and hedged assessments, back into her briefcase and runs her fingertips across the buttery leather and the embossed C.A.K. A wry, levelheaded twenty-something named Cornelia Anne Kennedy once carried this Coach bag to magazine editing jobs in New York and then to a job at PBS in Boston, where she was working when Walt was born. Of course, by then, she was Suskind, but, beyond the changes a first baby brings, she was still the same. She still loved springtime as she always had. When she was ten years old she started babysitting for the next-door neighbor in Connecticut—an almost impossibly positive and buoyant family. There she helped a lovely, graceful mom raise her five children and eventually watched her send her boys off to a camp in New Hampshire each summer. She'd see them come back altered, settled, their calves thickened, gazes clear, and handshakes firm, and she said if she has a boy someday she'll send him to that camp. She did, and that's where Walt now goes in the summers. It all used to fit so neatly—the things she learned to want, the ways to get there.

Then nothing seemed to work quite so neatly. She'd tried a few part-time jobs since Owen was beset, nearly a decade ago now—anything to clear some space, a little headroom to breathe. She married a man who can be intense—she loves that—and who chose, with her encouragement, a career that swallows up everything in its path and is dizzyingly visible. Everyone can see and keep tabs—this story, that book—and have an opinion. She's long needed an untrodden plot, something all her own to work and tend, that wasn't either my landscape or the country mapped by Owen's vast needs, which seemed to grow by the hour, even when she slept. There were days she wanted to run away. And when I saw it coming, I'd try to surprise her with a "run away with me" trip. So we could do it together—overnights somewhere, mostly. A few of those a year, and then back to it. No point in complaining—it is what it is. And the bar mitzvah, just a few weeks ago, was a great victory. Everyone now sees what we had glimpses of in the house, at dinnertime prayers, in passing utterances—that, beneath the surface, a deep inner life seems to be taking shape.

Forgot that one. *Inner life.* What IQ score would they give that, or the sidekicks concept? Huh? *The world and its goddamn yardsticks.* She checks her watch—it's time. A moment later, she and Bill and Suzie are settled in his office. She loves Bill, too, just like she loves Suzie. They really are like family, and there's nothing that they don't know. That makes the discussions go so smoothly; difficult for her, but facile.

"So what's latest?" Bill says, and Cornelia lays out a point-by-point assessment of five schools we have visited—three in Maryland, one in DC, one in Virginia—in the last three months. Each tends to have something valuable to offer—this one's work with computers, that one's art program. There's a school near Annapolis, more than an hour away, and twice that at rush hour, which has a strong academic program. The one in Virginia has the best teacher-student ratio.

Suzie knows all the schools well; their strengths and weaknesses, mostly in accord with what Cornelia has found. "Owen's a tough fit," she says. "Some of his skills are deep, especially when he gets one-on-one instruction, but so are his challenges."

They all nod. Everyone knows this. "If I could take a piece of each school, the part they do well that he needs, and put it all together," Cornelia says ruefully, "we'd be set."

"You could," Bill replies. "Do it yourself."

She's not sure if he's joking, so she chuckles.

"No, I mean it."

"Are you talking about homeschooling?"

"Yep."

"You've got to be kidding."

He isn't and neither is Suzie, who joins in. "You know, you're someone who really could do it."

Cornelia feels an urge to politely stand up, tell them some emergency has come up, and slip out the door. But she doesn't budge as Bill and Suzie begin to describe how she might manage it. Say *homeschoolers* and she thinks of religious fanatics in Oklahoma. But, no. Both describe how parents of spectrum kids are increasingly resorting to it. There are materials Cornelia can buy, classes she could take, Web sites to tap. Suzie would help. Bill, too.

It's indisputable that the whole team of half a dozen or so specialists who regularly work with him is about the best in the area. Now, two honored members are exhorting her to step up, on Owen's behalf.

"No one knows what he needs or how to get through to him better than you," Suzie says.

"Sometimes there's no other way," Bill adds.

Mostly, Bill and Suzie are talking excitedly across the table to each other—*then she can do this, or she can try that*—as "she" listens. And this person they're talking about—*what about her life?* That is, if this is the right path, which is by no means clear, especially considering the social isolation of homeschooling, when one of his key disabilities is his problem with social engagement. She'd be with him all day, every day. Literally. She sometimes thinks of autism as a beast that swallowed her son, one she battles every day, trying to retrieve him, to pull him out. She'd be swallowed, too, she and her whole life. And what rushes into her head? The goddamn whale in *Pinocchio*, Monstro, and she'd be Jiminy Cricket going into the belly after him. *Please someone get these Disney images out of my head!*

She snaps out of it, looks at the clock. They've gone over. She stands abruptly. "This is a big step—I need to think this over and do a lot of investigating." Bill and Suzie nod, looking tentatively up at her, both signaling that they hadn't thought much about how Cornelia would react to this. She knows they have come to see her as a partner, co-investigator, kindred—which, God knows, is rewarding. But we're not all talking about the same thing, here. This is their job, but it's her life. For them, it's a contribution; for her, total commitment. "Thanks, guys, really, I really have to think about this."

She slips out into the street and decides three things. First, she won't mention any of this to her husband, because he'll go into his motivational speaker mode, saying, "You can do anything," and it'll make her want to strangle him. Second, she needs to sit in the quiet car, alone with her thoughts. And third, she whispers to herself, "Maybe I could just drive away where no one can find me."

• • •

The teenage boys emerge from a thicket of bushes onto the small grassy area that serves as a stage.

They are thinly costumed, with swords, sheaths, and breastplates too snug for the bodies of fifteen- and sixteen-year-olds. There's a hubbub. Props need to be moved into place. The parents are here.

This is the "Glade Play," one of many productions put on each summer at Walt's camp. It's been going on for more than a century— the camp and the play—on this very mountainside overlooking a crisp, clean New Hampshire lake.

Walt is thriving so robustly here that it's hard not to wonder what's missing in his life inside our home. It hasn't been an easy few months for him. He was grounded for a month after we had Owen turn state's evidence against him. We didn't feel good about that. In fact, we didn't feel anything about it—a complete, parental blind spot. Owen's reaction when I pressed him about whether there was a party—his lips pressed together, like there was war raging in his mouth—was a clear sign that something had happened and Walt had brought him in on it: a hugely positive thing in their relationship. In our anger and worry over the party, we made a big mistake. For the first time, Walt had created a separate brotherly pact with his young accomplice and, in one move, we torpedoed it.

Not that it seemed to affect Walt all that much. He took the hit—"manned up," as he says—and then all but raced north to his third long summer at Pasquaney, a camp distinctive for being a throwback. It hasn't changed significantly since it was started in 1895. That was the Progressive Era, when there were many admirers—including the Yale men who founded the camp—of Ralph Waldo Emerson and values like self-reliance, selflessness, care for others, simplicity, trust, humility, and more self-reliance. Walt immediately took to the first and last virtues, and then filled in the rest, year by year. The change was stark, right off. When he won the award for best first-year camper at twelve, he didn't tell us for three days. All those years ducking stares built in him a desire to go quietly about his business; get the job done without fanfare—a quality often seen in siblings of the disabled. They tend to earn accolades—fueled, early on, by an adult-strength dose of survivor's guilt—but rarely want to receive them. What was indisputable is that living within our family's day-to-day improvisations, with a conspicuous father and conspicuous brother, impelled him to dive into a firm structure, calibrated over 109 years, of one-size-fits-all rules and rituals.

Which is where he stands now—in a white tank top with a blue "P" on it and long gray shorts with a blue stripe, made fashionable during the McKinley administration—looking across the hillside amphitheater to find us in the audience.

Our eyes finally meet. He nods, barely, and looks away.

No noticeable smiles toward parents are in order. This is serious business, seriously played. Specifically, *Henry V*—Shakespeare's drama about the young king who leads his nation into a war that, ultimately, ends in disaster.

Cornelia and I hardly know what to do with ourselves. We've sent Owen off to a regular camp in Maine, for artistic kids. They were blown away by his sketchbooks and, after many calls and memos to counselors and staff, it seems they'll be able to deal with his "behaviors."

On this splendid early-August afternoon in 2004, we can be just like everyone else. It's something Walt appreciates—*how could he not?* And we do, too. For him. For us.

The campers begin to play out scenes—not the whole play, but quite a bit—chosen, as was the play itself, by the camp's astute assistant director. He told Cornelia that he thought this play would be especially resonant with the kids because of the many obvious parallels to George W. Bush and the Iraq War, now a year and a few months along.

He's right. The wayward young king—his advisers gathered close—frets over his troubled relationship with his father and the merits of attacking France. Connections swirl in an orchestral weave: a 400-year-old drama that could have been written, names changed, in any *New York Times* story about last year's march to war; eternal issues of hubris, a young man's search for respect, and, ultimately, of Oedipal wreckage. I think as I watch the play start, how would I even begin to explain this to Owen, if he were here? You'd have to write a novella, quick, and then recite it through the voices of Disney characters. But it is precisely those constant calculations that we're free of—Cornelia and I, both—in this rare interlude. Our bodies rest on the steep slope of grass, free from a state of constant, low-grade tension of how to bind Owen to us and the wider world.

Of course, it's one hell of a play, lurching forward as Henry rallies his men to action in the St. Crispin's Day speech, saying that their deeds on this day of battle will create a story, told through time:

> *Then shall our names, familiar in his mouth as household words—*
> *Harry the King, Bedford and Exeter,*
> *Warwick and Talbot, Salisbury and Gloucester—*
> *be in their flowing cups freshly rememb'red.*
> *This story shall the good man teach his son.*

And, finally . . .

> *But we in it shall be remembered—we few, we happy few, we band of brothers.*

They grab swords, boys in their mid-teens, playing out the Battle of Agincourt in moves most of them honed on the kindergarten playground—trying not to laugh as they shove and swing—until the boy playing Talbot cries out and falls at the very moment of victory. Now, they're all back in character as celebration mixes with grief. The six of them, led by Walt's buddy, Robbie, as Henry—with Walt, as Gloucester, right behind him—lift the dead Talbot, a thin camper named Vikram, onto their shoulders and begin carrying him up the center aisle. The dell falls silent. Past and present, literature and life, snap together like a trap; a context, loosed from time and place, that feels like a glimpse of indisputable destiny. They're mostly not our sons, not at this moment; they're young men—soon to arrive at the age of those now dying in Fallujah and Kabul. Together, they begin to softly sing a dirge as they march:

"*Non nobis, non nobis, Domine Sed nomini tuo da gloriam*" ("Not to us, not to us, O Lord, but to thy name give glory"), the Latin prayer of humility and thanksgiving.

And it is we who suddenly feel humility, and thankfulness, that Walt has found such joy and release here. Parenting, it's often said, is about loving and letting go. Just like all the other parents gazing on, breathing lightly, we're doing our share of both.

"Look at him," Cornelia says softly, her breath on my ear, as Walt marches by, his eyes flat, fixed. And we both feel it—a familiar emptiness, sad and sweet, when you feel life's clock strike an hour. It prompts us to then applaud all the louder, the kind of cheering that tears at you. We want him to hear us. This is where he belongs, following whatever star he chooses, not bound by the gravitational field that envelops every house, and certainly ours. One boy, wandering so often in solitude, compels us to furiously shape our world to meet his needs; the other, among a band of brothers, now taking their bows, demands to be challenged and shaped by the wide world, with all the judgments and dictates and uncontrollable forces we fear.

We want that for him, though on this path his brother cannot follow.

•   •   •

I decide to first stop by the office—to hear the whole story.

The director of Owen's camp in Maine greets me through the screen door—"Come on in, let's talk."

He seems like a good-natured, middle-aged guy, more like a loan officer than a guy who goes to work in short pants. He called me yesterday, said I ought to drive up.

"We just can't handle him," he says. "He's much more distracted than we figured. So much is going on in his head. He's gentle, that's not it. The counselors are just kind of overmatched."

I don't argue. "Well, he made it five days—could be worse," I say, trying to salvage an upbeat anything. Then I think of what Owen must be feeling and I feel like an idiot. We overreached, thrown off by the insanity of this damn thing, where he can give a bar mitzvah speech like that and then vanish inward on a whim, and barely know where he's standing. Of course, they were impressed by the sketch-book—*who wouldn't be?* I probably oversold Owen, and now he's been whacked.

"Have you told him?" I ask.

"We told him to pack up his things."

Owen's sitting on his trunk outside the cabin when I walk up.

"Do I have to leave?"

"Yup, buddy, that's why I'm here."

He gets up and stands there, not budging. Something's on his mind, churning. I know, by now, not to interrupt the silence.

"I'll leave only if you promise someday I can come back."

I'm caught short. I have no expectation they'll let him return.

"You bet."

God, I hate lying to him. He believes everything you say. Lying to him is like a crime.

We don't say anything in the car for five minutes, then ten. He's just looking out the window, the same look he had after the faux graduation from the Lab School. The Maine coastline is passing by. It's now fifteen minutes.

He starts singing.

Come with me, and let's go wander
Far beyond the wild blue yonder,
Out where stars roam free.
Though the journey's far from breezy,
Stick with me, I'll make it easy.
You can depend on me.

Oh, brother. It's a song from *Home on the Range*, the Disney movie Owen saw numerous times last spring. The plot involves Roseanne

Barr and Dame Judi Dench voicing cows who are trying to save their Patch of Heaven farm by outwitting an evil cattle-rustling speculator. There are quite a few well-developed sidekicks, including a character named "Lucky Jack," a wise, irascible jackrabbit.

Owen knows the movie was not well received but doesn't care. He loves it and adores the sound track of prairie ballads sung by Tim McGraw, Bonnie Raitt, and k.d. lang. He watches it. He lives it.

With my mind wrapping around the selection of this song, it takes me a moment to realize what's different. He isn't singing in the voice of one of the characters.

It's his own voice. A completely different tone than he usually sings in.

Yeah, there's a long road before us,
And it's a hard road, indeed.
But, darlin', I swear,
I'll get us there,
Wherever the trail may lead.

It's a long road before us, a hard road, indeed.

For the next five hours, as we travel west across the northernmost reaches of the Appalachian Trail, he sings that song maybe twenty times—all five verses.

Finally, as we close in on Fairlee and the lake house, I'm reduced to pleading.

"Owen, you've got to stop. You're killing me."

He looks over.

"Okay—let's have a discussion. Tell me why you're singing that song; why do you like it so much?"

"Because it's a journey song. I like journey songs the best."

• • •

Cornelia and I talk that night on the dock. She's upset about camp. Owen's not happy. Can we fix it, make it right? This is our model— she cobbles together a plan, I sell it.

A week later, I'm on the phone with the camp's director. I tell him what Owen said when I picked him up—about wanting to come back. It's a long call, in which I go from cajoling to penitent to understanding to outraged, and then back to penitent. Owen had been to a few summer camps over the years, but always with an aide, a "shadow," that we'd hire to guide him along. This was our mistake, I tell the director—sending Owen this time without one—but in the past few days we've found one, a shadow who could come back with him. I've worn him down. The man just wants to get off the phone.

So, for the last two weeks of the summer Owen returns to camp with Frank—a high school senior who was one of the Boston kids we see each fall at that Vermont dairy farm. The two boys have known each other since they were little kids. Frank knows all of Owen's moves, movies, and passions.

The first week is fine—Frank follows Owen around keeping him on task. It's like he has a private counselor and cruise director. He pushes Owen along through sports and arts and crafts, and facilitates conversations with bunkmates, especially cueing Owen to do voices, like Mr. Burns and Smithers from *The Simpsons*, which other kids love. In the finale of a camp-wide relay race, an obstacle course, counselors carry campers—usually the smallest kid in each bunk— the last few hundred yards across the finish line. Owen gets that slot, and Frank—a big guy, Owen in his arms—brings victory to the cabin. He later tells us: "I've never run so fast as when I carried Owen." Cornelia and I laugh for days over this: the story of our lives.

But Frank won't be able to carry Owen for the main activity of the final week—a talent show that all the kids are exhaustively preparing for. He asks Owen if he knows what he wants to do. Owen says he does—he's going to sing a song. That's all. Does he need any musical accompaniment? Nope. Frank asks about a hundred times for more details. None forthcoming, not even what song. Fellow counselors are wondering, concerned. The other kids are all practicing. The shows, skits, musical offerings are due to be elaborate, as would be expected at a camp for the "gifted and artistic." Frank only tells them, "He just says he's going to sing some song."

After the session's final dinner—and before the closing campfire—about 150 kids, counselors, and staff gather in a large, corrugated-steel rec center with a wide stage. Owen's sitting next to Frank and the kids in his cabin, dead center in the thick of the crowd, all T-shirts and crossed legs. Two-thirds of the way along, the stage director walks over with her clipboard, motioning to Frank. "Owen, you're up."

A minute later, he's on the stage, mike in hand, looking out at the sea of campers.

Inhibitions are reasonable things. No one wants to show themselves to those who won't be appreciative. No one wants to be embarrassed, or ridiculed, or fall flat on a stage. Owen's brain doesn't work that way. In a way, it's a cleaner transaction. The feeling comes or it doesn't. When it does, he seizes it.

And that's what he's doing, trying to summon it, as his eyes, scanning for patterns, examine the throng of faces, some of which are now slipping into "uh-oh" anticipation that a stage-fright debacle is unfolding, with the weird kid who talks to himself. But whatever his eyes scan as the seconds tick by, they're also looking inward to the place where about the same number of characters—a community of about 150 or so, sidekicks mostly—live alongside some adult-strength realizations about isolation and loss. If it works, these two communities will connect.

He finally brings the mike to his lips.

Once we cross that far horizon,
Life is bound to be surprisin'
But we'll take it day by day.

Of course, it's "Wherever the Trail May Lead"—his theme song for this difficult summer—which he now sings as a torch song, a revival. Belts it out like there's no tomorrow. And for him, there really isn't. Being unfettered in this way, living so fully in the present, is one of the flip sides of "context blind."

To a camp of arts kids—each a hothouse flower of some talent or another, thinking incessantly of blazing tomorrows of stardom and whether they'll be *the one* who makes it—he looks courageous, free.

And halfway through they're up and whooping, on the way to a standing ovation.

They don't know what he's been through. He wouldn't be able to tell them if they asked. But the deep bow he takes, as cheers wash over him, is, itself, a novella.

• • •

Cornelia walks up the stairs to check that both kids are asleep before she ascends to our third-floor bedroom and turns on the lights. I can see the soft, yellowish glow through the skylights of my backyard office. I watch for it—we've discussed this in advance—and head over to the house and head upstairs. We talk in whispers so the kids can't overhear us. Seems wrong to talk about this in any other way.

The fall has been a difficult one for her sister, Lizzy, who's battling a particularly virulent type of breast cancer. Cornelia has traveled from Washington to Connecticut several weekends in September and October.

Lizzy is the single sister—the one, among five girls and three boys, who never married. But she's also been a jaunty, world-wise aunt for all of our kids, twelve cousins in all, generally ranging in age from mid-teens on down.

And none of the kids know all that much, just that Lizzy has been sick for about a year, but she's fighting it.

Certainly, there's plenty of signaling that goes on, like when Lizzy was called to the *bima* near the end of the bar mitzvah service to read a passage of Khalil Gibran, which she prefaced—looking firmly at Owen from the podium in her blue dress and brown wig—with: "Owen, you are a model of perseverance for me . . . and for that I thank you."

Mostly, though, things are not said—even among the adults. Because what is there to say? Lizzy's drawn from a tough lineage; you could all but see her managing potato diggers on the rocky Irish coast. She asks for nothing. Never has. She's seeing the best doctors. She's fighting it.

Over the past decade of visits to befuddled autism doctors with their best-case predictions, Cornelia's tolerance for protective hopefulness has steadily eroded.

She has worked hard to see things as they are; not as she hopes they might be. I'm able to do that in my work. In my life, not so easy.

We sit on the bed in a dim light. "I don't think she's going to make it through the weekend," Cornelia says, now all cried out and matter-of-fact. "I need to be there." I stroke her head as she falls into sleep.

Late the next afternoon, Friday, she quietly gathers a few things in a small suitcase, grabs her purse and phone. We hug in the foyer. I tell her to send my love to her sister. She says I should just tell the kids that she's gone to see Lizzy and that she'll call. As she opens the door, we hear someone bounding down the steps.

A moment later, Owen is standing in the foyer, a CD in his hand.

It's his most precious possession—the soundtrack to *Home on the Range*.

He hands it to Cornelia. "Play her song six. Tell her it's from me."

• • •

Lizzy, a social worker, is in her apartment in Bridgeport. Nurses and family members are coming and going. But now it's just she and Cornelia, who has settled in. Lizzy's just forty-nine. For years, she and Cornelia, one slot behind her in the birth order, shared a bedroom. Now they're sharing one again.

And Cornelia is there to boost Lizzy as her strength ebbs away. Exhaustion is overwhelming her, like the crush of heavy waves. She hugs her little sister, the fear and uncertainty finally overwhelming her. "I'm not sure how I'm supposed to feel," she tearfully tells Cornelia.

Right to the end, the *supposed to*s tug at her, like they do all of us.

The sisters cry for a time, and then Cornelia tells her that Owen sent something for her.

Lizzy lays back in bed as Cornelia puts in the CD. "He told me to play this song for you."

The song washes over them both:

Yeah, there's a long road before us,
And it's a hard road, indeed.
But, darlin', I vow,
We'll get through somehow,
Wherever the trail may lead.
Can't tell you when we'll be there—
It may take all our lives.
We're headin' for that great unknown.

We'll soon be walkin' free there,
But 'til that day arrives,
At least we won't be travelin' alone. . . .
And there's a long road before us,
And it's a hard road, indeed.
But, darlin', don't fear,
'Cause I'll be right here,
To give you the strength you need . . .
And through the whole ride,
I'll be by your side,
Wherever the trail may lead.

Lizzy listens to the song, sent urgently by someone with no idea what he's supposed to feel either, and heaves up sobs, a release from burdens.

"Tell Owie thanks," she whispers to Cornelia. "He's always been my angel."

A few minutes later, she drifts into a sleep, which soon deepens into a coma. She never really awakens. In two days, she's gone.

• • •

On the Monday after the funeral, Cornelia tells Owen to pack his book bag and bundle up. It's early November and they begin their morning walk, about half a mile, to a Baptist church near Chevy Chase Circle.

There's a room in the church basement that wasn't being used. Cornelia rented it for five hundred dollars a month, with the proviso that she could paint it.

Walt is now an tenth grader at Washington's Sidwell Friends School. He and a buddy from Sidwell, spend a Saturday painting the cinder blocks to Owen's specifications.

Dr. Dan Griffin, a PhD psychologist we've added to the team, suggests that Owen name it.

He did. So on this morning, like every morning since early September, they hang their coats on hooks in a small room—ten by sixteen with a single window—now officially called Patch of Heaven School.

A school to try to teach one hard-to-teach boy—run by his mother. If we needed any more proof—a final nudge—the summer provided it. It is now overwhelming and indisputable: Our son has turned his affinity for animated movies, mostly Disney, into a language to shape his identity and access emotions that are untouchable and unmanageable for most teenagers, and even adults. But he'll have to go further to learn basic skills—reading, math, general knowledge, how to listen and respond—if he is to make it to a high school that can usher him forward. To attempt that, we'll have to work with, around, and through his enveloping passion for those beloved movies. The question has finally been called: exactly how much can you learn—about what's real, in the real world—from a Disney movie?

Cornelia and Owen settle among the freshly painted cinder blocks to search for an answer.

chapter seven

MAGIC FORMULAS

Owen looks at the picture he drew of Iago, taped securely on the face of his gray metal locker, and feels the parrot's voice run through him.

He has developed secrets about Iago. Only he knows them. It's the fall of 2005, a year into the experiment called Patch of Heaven School—and a secret world is taking shape inside of him. But it's only for him.

Owen makes the Iago scrunch face and murmurs, "Okay, okay, now listen, Jafar," under his breath, though he's barely making a sound.

"No self-talk, Owen—all talk is part of *conversation*," Cornelia says, hanging her coat in a locker—her locker—adorned with a picture Owen drew of Big Mama from *The Fox and the Hound*. "If you *want* to talk about Iago, let's talk together about him."

He looks at her, trying to make up his mind. "No, I'm okay," Owen says. And then he plops down onto the navy sofa, next to a blond-wood desk and file cabinet, on top of a French blue carpet with a white swirl design, all of which Cornelia picked up in a buying spree the previous fall at Ikea.

When she bought her L-shaped teacher's desk at The Container Store, she saw them: two lockers being used as props in a back-to-school display. She begged the sales clerk for the items. "Sorry ma'am, those are not for sale," the clerk responded. Cornelia persisted, calling every few days for a month until they relented.

The two five-foot-tall, standard-issue school lockers are now her key props in making this feel like a real school, instead of just a place Owen goes every day with his mother.

After a year, many moving parts, assembled piece by piece, are in place to preserve this spell. From the dry-erase board to her demeanor, Cornelia does her best to hang the role of mother on the hook every day. Once they're in the room, she assumes a tone and focus that is noticeably different from what Owen sees in the kitchen. She needs to be caring but demanding, not available for fun, unless otherwise noted, but quite interested in results, and ready to allow Owen to sometimes struggle to find an answer. In short: *teacher*.

But not one who looks befuddled or impatient when Owen does what he's long done—which is become distracted and inattentive in somewhere between one and two minutes and turn to self-talking. Depending on which chair you inhabit, she's either a dream or nightmare: a teacher who sees all and knows all—as only a mother can—who is on top of the student, her one and only student, every minute of every day.

This one-on-one intensity happens to be what works best with kids on the autism spectrum, whether it's Lovaas-style behavioral training—which has recently been borne out by research—or Greenspan's hyper-interested and encouraging Floortime. Cornelia mixes them together. There are, no doubt, rewards for good behavior and completed tasks. There is also intense, enthusiastic focus on how Owen sees what's before him on the lesson plan, as well as interest in his many tangents—if, that is, they relate to the things that *must be learned*.

Because that's what they're here for: to master what must be learned to get into a Rockville, Maryland, high school that we've been eyeballing for students with special needs. He has a ways yet to travel to be ready for that school, but his progress, after a year of homeschooling, has been surprisingly good. And while Cornelia is ready to do anything to achieve this goal, she's trying to be mindful of not letting this effort damage the only thing that ranks above it: the mother and son relationship. This kind of in-your-face exposure, every day, could do that. So, she keeps things moving—lots of field trips and an array of surrogates and specialists are all now part of the curriculum.

On the schedule for today—Monday, September 12, 2005—there's a midday visit to the Smithsonian's Museum of Natural History in Washington, DC, then an afternoon visit to Dr. Dan Griffin, Owen's innovative play therapist. Tomorrow at eleven, Christine Sproat, Owen's occupational therapist since he was five, will pick him up for rock climbing in Rock Creek Park. After two hours of classwork on Wednesday morning, Cornelia and Owen will be gone for the rest of the day—swimming at the Bethesda, Maryland, YMCA with Joanne, an instructor who herself has a child with disabilities; then, after lunch, there's a piano lesson with Ruthlee, the semiretired Ivymount piano teacher, at her home. And finally, Owen has a private session with his psychiatrist, Dr. C. T. Gordon, who also runs a Thursday afternoon social skills group, where he tries to teach Owen and two other boys on the autistic spectrum basic skills of social interaction.

The day after Dr. Gordon's session, Friday, Jennifer, the speech therapist, will come to the room, for an hour on speech skills and then take Owen out to a nearby corner of shops for pragmatic exercises, like ordering lunch in the line at Subway. Suzie Blattner, Owen's academic tutor since he was four, makes a visit each week, as much to tutor Cornelia in the basics of teaching as to work with Owen on his reading and math.

The most important two hours of any day, though, is the morning session, where Cornelia presses Owen to focus and retain information, like she's doing on this crisp autumn morning.

And it's succeeding largely because, after a year in this room, she's become more of an expert at working the magic formula: find hooks in animated movies to enliven, illuminate, and engage. She knows his language. Once you sit in his head, and look out through his lens, it's a matching game. With a goal of education or therapy, or simply finding ways for him to communicate, look for where the many Disney hooks rest in him—the sweet spots where he's taken the narratives deep into his psyche—and use them to pull him out. She does it. She and I have directed his therapists on how to do it. And it's working.

"Okay, Owen, we're going to do pirates, now."

He nods, and looks intently at her. She knows what's coming.

"All right, go ahead."

"Now, you listen to me, James Hawkins," Owen starts, one eye shut, as though patched, in Brian Murray's (Bill's brother) voicing of John Silver from Disney's 2002 *Treasure Planet*, an outer-space version of the classic *Treasure Island*. "You got the makings of greatness in you, but you got to take the helm and chart your own course. Stick to it, no matter the squalls! And when the time comes, you get the chance to really test the cut of your sails, and show what you're made of! Well, I hope I'm there, catching some of the light coming off you that day."

Takes roughly twenty-six seconds. Cornelia laughs—how could she not—Owen is suffused with such joy when he recites this resonant passage; a charge runs through him, voltage peaking with "the light coming off you that day."

It's as though his whole being snaps in coherence. The clinical term is he's *integrated*, both in his senses and, importantly, his emotional core. And now he's ready for a wide-ranging discussion, first about when the movie is set—"in the future, I think, but kind of a past and future both," he says.

Cornelia follows up, "Because, Owen, they're in a ship like the pirates sailed in which era?" And he's not sure, but *he wants to know.*

That's the key. So she opens the text—a book called *Pirate*, one of the best-selling Eyewitness Books for kids and young adults. They read about the so-called golden age of piracy in the eighteenth century, with colorful characters ranging from Edward Teach ("Blackbeard") to William Kidd to the Barbary pirates off the coast of North Africa, whom President Thomas Jefferson declared war on in 1802. Of course, these pirates were models for everyone from Long John Silver to Captain Hook to every character in Disney's 2003 *Pirates of the Caribbean: The Curse of the Black Pearl*.

A half hour later he knows about everything from what goods ships carried in the 1700s to what Jefferson believed in, and even what's on his tombstone at his home in Monticello.

Then there's a break—she knows when he needs one, and when to call him back—and then they do computer training for a half hour, specifically focusing on how to define and paste text. Cornelia has been teaching him rudimentary computer skills, including how to use spell-check, which is a godsend for him.

Next stop, math. Every day Cornelia starts with Owen's strong suit: pattern recognition, traditionally a sweet spot for autistic kids. Today, it's a work sheet with, 8, 16, ___ , 32, ___ , ___. He handles it, writing in 24, 40, 48, then writes the rule: *Increase by Eight*. He does a few more of these, but mastering this is not all it seems. It's called the "Swiss cheese effect," how strengths and weaknesses can sit side by side. With most kids, it's a solid block of cheddar; with spectrum kids, they're grasping the material, and then you fall into a hole. Ask him to do basic subtraction—such as how much change is he owed from a dollar—and he can't do it.

It's the same brand of conceptual thinking that makes word problems a nightmare. There's no pattern to recognize, just words, each decoded, pronounced, and understood, but, for Owen, coyly concealing the threads of connection that allow for a speaker's intent to be turned into an equation.

So, Cornelia gives him an equation: 3 + 6 = 9. Okay, he knows that pattern, and can count the digits in his head. Now, Owen, she says, write it up as a word problem.

He sits for a moment.

"I can't. Mom, can you help me?"

She shakes her head. "You can do this, Owie. Give yourself a minute."

A minute passes, then another. His eyes are wandering, as if a bird flew through the room. He's trying to put something together.

He writes, *Lucky Jack had three sticks of dynamite. He found six more at an old house. How many sticks of dynamite did he have altogether?*

Great praise flows forth—yes; it's a mother's praise and a teacher's praise. Plus, this teacher is allowed to hug him.

Okay now. Let's keep it going.

Cornelia writes the equation: $19 + $10 = $29.

Owen smiles.

Now he's quick, like he's been noodling this already: *Iago has $19 he finds in a treasure box. With $10, how much money does he have now?*

This is fifth-grade work. He's fourteen. But it's progress.

He laughs and waves his arms.

"What's so funny?" his mom asks.

"Nothing," he giggles. "It's just funny."

• • •

Cornelia doesn't know what just happened, not really. No one does. But back at home late that Monday afternoon, Owen slips into the basement, which is still his refuge.

In a flash, he's on the Internet, on Google. He types with one finger—Aladdin Script—and after a few clicks he hits a bootleg script site. Enthusiasts watch the movie, over and over, and produce a script. It's not the actual shooting script, but it is identical in every way except that the notes on scene setting and character cues are not up to the real script's precision. Owen uses the very computer skills he worked on that day to scroll the script's length defining it all, hits CONTROL C to copy, and then—creating a Word file—pastes it. He's captured the script for *Aladdin* and taken ownership. For Owen, this is like absconding with the Dead Sea Scrolls.

He scrolls through this with confidence, steady and sure, just like a practiced reader skims familiar text. All these words are already in his head.

When Owen first decided a year before to put Iago on his locker, Cornelia and I both asked him about it. *Iago, as the signature character for his school locker?* Owen explained that Iago was different from all the other villain sidekicks. "He's the first villain sidekick in Disney who provides 'comic relief.' And anyone with a sense of humor has to have some good in him." In the ensuing year, he's said this over and over. Almost word for word.

Now, he's doing something about it. He arrives at an early section of the script—where Aladdin, imprisoned in a dungeon, meets a fellow prisoner; in fact, it's Jafar in the disguise of an old, enfeebled man. The movie's plot first unfolds, as the old man tells Aladdin about the legendary Cave of Wonders and how he needs someone with "strong legs and a strong back" to enter the cave and retrieve the Genie's lamp. Aladdin agrees and then the old man opens the dungeon's trapdoor and leads them out on their mission.

At the top of this section, where Jafar first appears in the old-man disguise, Owen opens a space and begins to type:

SMUGS: LISTEN, BOY, I'VE GOT A WAY OUT OF HERE.

The old man is no longer Jafar in disguise. He's a fresh character, with his own personality.

Now, on fresh terrain, Owen begins to construct a new scene:

IAGO DUCKS INTO THE DUNGEON TO CHECK ON
ALADDIN, WHO'S SOON TO BE EXECUTED.
SMUGS: THERE'S A TREASURE BOX HIDDEN DEEP IN
THIS DUNGEON.
IAGO: A TREASURE. OH BOY, OH BOY. THAT SOUNDS
LIKE MY KIND OF THING.
IF IAGO HELPS ALADDIN AND SMUGS ESCAPE, THE
OLD MAN SAYS HE WILL SHARE THE TREASURE
WITH THE PARROT.
SMUGS: YOU ARE NOT EVIL IN YOUR HEART. YOU
JUST WORK FOR AN EVIL MAN. THIS TREASURE
WILL HELP GIVE YOU YOUR FREEDOM.
IAGO: HOW DO YOU KNOW I'M NOT EVIL?
SMUGS: BECAUSE YOU ARE FUNNY. AND ANYONE
WITH A SENSE OF HUMOR HAS TO HAVE SOME
GOOD IN THEM.
ALADDIN: YOU CAN BE ONE OF MY SIDEKICKS AND
MY FRIEND.
IAGO: I HAVE ALWAYS WANTED A REAL FRIEND.

He's never written dialogue before, though his head is filled with it. What's running through his noggin is now on the page, as though this was the way the movie might have been, maybe should have been.

Even years later, when he told us about this night when he changed this *Aladdin* script, he explained that there was a problem to be solved. He'd long ago turned this parrot into someone he could confide in, something I'd discovered from under the bedspread that night many years before. How, though, could a villain's sidekick be Owen's dear friend. At some point, after umpteen viewings, this insight about good and evil, and one's capacity to change, took shape. Did he know when? Not exactly. Did he impute it by observing real people in real situations? He can't say. All he knows is that he secretly changed this plot, so a villain's sidekick could switch sides, free prisoners from a dungeon, and help a hero fulfill his destiny.

• • •

It's not until a few weeks later that I see a pile of printed pages sitting next to the kid's basement computer. It's the script from the 1990 Disney movie *The Rescuers Down Under*. I'm surprised that he's printed it out—he's never done that before. But the page on top is odd, and the formatting is off.

I see a passage of dialogue where Frank, a frill-necked lizard that Owen has placed high in his sidekick's pantheon, is describing how well he knows the movie's hero, a boy trying to protect a giant eagle from a poacher named McLeach.

> FRANK: I DON'T KNOW HIM DEEP DOWN—I'M NOT
> A *SYKIATRIST*, IF YOU KNOW WHAT I MEAN—BUT
> I KNOW HIM PLENTY WELL. AND ONE OTHER
> THING—I ALWAYS TELL THE TRUTH. ANYWAY,
> MCLEACH TOLD HIM AN EVIL FIB THAT THE
> GREAT BIRD WAS DEAD, THAT'D HE HEARD IT
> SOMEWHERE, AND THEN FOLLOWED THE BOY
> AS HE RAN TO FIND THE BIRD.

The dialogue goes on for many pages. There's actually one altered scene and two new ones that, together, solve a problem at the heart of the movie: a major central scene that doesn't really advance the plot in which Frank—a significant character providing comic relief—appears and vanishes without any discernible purpose.

As I flip the pages, I feel a sensation of relief and fatherly pride, and a kind of deep sadness, all knotted together. I get a glimpse of an inner world that's richer and more complex than I could have imagined, and at the same instant see its narrowness: that he can only do this in the voices of forgettable characters from a little-known movie.

Yet there's joy to it, to the dialogue; that's unmistakable. And that's just pure, good: this clearly makes him happy.

That night, as Cornelia and I pore over the script, we start to become more hopeful that this is a first sign of a change: that he may be breaking free from the brittle literalisms that he wears like a snug suit of clothes. The Disney scripts have been built—by him and us both—into a scaffolding where we can see him, and meet him, and increasingly nourish him with basic learning. Though we won't know about the Iago script for years, we now know of this surprisingly intricate rewrite of *The Rescuers Down Under* displaying the same urgent capacity.

He's not reciting or mimicking here. He's creating. Whatever change in him is driving it, he's beginning to reinvent these beloved narratives, actually altering the landscape where he spends so much of his life.

Sitting in the kitchen at midnight, Cornelia examines the script with a trained eye, finding references from schoolwork that he's used in crafting the scenes, including the problem that most of the movie's main characters are mice, which frill-necked lizards eat. This is something Owen learned—after Cornelia used Frank to prompt a lesson about lizards—that he deftly handles in his rewritten dialogue:

> ONE OF THE THREE MICE QUIPS, "THANK GOODNESS
> WE'RE NOT BLIND."
> FRANK JOKES BACK, "AND THANK GOODNESS I'M
> NOT HUNGRY."

She rolls her eyes and puts the script down on the kitchen counter. "He's running his own little home school in the basement.

Wonder where he learns more—days with me or nights alone."

"It seems like they may finally be working hand in hand," I say.

"Well, that's the hopeful view," she answers. "But how do I get him to write this lucidly about anything *other* than animated movies, or the voices in his head?"

I ask if we should look for an opportune moment to talk to him, to see if he can explain some of his underlying emotions, like we did when we found the sidekicks sketchbook.

"No, you do it. That's more therapy. I'm his teacher," she says wryly. "And I've got to be up early for school."

Soon, I'm sitting alone at the kitchen island with the script. My first thought is to put it back right where I found it so Owen won't know I saw it and I can pick the right time to talk to him about it. Or perhaps just not let him know I ever saw it, like I'm covering my tracks after a source passes me a government document. And that thought—the wrong thought for this moment—makes me recoil.

I deal so much in secrecy that I'm sick of it. The federal investigation from last year ended, leaving my lawyers to battle over my right to keep the documents. They're sure I'm being wiretapped, though there's no way to confirm it, and I've started a new book about how the response to 9/11 reshaped the country and its government. That means for the past year I've been walking between sunlight and shadow, talking off-the-record with intelligence officials and operatives—professionals in the game of conceal and mislead—trying to fit bits of gleaned information into patterns that frame larger truths.

But I own this kitchen in this house; I have a right to know what's happening on Owen's secret matrix. We have to stop walking on eggshells with him, afraid if we press him, at the wrong moment, he'll close up, like some reluctant whistle-blower.

After school the next day, I simply hand him the script.

"I read the changes you made to this script, Owen," I begin.

He looks at the script and at me. I know I'm crashing into his secret world, a place he wants to control, but I have to know what goes on in there to know him.

He pulls back. "I still love *The Rescuers Down Under*! I didn't do anything wrong, did I?"

I'm caught by surprise—he feels like he's betraying his beloved Disney by changing their script.

I tell him it's okay, that the 1990 movie, and its script, won't change.

"You're starting to create things that are yours—like the way you helped Frank become more interesting and alive."

We're standing in his room. His jacket is off, the backpack's on the floor. It's late afternoon. Our Friday ritual of visiting the video store and grabbing pizza will soon begin.

We just stand there for a moment.

"Frank wasn't appreciated. Some of the sidekicks aren't," Owen says. "I made it so he's more important in helping the hero fulfill his destiny."

He pauses. There seems to be some other thing he's thinking. I wait.

"Dad, Frank had more he wanted to say."

• • •

The children arrive with dusk, one after another, filing into the foyer of our house, their parents close behind. They're tallish for Halloween, all fourteen-year-olds, but dressed in precise, elaborate costumes that carry no trace of horror or teenage angst. A few dress as Disney characters, a couple are simple ghosts, and there's even a princess. Their host, dressed as Lucky Jack, the wisecracking jackrabbit sidekick from *Home on the Range*, tells everyone to get hot dogs, and to make it fast. "We need to get out as quick as we can," Owen says. "This is our night."

He's not normally so forceful, so much in charge. But this is his annual Halloween party, a tradition, now six years along. He plans it, months ahead, down to the minute. It's his favorite night of the year, every year. And his guests are appreciative. They don't get invited to many parties. With the exception of Nathan, Owen's stalwart "typical" friend from next door, they're all autistic.

To say Owen is friendly with all of them demands an alteration to the typical notion of friendship. There are a few from Ivymount, some of whom he had playdates with over the years. A few he sees only on this night, once a year. But he thinks about them all, often giving them sidekick identities, and they're all invited. As Owen says, "No sidekick gets left behind."

From the start, Cornelia and I always make these Halloween parties for both children and adults. By now, we know all of these parents. We recognize in each other, without words, the pressures of never letting a child out of sight, of watching them, intently, for clues about what's happening deep inside, of being uncertain, always, about what the future may hold.

Finding others who understand all this merits celebration—so, there are bottles of foreign beer, wine, and quesadillas, chips, and guacamole to complement the hot dogs. "Why doesn't everyone relax," Cornelia says, as she collects the kids' dirty plates. "I'll take the gang out with Walt," I add. "Everyone can have an hour off the clock." This draws knowing nods. Yes, that'll be just fine.

Susan, one of the moms, takes me aside. Her daughter, Megan, a pretty dark-haired fourteen-year-old, has no speech. She's dressed as a princess—Ariel—for many years; she has been her favorite character. "You know Megan's rarely away from me, and she doesn't know her way around here."

"She'll be fine, Susan. We'll keep a close eye on her, both of us." Walt, downing a hot dog a few feet away, offers a got-it-covered nod.

Moments later, the troupe is out, crunching leaves underfoot, with

Owen in the lead. Among these kids, though, it hardly matters who leads or who follows. They do not size each other up the way most kids tend to, looking for an advantage. So what if this one moves his arms in fits and jerks, or that one carries on a running dialogue under his breath. What does it matter if the pretty young lady can't speak? It's like that old Baptist hymn about heaven: "There'll Be No Distinction There."

And, for them, tonight is heaven, America's feast of self-invention. That's something the autistic kids, facing an onslaught to their hair-trigger senses and disapproving stares, know how to do: how to hold tight to their favorite stories, to live within them, until they can reimagine themselves in a world renewed.

The streets of exhaustively carved jack-o'-lanterns, fence-post cobwebs, and inflatable skeletons are like one block party after the next. It's a neighborhood of old brick houses, filled with Washington, DC's professional class of civil servants and advocates, lawyers, and journalists, including a few with theatrical pasts. Several haunted houses, every few blocks, have drawn trick-or-treaters from surrounding neighborhoods.

They move easily in this costumed crowd, weaving through a landscape that, to them, now seems properly imaginative and festooned.

Here—just as when he visits Walt Disney World—Owen does no self-talking or scripting. There's no need to conjure a movie through recitation. He is walking within it, smiling and hyper-attentive.

So, it's Lucky Jack who first notices what's gone wrong.

He turns to Walt, wide-eyed. "We've lost Ariel."

Walt grabs my sleeve. "Megan's gone!"

A moment of sheer panic. She could be anywhere; the street is jammed. There is a dark forest—Rock Creek Park—nearby. "We need to find her," I blurt out, "and someone needs to stay with the other kids."

Owen—who often averts his gaze—locks eyes with his brother.

"Tonight, you're the hero," he says, evenly. Walt nods. The competing worlds of these two boys—Owen, in tandem with his mother each day, fighting against and alongside his imagination; and Walt, who's now a popular high school football player, big and charming, with boundless ambitions—collapse into one. Walt breaks into a sprint, swift and sure, and vanishes into the crowd.

The throng seems to thicken. Walt is gone two minutes, then five.

"She can't speak," I say softly to myself, as my thoughts race: *she doesn't know where she is. She could be lost in the woods. We may have to call the police.*

Owen looks at me intently, like he's trying to get behind my eyes.

"Don't worry, Dad. Walter will be the hero," he says.

"Owen, those are movies. This is real life!" I respond.

He pauses, searching through *The Little Mermaid* for a handle. "Walter is a lot like Prince Eric," he says about the movie's hero, before matching a few key characteristics. "Walter's fun loving and courageous, like Eric. Right?"

"Yes, Owen. I suppose so." Talking about a Disney movie is just about the last thing I want to do right now.

He puts a hand on my shoulder as another minute passes. The kids are getting restless. I'm running through what I'll tell Megan's mother. Then, all together, we see it—Walt emerging from the crowd, holding Megan's hand.

Ariel is welcomed back to the group. Owen doesn't notice. He's looking at his brother. Walt and he high-five. "You're the hero, Walter," he says, "and the hero can do anything!"

• • •

Two weeks later, a dinner table conversation turns to a usual subject: Owen's relentlessly stated desire to bring back hand-drawn animation and start "a new golden age of hand-drawn."

We all listen. He's passionate about this, the spoken corollary to a house full of drawings. It's been three years since the drawing mania began, which means three sets of birthday and holiday cards for Cornelia and me. Walt has his own collection, too. Everyone wants to display them—they're very personal works of art, with a character selected for the occasion, and written sentences of strong emotion from someone who has trouble expressing his feelings in speech.

Then there are the sketchbooks, rising toward the ceiling. There are dozens of them. We still don't fully understand the nature of Owen's joy, as he holds the pencil for hours, creating increasingly precise renderings of his sidekicks, now with an occasional villain or hero. What we can see is that his face, as he draws, usually mirrors the expression taking shape on the pad. The selection of what he draws—from the pantheon of hand-drawn characters—also often seems directed by what he wants to feel. Like the voices, it's a form of emotional language.

The rest of the world, of course, is moving in the other direction. Since Pixar's *Toy Story* hit theaters in 1995, the wave of computer-animated films has grown, unabated. They don't seem to have the same effect on the autistic spectrum kids we know, though our random sample is modest. Owen watches them, and some he's enjoyed, but they tend to leave him unrequited, so he returns again and again to the classics or embracing the few hand-drawn, like *Home on the Range.*

Cornelia and I hypothesize that the three-dimensional realism of computer animation may be too much like the overstimulating reality he faces every day. But there's more to it. The hand-drawn characters tend to be more vivid in their expression of emotions; it's precisely that exaggeration that breaks through to Owen, and did since he was small. That bond, from the days when he couldn't speak, has endured. "I can feel those characters," he says.

So, in the year since his bar mitzvah, this has become Owen's chosen mission—the "return of traditional hand-drawn animation, especially from Disney." He says that quite often, just like that—at least once every day or two. It's almost a matter of civil rights for him; this chant, his version of "we shall overcome." It's not only that he sees, like most kids, what's coming out in theaters and on DVD; he trolls animation Web sites online. He knows his hand-drawn world is shrinking.

Cornelia and I are deeply sympathetic, of course, and have an identical response: "Don't worry Owen, hand-drawn will return." He believes what we say—both his neurological grace and affliction— even as, in this matter of his deepest passion, and sole area of investigation, he recognizes that the prevailing judgment is otherwise.

Over dinner—a nice dinner in the dining room—we offer our "trust us, it'll all be fine," response; Owen digs in with a series of *but whys* (why did computer animation take over) and *but hows* (how will hand-drawn be revived).

Walt watches the back-and-forth enveloping another dinner. I know the events of Halloween night still echo in him. We talked about it a few nights ago, how Owen looked to him to find Megan; a kind of nightmare we've all had from time to time, about losing Owen, about him being hurt; and how Walt—who grew up wanting to be a fireman—felt that night ushering the silent girl to safety.

It wasn't a long talk. Walt's a busy guy. He's a fully loaded, seventeen-year-old, testing the limits in the traditional trial and error, with plenty of adventures under way, beyond our purview. But the events of that night, and Owen's hug, seemed to jerk him back.

"Listen, Owen," Walt says, cutting off our "don't worry" duet. "They're practically putting out two computer-animated movies a week. If you want hand-drawn animation to come back, you've got to step up. Lead the charge. You've been into this animation your whole life. You got any movie ideas in there?"

Owen nods, showing he's heard Walt, loud and clear.

His brother, his hero, is issuing a challenge. This is new terrain for Owen. He makes a face—lips pursed, chin out, eyes cast down—which we all know as a summoning expression, like the running start to a jump.

"I have one idea," he says, tentatively. "Twelve sidekicks searching for a hero. And in their journey, and in the obstacles they face, each finds the hero within themselves."

Walt lets out a whoop. We grab our glasses. Owen didn't offer a title to his movie, but—as one—we all clink and toast, "To *Sidekicks!*"

• • •

Owen and I walk gingerly down the steps of a side entrance to Dr. Dan Griffin's basement office in Takoma Park, Maryland. It's a particularly cold and stormy afternoon in December 2005, the week before Christmas. A massive ice storm has just crept up the East Coast. But in all weather, this basement office has become a refuge, a safe place for Owen.

Dr. Griffin welcomes us with hugs, as always, and we settle into our usual chairs. Cornelia made a shrewd management decision when she started homeschooling, telling me the weekly appointment with Griffin "is your time."

Owen started seeing the psychologist when he was thirteen, and Cornelia has been there many times herself. But she needs the break and, from the start, Griffin's hyperkinetic, sometimes scattered style fits well with mine.

More than any other therapist, this psychologist takes hold of what, in essence, was a kind of "Disney therapy," or more broadly, what might be called "affinity therapy," that Cornelia and I, with Walt's assistance, have been conducting for years in our home. He is regularly updated about ways Cornelia is using Disney scripts as a bridge to teach Owen broader knowledge, and creating a tailor-made educational toolkit at Patch of Heaven school.

In Dan's office each week, we are trying to use the scripts to teach him social and life skills. One difference: neither Cornelia nor I are trained educators or therapists. But he, on the other hand, is a highly trained specialist, who'd been handling a flood of autistic spectrum kids, among a jammed patient roster, for fifteen years.

Like many other therapists we'd seen, Griffin was initially a little concerned about Owen's intense affinity for Disney movies, but unlike the others he became intrigued. Griffin kept session notes which years later he shows us, and expands for us into a fuller account of his thoughts at the time. It is our first uncensored view of how a knowledgeable outsider sees us:

In talking early on to his parents about how Owen spends his time, I picked up that he really loves Disney movies—especially classic Disney, from the '40s and '50s, and hits from the early '90s. They told me that since he had been very young his favorite activity was watching Disney movies and poring over them and then reenacting scenes. He'd had entire scripts memorized, and he could act out every part, and every voice. The intense narrow interest struck me as typical of many autistic kids. Other kids I'd seen had been very interested in cars, or Pokémon, or arcane areas of science and history. But Disney movies are different because they involve relationships and carry emotional complexity.

I decided I would experiment with trying to incorporate this interest early on, simply as a way to connect with a child who had difficulty engaging or expressing himself with pragmatic speech. I started by telling him my favorite scenes from old Disney movies and asking him to reenact them. It was something I could talk to him about. For example, I asked him if he knew the scene in *Hercules* when Phil is getting discouraged and made fun of as a trainer. He knew the scene and I was struck by how perfectly he remembered the script, and was able to recreate the voices. But even more surprising was how accurately he mimicked the emotions. In one scene, for example, Phil is disgusted with himself and Hercules is encouraging him not to quit. Owen seemed to really inhabit Phil's despair and Hercules' compassion and encouragement. Owen infused the dialogue with real feeling, as if he truly grasped the emotional significance of what was at stake. This kind of emotional acuity is generally not supposed to be an autistic kid's strength. What I thought was especially cool was that he could shift from Phil to Hercules and capture each of their emotions.

One of the parents—I think it was Ron—mentioned to me that he had been given advice from several professionals to discourage Owen's obsessive interest because it's self stimulatory and avoidant—meaning he would use it to avoid social interaction and instead retreat into fantasy. I understood that that would be the professional consensus, but I remember thinking, and maybe even saying, "I'm not so sure." Another option would be to use the movies as a reward for Owen behaving in desired ways, but I thought we could use them in a more integrated way. Often with kids like Owen you are only teaching them to survive in social situations, but his love for Disney could provide the extra spark to help him not just engage competently or without disaster but to actually want to engage. I had this hunch because he and I were so much more connected when he was acting out Disney. When we talked about the movies it felt so much less like work and more like joyous cooperation. It really made him happy to perform, and he seemed happy that I was interested. It was like night and day, compared to my other interactions with him. Before I'd seen him perform, he was polite, respectful, but he seemed "autistic" in the traditional sense—not consistently "there."

But when he was performing, he seemed totally alive and present.

My epiphany came during a session with me, Owen, and Ron. We were working on how you ask a follow-up question in a conversation. It seemed like a good skill to work on but we weren't getting anywhere. Ron and I were playing the role of reporter and interviewee. We were plodding along dutifully, and Owen was obviously not interested. In an effort to wake us all up Ron and Owen broke into a Disney dialogue. It was a scene from *Aladdin* involving Jafar, and I was blown away at how good Ron was at acting out the scenes. What struck me was, not only did Owen come alive, but Ron came alive in a way I hadn't seen before, and the connection between them was electric. I noticed so much joy, intensity, spontaneity, laughter, and they seemed much more organically connected. The room crackled with sparks of delight.

• • •

The aha moment that Dan refers to actually happened with me and Owen at a session three months ago, in September 2005. The very next session, I gave Dan a full description of Owen's views about sidekicks and heroes, his role as "the protector of sidekicks," and how he seemed to be using this narrative construct to shape his identity. He was clearly transposing his deepest feelings, his fears and aspirations, on the sidekicks.

By early October, after several sessions riffing Disney with Owen, Dan came up with an ingenious plan for Owen to protect and advise a sidekick. After a few discussions, we decided on Zazu, the proud but naive hornbill charged with protecting young Simba in *The Lion King*. Owen, in an exchange, said, "Zazu has a lot to learn."

It was decided that Owen would teach him . . . as a way of teaching himself.

Hence:

Educating Zazu

I, Owen Harry Suskind, agree to undertake the challenging but critical task of providing stimulating educational experiences for my good friend Zazu. This project will take a good deal of work and preparation, but should be a lot of fun and also immensely beneficial to Zazu. I agree to do this for the academic year of 2005–2006.

Areas of Zazu's learning program shall include, but will not be limited to:

1. Life in the world
2. How to concentrate
3. Following directions
4. Health
5. Asking questions
6. Making friends
7. Fun
8. Loving people
9. Science
10. Helping others

Signed, _____ Owen Suskind

Witness _____

Witness _____

Owen signed the contract with much fanfare. Dan and I signed as witnesses.

• • •

We start today's therapy session in early December, with talk of Zazu and his progress. Today, the focus is on Contract Item 6: MAKING FRIENDS.

Owen doesn't have friends, other than through carefully structured activities: he sees Nathan, our neighbor, one evening a week at our house for an art class. Their meetings are facilitated by a twenty-something media-arts guy from the Lab School, a large, happy Wisconsinite, who helps the two boys make a short animated flipbook. In Dr. Gordon's social skills group, he also sees Brian and Robert, two autistic spectrum boys who are also really into movies.

But when advising Zazu he suddenly seems full of advice about how to make friends.

"To make a friend you have to be a friend," he says, picking up a line that's used at Walt's summer camp; it's something Cornelia has said to him a few times but never heard him repeat.

"And you need to be interested in what they're interested in," Owen has added. "And then they can be interested in what you're interested in."

These are sentences Dan might have heard kids say many times in his career. But what makes this moment special is that Owen seems to infuse the advice with feeling. Instead of just repeating these chestnuts about social skills, Owen seems to really be owning them. Dan keeps up the momentum by bringing up the "Second Question Rule"—for keeping a conversation going with a more narrow question: "When did you do that? Who else was with you? How did that feel?" We practice a few of those, all three of us.

Owen mentions how Zazu has trouble with Contract Item 8—Loving people—because he's "ashamed about how he failed Simba," who slipped away from the hornbill's watchful gaze and got into trouble—trouble that eventually led to Mufasa's death.

For the past few months, Dan—who has two small children—has been brushing up in his off hours on Owen's favorites. Dan takes the risk of asking Owen to elaborate about the fairly complex dynamic between Zazu and Simba—when you fail to meet your own expectations, and disappoint someone you care about, what does that feel like? As Owen is thinking, I mouth "P-h-i-l" to Dan. He knows immediately which scene I'm thinking of, and asks Owen if this is what happens to Phil in *Hercules*:

Owen starts to laugh. "Can I do it?"

Before we can nod, Owen's off and running, doing all the parts in a scene where Phil is trying to tell a crowd of doubters about Hercules' potential:

> PHIL: THIS KID IS A GENUINE ARTICLE.
> MAN: HEY, ISN'T THAT THE GOAT-MAN
>   PHILOCTOTES WHO TRAINED ACHILLES?
> PHIL: WATCH IT PAL!
> STRONG MAN: YEAH, YOU'RE RIGHT. HEY, NICE JOB
>   ON THOSE HEELS! YA' MISSED A SPOT!
> PHIL: I GOT YOUR HEEL RIGHT HERE! I'LL WIPE
>   THAT STUPID GRIN OFF YOUR FACE! YOU—
> HERCULES: HEY PHIL! PHIL! PHIL! TAKE IT EASY,
>   PHIL.
> STRONG MAN: WHAT ARE YOU, CRAZY? *SHEESH.*
> HEAVY WOMAN: YOUNG MAN, WE NEED A
>   PROFESSIONAL HERO. NOT AN AMATEUR.
> HERCULES: WELL, WAIT. STOP! HOW AM I
>   SUPPOSED TO PROVE MYSELF A HERO IF
>   NOBODY WILL GIVE ME A CHANCE?

Dan would later cite this moving moment in his memo, and talk about how surprised and touched he was that Owen could access the emotions of Phil, Hercules, and the three other characters in that scene.

A typical birthday boy at age one

And mugging for the camera at two

Owen vanishes by age three,
right before our eyes

Exhausted, terrified, and in a daze,
we hold tight to a silent child

We each play our roles. Cornelia nurtures, teaches, and stands behind him, no matter what comes his way.

Behind the scenes I'm a clown, doing voices, tugging him along. In public, a very different face.

"Context blind,"
like many of those
with autism, Owen
(with brother, Walt)
is utterly in context,
relaxed and engaged
in his favorite place:
Walt Disney World.

e begins to first
peak in Disney
dialogue and then,
few years along,
stages elaborate
role-playing: with
his cousins here,
from *James and
the Giant Peach.*

Disney scripts are used in the
curriculum at the homegrown
"Patch of Heaven" school.

y high school,
Owen's using
movie themes
and morals to
learn and survive.
(With Walt on
visiting day at
Camp Pasquaney)

Across nearly two decades, members of "Team Owen" slowly built his skills (Suzie Blattner tutoring him at seven); and then (with Dan Griffin) helping him gain the confidence to meet the world.

Owen watches Walt's every move, subtly mapping his life along his brother's path. Walt, though, says Owen's "my best teacher."

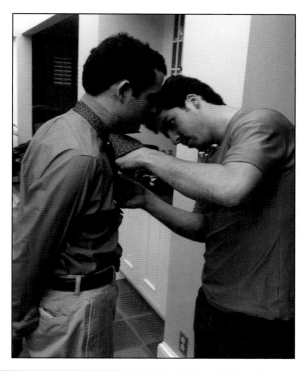

Owen meets one of his heroes, Disney animation legend Glen Keane, who tells him "it's the stories we need."

Now having channeled his passion into art—painting interpretive versions of iconic characters.

A happy young man with his girl (Emily Jathas) and his dog (Gus)

As that day's session ends, Dan pulls me aside. "Autistic kids like Owen are not supposed to do that—this is getting weird in a very good way."

•   •   •

Cornelia ducks into my studio office behind the house and puts Owen's black-and-white composition book on my desk. It's late February 2006.

I can tell it's a good urgency—to report something hopeful.

"Read this. Last entry."

I open to the book's last page. She asked Owen to create a story, with himself as the character.

"A boy is fearful of his future and what his life will be like . . ." the story begins. It has a few twists along the way, as the boy wanders into a forest and finds a stone, a magic stone. Tilt it toward the sun and it becomes a mirror in which the boy can see the future. The boy loves the stone. He sees many possible futures for himself, all of them exciting. But then crossing a river the boy slips and loses the stone.

"But it's okay," the story finishes. "He doesn't need the stone anymore, now that he knows his future will be bright and full of joy."

"I think he's ready to go," she says.

"I think you're right. Are you ready for someone else to take over?" I respond.

She smiles. She talks about how she was dreading this, before it began, how it'd devour her life. "I realize I'm going to really miss it. Just the two of us, making our way. But he's ready. This is what we've been working for—for him to join the rest of the kids."

The next week—the first week in March 2006, a few days before his fifteenth birthday—we tell Owen that he'll be interviewing at the school we've been angling toward in Rockville, Maryland, called the

Katherine Thomas School (KTS). It has a new high school program, which was just started last year by the former assistant director of the Lab School's high school, Rhona Schwartz. The school, which Schwartz is the director of, is much like the Lab, but more inclusive of more types of kids, with about one-third of them on the spectrum.

It's very small—only about forty kids—but due to grow, or so Rhona Schwartz, tells us on our visit with Owen. She takes us on a tour. It's a spacious building, only half-full, and we can see Owen, nodding, checking the boxes of what represents school to him: classrooms, library, science lab, music room, art studio, gymnasium, and principal's office, where we settle for a chat.

Rhona, having worked under Sally Smith, knows just who she's looking at with Owen. The school, set up to handle ninth through twelfth graders, currently has only the first two grades filled. In the fall, Owen would be in the third class of ninth graders, she explains. "Would you like that, Owen?"

"Yes!" he says, with a plastered-on smile. "I think this is the place for me!" We all chuckle. I've never seen him in this mode, like a salesman looking to close a deal: settled, clear-eyed, sort of charming. Cornelia's looking bemused, behind which she's thinking what I'm thinking: *he must* really, really *want this*. Rhona tells Owen and us that he'll come back for a day so he can be observed, "just to make sure this is the right place for you."

We next talk to Schwartz after Owen's observation day. It's a disaster. She tells us he was walking the halls, pacing, flapping his arms, doing "lots of stim." He passed by a classroom where he spotted his friend, Brian (from the social skills group) and just strode right in, in the middle of a lesson, loudly telling Brian he's coming to this school.

It's all, suddenly, hanging by a thread. We rush right over. Cornelia explains he must have been very anxious. "This is not the way he usually behaves . . . I'm with him every day," she says. "He must have been very nervous and trying too hard." He certainly seemed settled on his visit with me, Rhona says. She'll give him another tryout.

During his second observation day, Owen's a little better, but not there yet. But then, after a third observation day, Rhona reports he's "significantly better." These three days stretch over four weeks. For us, it's a month of sheer hell.

But he's in. We pass the good news to Owen, and he's ecstatic. "I really love this school," he says. With the homeschooling, we always worry about the so-called social piece, with his loss of daily peer interactions, spending so much of his time in one-on-one sessions with adults. Over the past two years, Cornelia and I have tried to schedule as many organized activities with other kids and "playdates" as possible, even if the pool of potential friends is small. And they mostly are just that—potential friends. The hope—ours and his—is that in the mix of high school, with kids like him, he'll finally make friends.

We credit the anxiety of his visitations to performance pressure, just Owen wanting it so badly.

And, soon enough, the items from Patch of Heaven—the desks, the file cabinet, the white board—go up on craigslist. Cornelia ends up donating everything to a mom who is homeschooling her kid in Cedric's old neighborhood, rather than having him brave the schools in their part of town. She doesn't want the lockers, which Cornelia leaves at the local church.

They have served their purpose.

•   •   •

Owen gets up on a bright June morning, slips out of bed, and puts a video into a small television with a built-in VCR. In this period— already dominated by DVDs, Netflix, and video streaming—the set's a throwback: it's of the same generation as the one we used when he and Walt were toddlers in Dedham, Massachusetts.

And that's the way Owen likes it. The familiarity, in the shape and function, is a comfort to him. The video presentation is slightly different than the DVD, all but imperceptible variations in the framing and pixilation of the picture. He sees it though. And then there's the rewinding. You can rewind a VHS tape to the frame, and work the controls, *pause, reverse,* and *play,* to isolate the tiniest shifts in an expression, or the way a mouth shapes around a word.

He still does that sometimes, though he doesn't need to, using the screen as a mirror, to mouth words or get the movements of his body just so, matching the screen. Or just running a few seconds again and again—a moment of surprise or fear or tenderness—to feel whatever sensation the character is feeling, over and over.

It's nice that this portable TV is in his bedroom—a concession he just won this year—so he can put in a video, grab the remote, and slide back into bed. Lately, he's started something new: watching certain scenes, with the sound low, in the early morning to prepare him for the day ahead.

This morning, it's *Aladdin*, and, sitting up in his bed, he points the remote and presses FAST FORWARD. It takes a minute—he picks the fast option, where the movies races by—until he nears the end.

It's the scene after Jafar and Iago are vanquished, and all the plot-lines are swiftly resolved. Aladdin has to decide what to do with his third wish—turn himself into a prince, so he can marry Jasmine, or free the Genie from servitude, as he'd promised. The Genie suggests the former, saying "this is love—and you won't find another girl like that in a million years." Aladdin chooses the latter: "I wish for your freedom." This sends the Genie into whoops and flying loops of cele-bration:

GENIE: OH, DOES THAT FEEL GOOD! I'M FREE! I'M
FREE AT LAST! I'M HITTIN' THE ROAD. I'M OFF
TO SEE THE WORLD! I'M . . .
*HE IS PACKING A SUITCASE, BUT LOOKS DOWN AND SEES
ALADDIN LOOKING VERY SAD.*
ALADDIN: GENIE, I'M—I'M GONNA MISS YOU.
GENIE: ME TOO, AL. NO MATTER WHAT ANYBODY
SAYS, YOU'LL ALWAYS BE A PRINCE TO ME.

Owen hits REWIND. Watches it, again. And then one more time. Beside him on the night table is a pile of cards he's been drawing over the past few days. Nearly a dozen of them. They're thank-you notes to his therapists and the assorted others—his music teacher, art teacher, swimming coach—that's he seen each and every week for the past two years at Patch of Heaven. His team.

Each note carries the picture of a sidekick.

Dan Griffin, the psychologist, made him a flip-book of laminated index cards, each carrying the picture of a favorite Disney character with a lesson—listen to others, smile whenever possible, don't worry about what you can't control—that he carries with him everywhere. As a gift, Owen gives Dan a precise rendering of Rafiki from *The Lion King*, with a note that says, "Dear Dan, I want to thank you for helping me make friends and for being popular. You're my great wise man."

A carefully selected picture, with an inscription, has been fashioned for each of them. Tony Riel, the media arts teacher from the Lab School, who visits our house one evening every week to teach Owen how to turn drawings into flash videos, gets a vivid rendering of the royal blue Genie . . . who is, after all, a sidekick.

C. T. Gordon, the psychiatrist who takes Owen and the other boys on nature hikes, as he helps them create stories that'll reveal their inner feelings, is granted the role of Cornelius, the wise old mentor from *Once Upon a Forest*, a 1993 Hanna-Barbera animated movie. Cornelius leads the "the young furlings" on their adventures through the woods, teaching them as he goes.

Sharon Lockwood, a gentle speech therapist/psychologist of late middle age, watches movies with Owen and analyzes scenes that can be applied to life and help him work through anxiety. In some ways, she's the most maternal of his therapists—a woman of soft-spoken deftness and compassion—so she gets the character often applied to Cornelia: Big Mama, from *The Fox and the Hound*.

And on it goes. Each one is placed in the pantheon.

By early afternoon, they start arriving—the whole cast—with their husbands or wives. In some cases, they've brought friends. It's a warm day, and the flowers are in bloom in our backyard. Dan, an earthy Italian/Irish musician who also cooks, brings a pepper and sausage dish. Sharon, with her husband, a psychiatrist, bears a fruit salad that fills a large carved watermelon.

Cornelia passes out Patch of Heaven yearbooks, a small hardback book of about twenty pages, that she designed and had printed online. In it, they're all pictured with Owen, above captions of the things they did for him and with him.

And at the center of it is Owen, watching them all, at the very slightest remove, as they drink and balance paper plates, talking with animated zest—in a swirl of pairs and clusters, moving to and fro on the backyard's flagstone patio. He sees the sunlight is reflecting off them in several interesting ways, especially off the women's earrings and the men's wristwatches. One usually laughs before the other, like they're going in some sort of order, but then they switch. No one is wearing red. The women sometimes touch the men's arms, but not the other way. There are birds chirping from a tall branch. A car is passing far off on the street. Christine moves like Grace, the pretty, goofy cow in *Home on the Range*. He's glad he picked that character for her card.

"Owen. Owen? It's time." It's Cornelia. Coming out the back door, with plates for cake in one hand, she hands him a folder with the thank-you cards.

He passes them out. He doesn't say much—just a cheery, "Here's your card!" But he doesn't have to say anymore. The cards speak for him.

Years later, once he became able to reminisce about these days, he told me, "I was excited about going to high school. It's something I really wanted. But I was scared about what I'd do without all of my therapists and teachers. They all knew who I was."

As he watches them read their cards, and he looks from one face to the next, there's something Owen knows he can now feel, powerfully: that this is a party for him. That's who they're all here for. He's on his way to a high school, just like Walt. A real high school, with all the things a high school has. And everyone here helped.

He hears Aladdin's voice; it's in him. He's not a hero, no. But he sure will miss them. Twelve sidekicks, all smiling in the sun.

chapter eight

LUCK FROM UNLUCK

Cornelia looks over at her passenger sleeping in his down jacket, the packed feathers inside the collar providing a soft ledge for his cheek. Vibrating between the knees of his tattered jeans is a loaded-to-bursting backpack—the signature item of any American high schooler, anywhere.

He sure does look the part. And not just when he sleeps. He does his homework after dinner in his room with the door closed. Most nights he calls one of his two friends, just to talk, and then usually calls the other. He moans, "just five more minutes," when his mom wakes him up for school.

It's 8:07 on a brisk morning in early November 2007, about ten minutes still before the exit off the interstate for Rockville, Maryland, where Owen, now sixteen, is a few months into his sophomore year at the Katherine Thomas School.

He usually doesn't sleep during the half-hour drive each morning. But he was up late last night—there's a big math test today—and hearing his light breathing, safe in this warm womb of the car, warms Cornelia, too. He does seem happy and engaged—and that's what she's hoped for. Owen's mom has concerns, all sorts of them, old ones and new, and questions about how the traditional challenges of adolescence will present themselves, or not, in a teenager whose body is growing fast while his mind—his feelings, his intellect, his identity—remain, as ever, largely beyond view or reach. But Cornelia's worries are steadily unwinding, with each morning drive or afternoon pickup, as is a knot in her stomach that she's carried so long it now seems like a traveling companion.

The Volvo could drive itself; she's made this trip so many times, and she nudges him awake—"we're here, honey"—as they make the last few turns toward school.

"Ready for your math test?" she asks, never much of a math student herself. He's in algebra, a course they stretch across two years. His father helps him with that.

"No, umm, I'm good, Mom," he says in a grumbly exhale, his voice low and oddly unaffected, as it is sometimes right when he wakes up, almost as though, coming out of sleep, his body forgets he's autistic. Just one of those mirages, she knows, moments when a spectrum kid does something so typical—could be a look, a word, a gesture—that it seems like they've suddenly emerged from a spell. Of course, it just tees you up for a hit. This autism is no spell—it's a way of being. And, by now, Cornelia has built retaining walls against such surges of uplift.

The car eases into the drop-off line, and he opens the door. "See you after school, Mom!" he all but sings, all chirpy. And a voice in her head says . . . *wish he could use that other voice in the halls.*

But who's she to say? She doesn't know much of what goes on in those halls, and that's the way it should be: at some point, a boy must grow away from his mother. What book doesn't say that?

A few minutes later, she settles into a booth at Panera Bread at a mall not far from the school. She has about forty-five minutes before Rhona Schwartz, KTS's director, is due to meet her here. So, over tea and a muffin, she answers yesterday's e-mails and sends off a few texts to her sisters. Cornelia's been given a big slice of her life back since the homeschooling experiment ended almost eighteen months ago, and it couldn't have come at a better time. Or worse. Earlier this year, Cornelia's middle-age brother died of cancer—just like one of her sisters had in 2004. And then her father passed away two months ago. It was cancer as well. Cornelia's battered and a little numb. She couldn't have been there 24-7 for Owen, not this year. He found a home, a lifeboat, at KTS just in time. It was lucky. Luck from unluck.

She reaches into her purse for a half-dozen folded pages: Owen's year-end evaluations for last year, ninth grade, in all his subjects.

Cornelia looks at the date: May 2007. Sure, it was a bad time after her brother, Martin, died. But did she even read this? It wasn't just Martin. She's been the recipient of so many bleak progress reports on Owen over the years that she can barely bring herself to look at them anymore.

But she needs to cram. Rhona will be here soon enough. Her eyes scan for the key parts—direct assessments of Owen—and finds herself surprised. They're generally positive: he's sometimes distracted, needs prompts, works hard, and has trouble with abstract ideas, especially in math. But it's very much him. In English, he did not test well, but "seemed to especially enjoy voice acting the characters in our reading."

Cornelia reads on. In computers, his work in class was inconsistent, but "he was able to give a very nice presentation on Disney sidekicks"; in drama, "he displayed remarkable skills at character development." And, "as an actor he was beyond creative in his demonstration of technique."

One teacher wrote he started the year with "limited independent work skills and frequent pacing" and ended it with "minimal prompts and pacing" and working independently.

Cornelia folds the sheets and carefully returns them to her purse. After thirteen years and four schools, this may be the first positive report she's ever received. She doesn't want to embrace hope that'll soon enough be dashed. But what's here is indisputably forward motion. His conscientiousness and effort come through in almost every assessment—always doing his homework, giving it his all, even in the subjects where progress is slow. Whatever worked at Patch of Heaven in terms of building his skills, integrating schoolwork with his blast furnace imagination, and teaching him to manage anxiety, he's self-propelling now. One theme found in each teacher's comments is his desire to improve. He really wants it.

She hears someone with a New York accent approaching and looks up. Rhona Schwartz gives Cornelia a hug and slips into the booth, a travel cup of coffee already in her hand. She's a small bundle of readiness: short dark hair, large dark eyes, quick smile.

They've met a few times and get right into it. She has twenty minutes before she has to return to KTS. Rhona offers updates on how the nascent high school is faring in just its third year. With twenty-nine juniors, eighteen sophomores, and a strong incoming class of fifteen freshmen, the school now has sixty-two students. It's an eclectic mix of the learning disabled, with maybe a quarter of them on the spectrum, mixed with lots of Attention Deficit Disorders and Attention Deficit Hyperactivity Disorders, and a few students with severe medical problems. Some, understandably, have issues of emotional self-regulation, though the emotionally disturbed students go elsewhere. KTS has, in essence, become the school for kids who don't quite fit at any of the other special-needs schools in the area.

Most of the students are funded by Washington, DC, or Maryland as not appropriate for the public system, at a cost of nearly $35,000 each a year.

We're in the private paying group, along with about a third of the parents. But in a school this small, you can see the dollars at work. With a four-to-one student-to-teacher ratio, there are fifteen teachers; many of them are quite energetic, from artists to retired professionals. They use a typical high school curriculum, but one that's lightened and slowed down. Some kids, Owen among them, are on the trajectory toward earning a high school diploma; others are on track to receiving an achievement certification.

And Owen, Rhona assures Cornelia, is doing fine. *Really.*

She talks about his growth in the first year, but they both know the biggest breakthrough is that he now has friends. Owen knew one student coming in—a boy on the spectrum named Brian from his social skills group. Rhona describes to Cornelia in a cursory way how she matched Owen up with another boy, Connor, who has since become his other great friend. She knew that Connor, who'd been at KTS from elementary school, was a movie enthusiast, like Owen, and also gentle and cheery. Schwartz recounts that she approached Owen, even though he said that he already had a friend (Brian) and was fearful of losing that friendship if he tried to bring in this other person.

Rhona tells Cornelia that she has seen this before with kids on the spectrum; that they opt for control and sameness, rather than risk uncertainty and its pitfalls. She describes how she called Owen into her office and worked with him, using the overlapping circles of a Venn diagram, showing how the circles of Brian and Connor can overlap but remain distinct, and that both can overlap with Owen's circle. She had him color in the place where the three circles overlap in a color he likes. He picks green, and Schwartz tells him that's where friendship lives.

What Cornelia knows is that Owen, Connor, and Brian, who's also a movie fanatic, are now calling themselves "The Movie Gods." They have used movies to forge a trio. It's just about the best thing in Owen's life. After so many years of pining for friends, he now has two.

"I didn't know how it happened, how you found Connor," Cornelia says, softly, reaching across the table to squeeze Rhona's hand. "Thank you."

• • •

It's working, finally: a school for Owen. The key is that it's happening—classwork, friends for lunch, activities, the flow of a school day—in a controlled environment that suits him. It's not too controlled, but just enough. And modulated to what most of these students need. A chance to move at their own pace. And the pace is important, more so than for the typical kid at this age. Folks, plenty of them, know about this with learning-disabled kids. That's why they get extra time on the tests.

With a typical kid, the extra time wouldn't really matter. They process quickly, naturally. Either they figure out the answer or they can't, and then they move to the next question. With the learning-disbled student, the unevenness of how they process information, fit it together, means the extra time matters—it helps them work through their learning difference to get at their underlying intelligence . . . and show it on the test. For many autistic kids, you need to multiply—with the deeper complexities in the way they process information, either written or spoken, their underlying intelligence is often more deeply submerged or unevenly expressed.

That means there's some cat herding that'll go on, with kids moving at many speeds and in many directions in every classroom at KTS. But with enough time, they get there, often summoning some very improbable pathway to the right answer.

So, there's that, in terms of the academics. But similar dynamics apply to everything else going on in the building, to the small society that forms in every high school. What's different here, or needs to be? Everything here needs to be softened and slowed down a notch, including social matters.

Many of the kids carry a look-before-they-leap cautiousness, socially, a delay switch for time to demystify. And that translates into a gentleness; aggressiveness, after all, is often born of an overflow of confidence or frustration, based on comparative issues. On that last score, these kids don't form hierarchies in the usual way; there aren't ongoing battles for supremacy or rank, so typical of high school. Not that the underlying desires are any different. Their hearts beat strong and true, and maybe a bit more exposed than the rest of us.

And what we begin to see, day to day, is what Rhona tells Cornelia: that in this delicately controlled ecosystem, he's thriving.

• • •

Owen wakes up one morning in early December 2007 at 7:10. He's out of bed by 7:15, done with breakfast by 7:25 (a quick eater), out of the shower and dressed by 7:45, in the car by 7:50 (today, Dad drives), and at school by 8:20 A.M.

It was a day like any other, or so Owen would tell me a year later in quotidian detail. That memory, again. So much he can remember. Some things, he'd rather not.

And on this wintry day he weaves through the bustle on the way to his locker. Puts gloves inside hat, pushes the knitted ball into the jacket's arm and hangs it in the locker. Then he makes his way to homeroom, where he first sees Brian and Connor (they're both in his homeroom). All three talk about DreamWorks's new animated film, *Bee Movie,* which is just out for the 2007 holiday season. In their opinion, it isn't any good. Owen says he watched *Snow White and the Seven Dwarfs* last night, that it's been awhile since he's seen it. Still great. Brian loves it, too. Owen does Grumpy's voice. Connor and Brian laugh; they know it's Grumpy at the first word. They both chime in with other dwarf dialogue.

First period is music. Owen arrives and slides into his desk in the music room. His mind is moving this way and that. *Snow White and the Seven Dwarfs.* Grumpy. Why Connor likes the first Superman movie. Owen takes in the room. There are drums, a piano, and a few other instruments. Other kids soon arrive. There are five boys and two girls.

Owen doesn't mix with the kids. He's polite—always polite. But he keeps to himself. He has his two friends.

The boy sitting next to him—William—is a big, athletic guy, almost Walt's size. He's very popular. And he's bending over his desk toward Owen's.

"Hey Owen, something I've got to tell you," he whispers. "I know where you live."

Owen turns. He can't read the expression on William's face. He has a nice face, and he may be making a joke, but Owen's not sure. His dad always says, "If you think someone's making a joke, assume they are. Act like it is a joke, and you'll find out if it's not."

"You're trying to be funny?" Owen says.

William shakes his head. No joke.

"And, listen Owen, I know your parents. That's right. And I know something else. They don't love you. And they're going to leave you. One day, you'll come home, the house will be locked."

Owen is feeling panic rise in his chest. He can't lie, but he can't easily discern when others are lying to him. This is maybe the greatest peril many autistic people face, both kids and adults. They're believers. He knows what a lie is, of course. But he doesn't know it when he sees it.

"My parents do to love me. I'm a good person, with a big heart, and I love animated movies, mostly from Disney." He says with all the resolve he can muster, like he's lifting a shield.

It just exposes his flank. "Right, you're *always* talking about Disney. I know you love it. In fact, I know everything about you, Owen," William continues. "I told you, I know where you live. And if you tell your parents what I said, I'm going to come and burn your house down."

Owen goes through his day—world history, math, art, lunch,

science, gym, and English—in a daze. His eyes dart left and right, while his mind races around a continuous play loop. Could William really know Mom and Dad? If I tell them what he said, will he burn down our house?

. . .

In April 2008, Cornelia and I do the morning carpool together. Owen sits in the back, looking at the landscape passing by.

Owen's a mess. We don't know why. We just know that he is. We ask him how school is and he gets one of his plastered-on super-smiles, eyebrows up, lips tight against his teeth, and says, "School's great! Everything's a–okay!" He says it every time, just like that.

But he's not eating. He's not sleeping. We run in circles. Have been for months. Maybe it's his medication—possibly he's outgrown his low dose of Prozac. Maybe he needs a higher dose, or something else.

And he's not talking about Disney, not even when I do a voice. He won't respond with the counter. I'll do his favorite dads—Mufasa, King Triton—and my mimicked line hangs in the air.

Same thing for Monday afternoons with Dan Griffin. Disney's been tabled. Owen's responses are perfunctory.

We're in the car all together today because the school has called us to come in for a morning meeting. They didn't tell us why, just that Owen is behaving strangely, and they'd explain when we got there. We suggested that Dan come, too.

At 9:00 A.M., as the kids file into their respective first-period classes, we three—Dan has just arrived—file into a conference room. Rhona comes in looking grim. She's accompanied by Owen's social worker. (Each student at KTS is in a small social skills group— usually three or four kids—that's run by a social worker.)

Rhona gets right to it: Owen tried to poke a kid with a pencil.

No damage, didn't break the skin. "But this is so not like him," she says. "I know you guys have gone through a lot, with the passing of so many members of Cornelia's family. Is everything okay at home?"

Cornelia is stunned. "He tried to poke someone with a pencil? That can't be Owen."

Rhona nods in partial agreement. "That's been our reaction," she responds before laying out a few small details. It was in science and there were two kids who may have been "joking around" with him. "But nothing that would draw this kind of response."

I tell her that there are no big changes at home, at least none we've detected. How things might affect Owen are often unclear. Maybe there's some latent response to Walt having left this year for college. Maybe it's his medication.

Dan says that Owen seems grim in therapy. And not particularly forthcoming. He tells them that Owen seems to have replaced Disney films with relentless viewings of the first two Batman movies (which were from Tim Burton). Both are pretty dark. "Owen reveals things through his movies," Dan adds. "Maybe this is just a strong move into adolescent angst. Maybe something else."

We all talk more generally of the difficulties in reading teenagers during these years of rapid change, but how, with a typical kid, everyone has a fairly sound estimation of what the growing pains look like: separation from parents, testing boundaries, sexual awakening, disdain for the adult world. The basic Holden Caulfield menu one finds in *The Catcher in the Rye*. It's difficult to match much of that with a spectrum kid like Owen, at least with any real surety.

"What goes on inside of him is still, often, a mystery," I say, with frustration. "There are worlds in there—places we can't get to."

"You know, we love Owen here," Rhona says after a bit, to fill the silence.

"We know," Cornelia says, still trying to get a fix on an image of Owen—the world's gentlest child—going after another student.

"Just tell us anything you see. And we will, too. We'll see what we can find out about the pencil."

• • •

Around the corner and down a long hallway, Owen is sitting in music, trying to breathe.

William has brought in a friend, Tony, as his partner. The two of them wait for Owen each morning. The trap of torment, where revealing the threats against him will bring disaster, has held. Within it, there's so much room for them to improvise. Every day, there's a new twist.

"Hey, Owen, drove by your house last night," William whispers. "Didn't you see me? I almost burned it down last night. I was thinking you've been lying to me, that you already told your parents. Have you?"

Owen shakes his head, side to side. "I don't lie."

"Okay, then fuck you, too," one of the kids responds.

"I hate that word."

"Okay, fuckin' shit then."

He won't look at William's face. When his tensing body reaches its fullest, piano wire tautness, the other boy—Tony, who's sitting behind Owen—pokes him hard in the ribs. The wind flies from his lungs with an "oomph."

"Please stop," he says.

"*Owen, is there a problem?*" the teacher asks. The regular music teacher went on leave in the late fall. This teacher, a substitute, is a first-time teacher of music—he's overmatched in a subject that requires quite a bit of skill.

"No, everything's fine," Owen croaks.

He hears snickers next to him and behind.

Since William brought in Tony, Owen is seeing danger

everywhere—not sure who William will recruit next. The kid he poked at with his pencil in science yesterday wasn't even one of these two. It was just a kid who knows them and was starting to act a little like them. Owen felt like the mayhem was spreading, that the kid in science had caught wind of what was happening in music and was ready to join in.

The music teacher tells everyone to pick up their instruments. There's a year-end concert scheduled in a week and everyone works a bit on his or her presentation. As the period bell rings, Owen runs from the class and, when he's clear of them, starts pacing the halls, murmuring. "Come on, kid, come on. Fight back. Come on, you can take this bum. This guy's a pushover, look at him."

It's not Owen's voice. It's Phil—Danny DeVito's tough guy tone—from *Hercules*. He hasn't abandoned Disney. He's just taken it underground, not wanting to give the bullies any other weapons to use against him. He's relying on Phil, mostly. Phil talks to him, like an adviser. They have conversations, always in DeVito's voice reciting certain lines from the movie. This line—about this guy being a bum, a pushover—is one of the lines of dialogue Owen repeats a lot. Today, he adds the next line in the movie, a response from Hercules: "You were right all along, Phil. Dreams are for rookies."

And then he follows with Phil's finish: "No, no, no, no, kid, givin' up is for rookies. I came back 'cause I'm not quittin' on ya. I'm willing to go the distance; how 'bout you?"

And through the day, he mutters that stanza of dialogue under his breath, barely audible, a hundred times. It's the only thing that seems to drown out the dread.

• • •

There's a surprise in the pickup lane on an afternoon in mid-May.

"Walter!" Owen shouts and runs toward the car. Walt, five cars back in the pickup line, jumps out to meet him, and they embrace in the parking lot.

Owen hugs him with all his might. "Easy, buddy. You okay?"

Owen nods. "I missed you."

"I missed you, too."

There are a few honks from behind them and they jump back into the idling car.

"So, how goes. Everything good?"

Owen nods. "Are you done with college?"

Walt explains that they get out early in college—graduation's this weekend, and he'll be home for a few weeks, before leaving for camp, where he's now a counselor. The car inches forward. There are no U-turns. They'll have go through the line. Up ahead, there's a crowd. After-school pickup is carefully choreographed. To avoid injuries, and help along a few kids with physical disabilities, teachers or aides escort all students into the cars.

Owen sees William in the mix and his mind begins to race. This is his chance. Literal to a fault, he thinks that William said if he told his parents, he'd burn down the house. *But he didn't say anything about telling his brother.* For Owen, this is the cracking of a code, and he's already sketching in his head what Walt will do. William is big, but Walt is bigger, nearly two hundred pounds with muscles on muscles; in Owen's estimation, almost like Hercules. But thinking that creates a subtle turn, that none of the Disney heroes ever kill the villain, at least not in the classics. The villains are killed by their greed, or hatred, or, as in *The Lion King*, by their evil sidekicks. A hero never stoops to murder, even of someone who is pure evil. Walt eases his truck toward the front slot, as Owen watches him fuss with the radio. *Walt could kill him.* If he did, he'd no longer be the hero. And, slipping out of Disney calculus, he'd also be in very big trouble.

He looks out the passenger window and right at William, who catches his gaze and registers surprise. *What's this? His prey staring back at him?* Owen never meets William's eye. The adversary looks inside the car, sees a big guy who looks a lot like Owen behind the wheel, and backs away into the crowd of waiting students.

As the car pulls away, with Walt at the wheel, Owen feels his whole body let down.

•   •   •

As Cornelia and I load dinner plates into the dishwasher, we hear Owen, from the living room piano, practicing his song for tomorrow afternoon's school concert. We can't help but feel excitement. This is an earned reward. He's been taking a weekly lesson from Ruthlee Adler, his piano teacher, for five years. He can manage a few classical pieces, like the one he's now playing.

The next day, as we slip into our seats in the KTS gymnasium for the concert, I mention to Cornelia, how we knew he'd crush "Hatikva," especially after I told him that if he played it flawlessly he'd never have to play it again.

"I think that's revisionist history," she quips. "If I recall, we couldn't be sure he'd 'show up' for his bar mitzvah. But he did. It was such a warm place that day, a safe place."

The students enter and most sit down in chairs next to their parents. Some student-performers are up front; others will be summoned forward when it's their turn to perform. Owen's among the latter, due up near the end of the program.

But he seems tight and distant. He doesn't applaud when the others finish—he usually loves to applaud. Then, when his name is called, he just sits. Like he didn't hear it. We're sitting midway in a pretty good-sized crowd of about 120, so the concert director can't see him.

"Owen, you're up," I whisper. "They're calling your name."

He just sits, looking forward. One of the teachers up front spots him and begins to walk back. "Come on, Owie," Cornelia says. "This is it."

After a long pause he rises, and walks tentatively toward the piano, his songbook in his hand. He sits, opens it onto the music rack, and then nothing. Closer to the stage, right near the piano, a group of students, who will be singing next, look over quizzically at Owen.

Twenty seconds pass and he begins to play in a fitful manner. Owen struggles with it to the end. He jumps up and races back toward his seat, amid sparse applause. He's barely in his chair beside us when the next act is announced: an original song, written by "one of our most talented students." A large, handsome young man, who'd been standing by the piano, takes center stage. He seems self-aware and ebullient, a cockiness that's striking in a school like this because very few kids with special needs exude that kind of swagger.

But he brings it—a raucous song that really works, which he sings and claps masterfully, until the whole room is on its feet clapping to his beat and cheering. That closes the show.

I barely notice that Owen is frozen in his seat. I'm too busy looking at the kid. "Wonder what his 'issues' are," I murmur. "Looks like he's ready for MTV."

· · ·

"Do you want to cancel the party?" Cornelia asks me, tamping down exasperation.

"No let's do it. Look, a person's got to eat. So, I'll eat and get back to work."

She looks at me with pity, though she'd probably be just as happy if I stayed in the basement—where I've retreated to write the finish to the latest book because it's easier to nap on the couch than in my studio office. Like all books, this one is a battle to the end. On the first one, Cornelia joked, "It's as close as man will get to childbirth—you might as well enjoy it." Now, on book four, she's way past levity.

I look like death, and feel worse. She just gets to watch, make sure I'm fed, and wonder when her husband will return.

It's Saturday, June 7, and the kitchen might as well be zoned for a TV commercial—pots of every variety are simmering with ingredients gathered from across the globe (but all available at Whole Foods Market). There's a large rented table filling a wide expanse of the living room which was made possible after the couches and chairs were pushed against the walls. Cornelia's in a movie club, all women, except once a year, when the spouses are invited for a dinner party. That's tonight.

"Please be showered and shaved by seven o'clock," Cornelia instructs me. I nod sheepishly and slip downstairs.

I'm beginning to realize how you can lose yourself in this basement. It's cavelike, with thin, street-level windows that are shaded, and walls—stone, brick, and cement behind the wood paneling— that don't let sound in.

I've banished Owen to his room for the last few days—"Dad's taking over the basement"—and ordered him this sunny afternoon to ride his bike to a neighborhood market to pick up heavy cream for his mother. It's a make-work job. But it'll keep him busy for an hour.

I settle onto the holy sofa: Corn's first purchase as a single girl when we were dating in New York in the early 1980s. It's a high-quality product, holding up quite nicely after twenty-five years. We are, too. There've been stresses galore that have come to rest on this marriage, from the long, seesawing struggle with Owen to the moments of public battle when the latest books have been released into this toxic political environment. But the battles, if anything, have strengthened our bond.

And we're both feeling fortunate these days. No single reason, and many circumstances to the contrary—especially, in regard to Owen's strange and troubling behavior. But a kind of faith in possibility, in the way things tend to work out, is the cup we both seem to be drinking from. You do your best, and wait for a break. They come, luck from unluck.

Take Cornelia's father's decline last fall. It was precipitous, and as I was readying before a trip alongside Benazir Bhutto—for her long-awaited return to Pakistan—Cornelia intervened. Knowing her father wouldn't have long, she asked if there was any way I could postpone it. I did, albeit somewhat reluctantly, meaning I wasn't beside Bhutto that October as a suicide bomber attacked her parade motorcade in Karachi, killing 140 and injuring five hundred. She'd slipped behind a plexiglass screen at the last instant to work on a speech she was about to give; that's why she survived this attack. I wouldn't have followed her there.

Two months later, at the end of December, I sat with her in Quetta, the western Pakistan town controlled by the Taliban. We'd been chased that day by suicide bombers. It was her last major interview. She died nine days later.

By then I'd just gotten home for the holidays, after a difficult exit from Afghanistan, and was all but overcome with gratitude that the four of us were together, safe within the warmth of this house, this family.

In our long afternoon in Quetta, inside the fortress-home of a friendly warlord, Bhutto talked about her alleged corruptions, how she became prime minister, twice, of a patriarchal country, and about life's transactions: how it often boils down to credits and debts, who saved whom, who owes whom what. Whether for a family, or a nation, she said, that's where the trouble rests, a false calculus. "When things really work, though, it's because people realize that this is a lie, that, really, we all save one another. It's the way of the world."

So I decided, when I returned to America, to call this next book *The Way of the World*. There are probably better titles. But I get to choose and I felt that quote was so very true. True for the world?

Hopefully. But true for my own life and that of my family, the thing I know best? For sure.

The dinner is much more than the food—these are our good friends; there's drinking and laughter and jokes about how many days it's been since I've slept. By two A.M., Cornelia turns in and I slip back to the basement.

The book is running through my head—a puzzle of nearly five hundred pages, of characters and plot turns, Afghani kids and intelligence chiefs, documents and disclosures about how power often undermines principle. It's all laid down, nice and neat, but I need to manage a final summation of how they all connect, and connect us to something larger than ourselves in the next ten hours. A short passage of last thoughts, for literally the last three pages of the book, is due at noon. When all the pieces are fitted together, what does the puzzle reveal?

In the fitful early morning hours, the rich food and wine and insomnia catch up with me. I find myself grasping the toilet in the downstairs bathroom. I think this may be it—that Owen will find me here in the morning when he slips downstairs to watch a movie. When the misery passes—and certain death is averted—this harrowing image of Owen's discovery lingers and my de-puzzling turns to him.

What the hell is wrong with him? What holds together and what's missing? It's just basic reporting. What are the incongruities, the pieces that don't fit? Hold them up, turn them this way and that. They all belong somewhere.

I've overheard him talking to himself quite a bit lately; always, it seems, in Phil's voice. He's doing it quietly, under his breath, but you can tell its Danny DeVito's rasp. *Why Phil?* Well, he trains Hercules for battle, and is an aggressive little guy, himself. Is Owen—a kid without an aggressive bone in him—in some kind of confrontation, or headed for one? Why would he try to jab a kid with a pencil? It's not in his nature—that I know—so it must be driven by some circumstances, something that's making him incredibly tense.

As I run through the many moments I've seen him anxious, I think of that concert. He played that piece ten times at the piano in the living room with his eyes closed. And he never freezes in front of audiences. Look at the bar mitzvah. What are the differences between our living room—and even, more clearly, a crowded synagogue—and that gymnasium? Well, as Cornelia said, the bar mitzvah was a safe place. What was going on in that gymnasium? Mostly, I remember the performers—I really wasn't paying attention to anyone beyond Owen, Cornelia, and whoever was on the stage. Which brings me back to that one amazing kid who commandeered the room. And then, an attached memory of how Owen was sitting, looking at the floor when everyone else was up clapping.

• • •

A few days later, the book is at the printer's. I've gotten a few long nights of sleep. Owen has taken back his basement. We're on the sofa now, together.

"Who was that boy who did the last song? You know him?"

Owen wouldn't meet my eye. "No."

"Weren't a lot of the performers in your music class? Is he in there?"

He pauses. "Yes."

"So, he's in your music class for the whole year, but you don't know him?"

"Can I go now?"

"Not until you talk to me."

This went on for an hour, until Owen arrived at, "If I tell you once, I won't ever have to talk about it again."

I earnestly agree to this—a promise to him I've made, and broken, many times. "Yes, just this one time."

He sits for about five minutes in silence. And then it starts coming, fast, in a torrent. The whole story. It's cataloged in his head by the day. He doesn't want to say the words, what was said. I tell him I need to hear it all, every word. And then I'm repeating them back to him, feeling each blow, as though I'm being struck. "Burn the house down!" "Kill us!" And, "Kill you if you told us!"

He's not crying—he so rarely cries—but he's shaking, heaving it up. *And then, and then, and then,* spewing up each threat and curse.

Everything now makes sense, how the two bullies trapped him, toyed with him. He says he almost told Walt and he says it almost impatiently—like, *hey, I'm not a complete idiot, here*—but that he was afraid Walt would kill the kid. And I can see that whole scene in the carpool line, like it's happening. Thank God he didn't tell Walt. "But that must have been so hard. And you having no one to talk to."

And then, catching his breath, he tells me about Phil. He couldn't turn to us, so he turned to Phil. Of course . . . training him for battle. "I could talk to Phil—that helped me." And Lucky Jack, another training sidekick. And also Jiminy Cricket. "He said, let your conscience be your guide. And also, 'Go tell your parents. They'll understand.'"

I ask him why didn't he listen to Jiminy and tell us. "All these months you've been alone and terrified, every minute."

He puts his arms around my neck. I hug him, tight, and after a moment I feel his tears moisten my cotton shirt. "I was afraid they'd burn our house down."

Upstairs I hear the front door open. It's Cornelia. In a moment, all three of us are in the basement.

Her response is volcanic, then swiftly capped. She's moving fast and furious, like those women who lift cars to save their kids. The circle widens fast. That afternoon, Rhona Schwartz comes to the house. We don't have to tell her that Owen can't return to the school if the two boys who tormented him are there. He tells her himself. Cornelia adds one homicidal look and Rhona gets to work. They'll be gone by the fall.

C. T. Gordon, Owen's psychiatrist, is on a rare vacation, so we bring in the doctor on call, Dr. Lance Clawson, who is recommended by the school and plenty of others. He takes the lead. On top of everything else, Owen is now battling obsessive-compulsive disorder (OCD), as he replays the threats and swear words over and over, in his head, leaving him paralyzed with fear.

He gets medication for that and Lance sends us to a specialist, a therapist who starts Owen on a kind of cognitive behavioral therapy called ERP, for exposure response prevention. The idea is to expose him, bit by bit, to the horrific thoughts or words, but keep him calm and not let him break out into panic and paralysis. Over time, he'll become desensitized. This, in a manner of speaking, is what happens to neuro-typical people over the years, starting from the earliest ages—the on-rushing world numbs us and thickens the skin.

The axis of bombardment and desensitizing—and the need for ever-heightening shocks to draw a response—is what plenty of social theorists see as a dilemma of the modern, technological age: we live inside a Circus Maximus of violence, sex, and fear generally called the media culture. Owen, of course, has suffered a specific trauma. But its features—the lying, the threats, the curse words—are the types of mortal shocks we've tried to insulate him from.

Cornelia and I discuss this endlessly, night after night. On the one hand, we say he's just turned seventeen and he's in high school. He can't avoid the wider world, and neither can we. If things work out, it's the place he'll have to live. On the other hand, we're in a state of shock and remorse. Our fears, of how readily he'll be taken advantage of, a threat rising with each step toward independence, have been disastrously confirmed.

"I worked so hard to get him to this place, and now for this to happen," Cornelia says, late one night in July during a moment of reflection.

What do I think, over and over? What he wrote on the pad, that he'd be "the protekter of sidekicks." I always figured that was my job—to protect him. At that I'd failed.

We begin driving him up to an office in the Maryland suburbs where a middle-aged psychologist named Sherry has him recite each thing that the two boys said to him. As his body tenses, she eases him down. And then she starts the process once again.

Carl Jung's term is "the shadow." Or so Dr. Griffin told me the previous fall after a session where Owen was describing in effusive detail what drives many of the Disney villains: greed, lust, power, jealousy.

I said I'd never heard of Jung's shadow. Dan, as my all-purpose search engine on psychology, that night sends me a note:

> *Sex and the life instincts in general are,*
> *of course, represented somewhere in Jung's*
> *system. They are a part of an archetype called*
> *the shadow. It derives from our pre-human [sic],*
> *animal past, when our concerns were limited to*
> *survival and reproduction, and when we weren't*
> *self-conscious. It is the "dark side" of the ego,*
> *and the evil that we are capable of is often stored*
> *there. Actually, the shadow is amoral—neither*
> *good nor bad, just like animals. An animal is*
> *capable of tender care for its young and vicious*
> *killing for food, but it doesn't choose to do either.*
> *It just does what it does. It is "innocent." But*
> *from our human perspective, the animal world*
> *looks rather brutal, inhuman, so the shadow*

*becomes something of a garbage can for the parts
of ourselves that we can't quite admit to.*

*Symbols of the shadow include the snake (as
in the garden of Eden), the dragon, monsters,
and demons. It often guards the entrance to a
cave or a pool of water, which is the collective
unconscious. Next time you dream about
wrestling with the devil, it may only be
yourself you are wrestling with!*

Dan counts Jung as one of his important early influences. Of course, it's long been clear that Owen's been tiptoeing through the shadowlands, trying to get at it meditating on his favorite villains and darker human impulses. He knows people lie, cheat, bully, bruise, and even kill each other. These are elements in virtually every movie he's memorized. But he can only seem to wrestle with these human dualities in the controlled landscape of Disney, a place he can own, manipulate, and master.

The last six months are all about a loss of that control. He learns from movies—it's his way—but life isn't a movie that you can rewind, pause, and decipher from the end of a remote. It comes at you fast, faster than so many of the spectrum folks can manage. The dark side rose to meet him, face-to-face, each morning in music class. For no reason he could fathom, a carefully controlled life —by us and by him—was thrown into chaos.

• • •

Owen returns to school for his junior year, but he's quite tentative. He's bouncing around, still discernibly unglued.

The bullies are no longer there, but he's walking the same halls, sitting in the same classrooms. The residues are everywhere.

But so are a few precious counterpoints, namely Connor and Brian, who are waiting for him in homeroom, that very first day. It's a reunion of The Movie Gods.

They are each different, just like we all are, though they share some of the telltale traits: difficulty picking up social cues, rigidity in habit and intellect, difficulty taking the specific to the general, disorientation in unfamiliar situations, trouble with attention and receptive language.

Expressive language is a different story—and what bubbles up from within all three is a world made accessible through the moving image. Like the Venn diagrams Rhona drew the interlocking circles of The Movie Gods show plenty of overlap.

Brian's a "Thomas the Tank Engine" kid. The British-made children's series has only one human: the main character, Mr. Conductor, who was alternatively played by Ringo Starr and George Carlin. The rest are trains—Thomas, Percy, William, and so forth—that move along tracks as they play out modest human dramas, their emotions presented with frozen faces (smile, frown, surprise) right above the cowcatcher. It's precisely this structure and simplicity, the repetition of tracks and easily discernible emotions, that make it a favorite among kids with autism.

Connor likes Thomas, too, but he's *graduated*—if that's the right word—into the superhero-movies arena. There are plenty of those. He knows everything about everyone in those movies, just like Brian knows everything about Thomas.

Brian's interests extend beyond just the Thomas series. He's an aficionado of Mel Brooks's movies and, under an organizing principle of Judaism, he knows just about every Jewish actor in the history of movies. Connor, who's not Jewish, likes Brooks's movies as well—especially *Blazing Saddles*—but doesn't live for them like Brian.

And they both love Disney, which is where the Venn's borders of both boys overlap with Owen's. Owen is the aficionado in that area, yet they can all speak Disney, and are appreciative of his expertise, just as Owen is of Brian's mastery of Thomas and Connor's sweeping knowledge of dozens of superhero movies. But now, at the start of the third year of their friendship, the three circles are bleeding into one another. It's almost as though they'll venture into contiguous territory—movie territory, mostly—at the behest of a fellow Movie God, just like typical teenage boys do on a wider and decidedly more three-dimensional landscape.

As they meet that first day at 8:30 A.M., the restoration Owen feels is palpable. He hugs them both. The building feels different to him, he tells us later—"like it was last year with the bullies, but not." However, Connor and Brian are right where they should be, smiling and ready. Connor, a wide-set guy with curly hair, pushing six feet, cheers, "The Movie Gods are back!" And Brian, a dark-haired broad shouldered kid, about Owen's height, who smiles all the time—happy, nervous, confused, enraptured, doesn't matter—says, "All for one!"

They both want to know the same thing: has Owen seen *The Dark Knight* with Heath Ledger? Chris Nolan's second movie with Christian Bale as Batman has owned the summer, mostly because of the performance of Ledger, whose rendition of The Joker was so violent and troubling that some believe it may have contributed to the actor's death a few months before the movie's release in mid-July. His last performance was also mesmerizing. No one could take their eyes off the movie, with a villain who wreaks havoc for no apparent reason beyond the fact that "some men," as Bruce Wayne's butler Alfred (Michael Caine) says, "just want to watch the world burn."

Owen has heard it's dark and vicious, well beyond the two darkest movies he's embraced—the Batman movies by Tim Burton. The first with Jack Nicholson as The Joker, and the other with Danny DeVito as The Penguin, are shadowy and brooding, but carry their violence with a cushion of being comedic and unreal.

But, on his first day back, Owen is floundering, unsure of his footing. He nods, reaching across the Venn: "Yes, I'll see it." They're both overjoyed.

"Then, we can talk about it!" Connor exclaims.

That weekend Owen and I go to the Uptown Theater on Connecticut Avenue near our home, just a few blocks from Patch of Heaven's church basement.

I've never seen a movie like this with Owen and he's watching the screen with surprising intensity. The Joker kills a man by pushing a pencil into his brain through an eye socket. I can only think of Owen jabbing at his tormentor with his pencil. I ask if he wants to leave.

"No," he says, almost to himself. "I'm okay." Maybe this is what the ERP is about, learning to stay calm and detached while a thousand shocks are thrown your way.

I can't tell what he's thinking—this sort of thing he'd always turned away from—but now he's not. And, in my chair, the cinematic and the real are colliding. I've spent the summer doing interviews from the "Today" show to Jon Stewart's "The Daily Show" to Rush Limbaugh's radio show promoting my book, *The Way of the World*. Its main character is a U.S. intelligence chief who furiously treks around the globe in an attempt to prevent weapons of mass destruction from falling into the hands of terrorists. Their oath of using fear to undermine civilization's norms and create anarchy—to show our prized principles are matters of convenience, easily toppled—is identical to what Ledger's character pronounces in the movie.

> Joker: You'll see, I'll show you, that when the chips are down, these uh . . . civilized people, they'll eat each other.

And then this, to District Attorney Harvey Dent—a champion

of law, society's rule book to manage itself—who's lying, mangled, in a hospital bed.

> Joker: Do I really look like a guy with a plan? You know what I am? I'm a dog chasing cars. I wouldn't know what to do with one if I caught it! You know, I just, do things. The mob has plans, the cops have plans, and Gordon's got plans. You know, they're schemers. Schemers trying to control their worlds. I'm not a schemer. I try to show the schemers how pathetic, their attempts to control things really are . . . Introduce a little anarchy. Upset the established order, and everything becomes chaos.

The next day, Sunday, I hear Owen recite this entire passage in a flawless mimic of Heath Ledger's Joker.

I'm stunned. I ask him to do it again, and bring Cornelia over to hear it. She hasn't seen the movie, but the words are unmistakable in their impute—as is their connection to Owen's life.

We go out to the back patio where we can talk.

"He might as well be talking to the bullies," Cornelia says, outraged. "It's horrifying."

We talk for an hour. A warm September sun is beginning to set. Late summer bugs are buzzing around the flowers in a beautiful backyard Cornelia landscaped.

I suggest that reciting long passages of Heath Ledger is the way he's deboning the trauma, disempowering it. Just like the use of Disney over so many years, it's Owen's particular form of self-therapy, his compass and sexton. "Now, he's trying to deal with the darker stuff, in his life, in the way people can be."

"Yes . . . obviously," Cornelia says. "It's really about something deeper. A loss of control. Our loss, as much as his. We can't protect him. And I don't think he can protect himself. And that means someone I love so much—as much as life itself—is going to get hurt, again and again. And the movies are just movies."

•　•　•

At a hotel in Naples, Florida, we lay the cards on the table.

It's Christmas break and we figured a trip away with the kids was in order. It's nice to be together, all four of us. It's been a rough semester for Owen, though he's slowly getting back on his feet. Heath Ledger may have helped. Clearly, the therapy is working, slowly and surely.

And there's homework. That's what the cards are. Twenty cards, laid out on a little table under a hanging lamp in the hotel room— four rows of five. We have similar cards in our hand. It's a matching game, somewhere between Hearts and Go Fish.

The cards have curse words. Owen lays a card with the word SHIT on it on a pile of SHITS. "I need another SHIT," he says, sheepishly.

Walt starts to laugh.

"Owen, it's funny."

"I hate that word."

"I know, honey," Cornelia says. "But this is the way for the words to not have power over you."

I mention Lenny Bruce. Walt's on it—definitely, same idea. He says, "Take their power away."

Cornelia finds a match to BITCH. Owen shakes his head. "I hate that word."

Walt's turn. He's looking around the table. "I really need a FUCK," and then he cracks up. We all start laughing. Owen looks face to face, and starts laughing, too.

I think back to when Walt was five, right before we left Dedham. I came into his bedroom telling him it's lights-out time, which he wasn't happy about, and he tried out a new word he'd overhead. "Shit!" he shouted. I looked at him, kissed him good night, and slipped out, leaving him befuddled. It's since become an old family story, of how Walt was trying the word out for the first time, then figured he'd misused it.

I mention it when the next round of SHIT cards come up. And he nods, and smiles. "It was awhile before I tried using it again."

Though I'm sure Owen will never use these words, one unanticipated use of traumatic adversity—started a year ago, now, on that morning in music class—is that these words can be taken off the list of ugly realities that might exert power over him as he ventures into the world.

•   •   •

Monday afternoons are still mine, whenever I'm in town. In late February 2009, Owen and I are driving to Dr. Griffin's office for a 3:00 P.M. appointment.

The road forward is just proving to be daunting for him; the subtle play of light and darkness he's seeing in himself—like in all of us—bespeaks unmanageable danger. Just as Cornelia said last fall, when we sat on the patio—"we can't protect him" and he's realizing "he can't protect himself."

His conclusion: too many hurts, up ahead, to risk the journey. His compass is way off, whipsawing from Heath Ledger and his curse-word-therapy game . . . to Mister Rogers.

After getting back from our Christmas vacation, we start to notice this compass is pointing backward: a full-on regression. Anything that suggests growth, change, the adult world, or the future starts to become untouchable. High school, and the heartfelt vagaries of teenage life, with all its pitfalls and uncertainties, are unsettling. He's seen the wider world. He wants no part of it.

Cornelia maps the race backward, day by day. We've been trying to get him to use a cell phone. He discards it. Hides it in his backpack, power off. He's also reviving "Thomas the Tank Engine," and pulling out old picture books, from when he was a baby, from boxes under the Ping-Pong table.

If this keeps up, the very hopeful reciprocities with Connor and Brian will be disrupted.

Regression is ultimately a defensive reaction, like building a fortress, and retreating into it. Us telling him that he can't escape into little-kids things isn't working. We're part of the problem. He thinks we want to push him forward. That's understandable. We do.

If we can't advise him, who can?

Which is what brings me back to *Hercules'* Phil. That's who I'm thinking of as we drive to Dan's. Phil, after all, is who he turned to in that strangely dynamic internal conversation when he was afraid we may not love him, as the bullies said, when he felt he'd have to fight his way forward.

But there are many kinds of sidekicks, as—by now—we well know.

When we get to Dan's, I tell Owen I need to talk to Dr. Griffin for a minute, and that he should hang out in the waiting room.

Dan and I huddle, behind the closed door. We talk about Phil. He knows all about Phil. He knows about the regression. Basically, he knows almost everything we know, at this point.

"Okay, here's the idea. Have Owen solve a problem for a boy like Owen—fearful of the future—in the voice of one of the wise sidekicks."

Dan gets it immediately. He's pumped. "Which one?"

On the wall in a frame, above Dan's right shoulder, is the picture Owen drew of Rafiki.

I point to it.

He nods. "Definitely, go with Rafiki."

I call Owen in and everyone takes their places: Owen's on the couch. I'm on the wing chair next to him, and Dan's on his rolling desk chair, which he wheels right up close.

"All right, Owen," Dr. Griffin says, leaning forward, his hand framing the air before his face. "Let's say, there's a boy like you, different from lots of other boys, who's fearful of the future, of growing up, and wants to start going back to being a little kid." He pauses. "What would Rafiki tell him?"

Without missing a beat, Owen says matter-of-factly, "I'd prefer Merlin."

Dan stammers. "Umm. Okay, then. Merlin!"

"Listen, my boy, knowledge and wisdom are the real power!" Owen exclaims as Merlin, in the voice of Karl Swensen. And then he keeps going. "Now, remember, lad, I turned you into a fish. Well, you have to think of that water like the future. It's unknown until you swim in it. And the more you swim, the more you know. About both the deep waters and about yourself. So swim, boy, swim."

Dan looks at me, eyes wide. He's watched the movie plenty of times—but can't place that second part. I shake my head. Not in there. Yes, there's a scene where Merlin turns himself and Arthur into fish. That seemed to be Owen's trigger to update those lines. But where are the words coming from?

Dan asks Merlin more questions, and "a boy like" Owen receives advice, wise and gentle. And after ten minutes, I begin to realize that Owen has lived in an upside-down world, much more fully realized than we ever could have imagined. Now, we're in it, too. Merlin is speaking with a depth and nuance that Owen has never—and maybe could never—manage. At least could never manage without Merlin. Could it be that a separate speech faculty has been developing within him that was unaffected by autism? Or, maybe, in response to how the autism blocked and rewired the normal neural pathways for speech development?

Forty-five minutes later, Dan and I leave the room in a daze. Me, to drive Owen home. He, to reflect on and record the incredible moment in his case notes.

When I get home late that afternoon, I can't wait to tell Cornelia. She immediately gets it, sees the breakthrough, and wants to give it structure.

"Look, I know you can fake any profession, but you're not a psychologist. E-mail Dan—tell him to look for what's in the psychology literature about using voices like this."

In the coming days, Dan sends links to recent papers mentioning the use of something called "inner speech" in the development of executive function—that catchall term for reasoning, planning, problem solving, connecting past to present, and an array of other cognitive functions. First theorized by an early twentieth-century Russian psychologist, Lev Vygotsky, it starts as the self-directed, out-loud speech of young children—verbalizing as they make their way—and is internalized in preschool years, as a way kids "think through" actions. Studies in recent years indicate this inner speech may be impaired in autistic children, undermining, from early on, their executive functioning. In fact, when inner speech is artificially impaired in typical kids—something managed by disruptive noise or tapping—they perform on various problem-solving tests about the same as autistic children.

So many autistic kids memorize and recite scripts, there's a widely used term—"scripting"—that is generally seen by therapists and psychologists as repetitive, nonfunctional behavior, something to be reduced and remediated.

Certainly, we've done plenty of that, to help him control it in school and in public. But it appears that Owen, with our improvised support, has derived value in the scripting, itself, as a way—a seemingly successful way—to shape and develop this crucial inner speech.

His internal dialogue, in fact, seems to grow richer, year by year, dealing with not just executive functions, but emotional management and even emotional growth.

In sessions with Dan over the next month, Merlin (or Owen as Merlin) takes us on a tour of "inner speech."

Others step in as well. He selects the voices of certain sidekicks, generally the wise or protective ones, for different needs. Specifically, to help him deal with the challenges "a boy like" him is facing.

The insights are trenchant. Many are drawn, first, from a line of dialogue. But, as with Merlin's first emergence, they evolve well beyond the script. The voices of the characters—Rafiki, Sebastian, Jiminy Cricket—each have gentle guidance to offer. With each, it's the way it is with Merlin. Owen is accessing some latent speech faculty, where he can summon and articulate cognition that he doesn't otherwise seem to possess.

At home, Cornelia and I call it a back-to-the-future moment. In some ways, she points out, we're going back to the early role-playing days in the basement. Then, we had to stick to the script and find the right lines, on cue, to communicate. *Now, it's improv!*

As usual, Cornelia's bringing structure to the proceedings, helping all concerned. The improv idea enlivens Dan. In our therapy session, he sets up scenes that relate to Owen's life—being lost or confused, being tricked, being frustrated, or losing a friend. He then drops Sebastian in the middle of it, and asks Owen—as Sebastian—what he should do.

But the theater analogies go further. Cornelia, in sessions with Dan, also points out that we've broken through the theater's so-called "fourth wall." That's the invisible wall dividing the stage and seats, which the actors cross when they step down from the stage to interact—still in character—with the audience.

At home, it starts to become natural, a modern version of the old

Disney dialogue. At any given moment, when a challenge arises, we can ask Owen, "What would Rafiki say?"

An internal dialogue, that he's clearly been having for years, can now be taken and shaped by us.

• • •

Dan, meanwhile, digs around for theories and therapies that will support and illuminate what he's seeing each week. He looks at everything from narrative therapy—a technique of using stories to help shape a patient's behavior and attitudes—to personal-construct theory, which maps how, from the early ages, we develop constructs to provide a sense of order to the world, our place in it, and anticipate future events.

In springtime 2010, Owen is in the room for most of the session, but then gets breaks so I can fill Dan in on what's happening in Owen's life and we can discuss which characters might work best. The hour is intense. The breaks are almost like time-outs on the playing field, when Dan and I—coaching along the process—can huddle. Then we call Owen back in.

Merlin, not surprisingly, remains first among equals. The movie, *The Sword in the Stone*, is an eighty-seven-minute drama of an older man, Merlin, guiding a teenager toward life's deeper truths. It offers the cleanest structure. Merlin's sidekick partner, Archimedes, the owl, helps with young Arthur's intellectual progress (he teaches him to read), while Merlin provides guidance on his emotional growth and the shaping of his character.

But where does Merlin end and Owen begin? In a mid-March session, Dan feels around for the line between them, to see if Merlin can describe how and where he fits inside Owen. This, after all, is about Owen. He's the patient the psychologist is treating.

Dan thinks it through carefully. He figures he should start by addressing Owen.

Dan: Owen, can I ask Merlin a question?

Owen: Certainly.

Dan: Merlin, you're often able to unearth great insights. How do you do it? Where, exactly, do those insights come from?

Owen rises from the couch.

The response, in Merlin's voice, carries a tone of impatience bordering on anger: "You should never ask a wizard the source of his powers! It's the surest way for him to lose them!"

chapter nine

BLESSINGS, UNDISGUISED

A few minutes after Owen as angry Merlin turned on Dan, we're in the car, driving home.

It's been about a year since I last probed.

"So, buddy, have you thought any more about that movie of yours?"

Owen looks over at me, his eyebrows furrowed, and I'm thinking I may get my own dose of angry Merlin.

But I don't. It's his voice. He looks out the window. "I'm working on it."

I do this maybe once a year since he talked about his movie idea of twelve sidekicks searching for a hero. And, how, in their journey, and in the obstacles they face, each finds the hero within themselves.

I ask if he's written anything down.

"I do it inside my head."

I let this hang for minute.

"Sort of like James inside his head?"

"Not really."

"What's the lyric?"

"I don't know."

"Of course you do."

It's the signature song from *James and the Giant Peach*—the only one, of many, that Owen never sang. The omission was odd, in that it seemed to be the most applicable to his real life and real struggles. Cornelia and I took that as a sign that it touched him in some fundamental way, that it entered a secret place, and was sealed down there.

So, as we drive, I sing it:

My name is James.
That's what mother called me.
My name is James,
So it's always been.
Sometimes I'll forget
When I'm lonely or afraid,
So I'll go inside my head
And look for James.

Owen doesn't sing with me. He just looks out the window, his head turned away.

"Do you go inside your head and look for Owen?" I ask.

The car's quiet.

"Sometimes."

"How's he doing in there?"

"He's okay."

I feel a tumbler click.

"And how are the sidekicks."

"They're okay—they're with him. They're all in a dark forest."

"Has he found the hero within himself?"

"Not yet."

"Do you know how it might happen?"

He goes silent. It's about a fifteen-minute drive from Dan Griffin's office in Takoma Park, Maryland, to our house in Northwest, Washington, DC.

I figure I have ten minutes, tops. I make a point of missing a few lights. The hum and vibration of the car, passing landscape, closed windows muting sounds; not having to make eye contact, to read expression. The moving car has always been a sweet spot. Minutes pass. Now, closer to five left.

He starts to softly sing. It's the rest of the James song:

There's a city that I dreamed of very far from here.
Very, very far away from here,
Very far away.
There are people in the city, and they're kind to me.
But it's very, very far away, you know,
Very far.

We've come to our neighborhood. There's no time to delay.

"This city. Where it is?"

"California."

He pauses.

"Burbank," he adds.

It's better he's not looking at me, because he'd be trying to read my smile and that would break the spell. Lately, when friends or relatives see his sketchbook and ask if he wants to be an animator, his response is swift and routine, exactly the same each time: "I want to be an animator at the Disney Animation Studios in Burbank, California, and usher in a new golden age of hand-drawn animation."

I've got two more turns. When we pull up to the house, this window will shut. His sidekicks story, of him searching with his sidekick friends (the wise ones, the confused ones, the resourceful ones) for their inner heroes, is clearly some sort of mirror he holds up to think about himself, his identity. If their destination is also Burbank, maybe the symbolic and the real—the parallel planes of his life—are due to merge. But it has to be more than just arriving. The sidekick has to do something to summon this inner hero.

"And what happens there—in Burbank?"

"He and his friends make a movie about the sidekicks journey using traditional hand-drawn animation. It touches people and saves the world."

I'm confused. "Is that the movie or real life?"

"Both."

I pause for a minute, to think it through. I only get one shot at this.

"You mean an animated movie about the fictional boy and the sidekicks, in this dark forest trying to find their inner heroes, gets made by a real boy, which is how the real boy finds his inner hero?"

"Right, with hand-drawn animation."

"And that's you?"

"Right."

The car pulls to the curb. He suddenly turns to me with the plastered-on smile, the mask—chirps out an exclamatory "Okay?!"— and manages to leap out and shut the door in one swift motion.

· · ·

Walt sees his close buddy Mike Morris, another counselor, standing in the sun by the mail hut and sidles up to him.

"Sounds like that was quite an adventure," says Mike.

Walt's tired expression says it all. Mike, who's been his friend since he arrived here as a twelve-year-old, lets out a little laugh.

Mike's already heard from the other counselors that the weather took a toll on the group. Walt and another counselor led eight campers, all thirteen- and fourteen-year-olds, on a five-day "expedition" through torrential downpours, over thirty-five miles of tough hiking across muddy mountain trails and creeks that turned into rivers on wet nights and long days. Near the end of the trek, the sun broke through, and they marched triumphantly back to camp.

"Well, those campers feel like they scaled K2," Mike says, as he and Walt look across the returning hikers unloading their wet backpacks in the sun. "Nothing they can't do now. Look at them, they're walking on air."

Almost twenty-one, and a second-year counselor, Walt is starting to clearly see the forces that helped shape him, something that tends to happen around this age. There's nothing mysterious about it—old wisdom, now supported by plenty of research: *manageable adversity.* Not so much that you're crushed, like so many kids in Cedric's Washington, DC, neighborhood, but enough that it's a fair fight, a contest that tests more muscles of resolve and ingenuity than simply those employed to score an A on some exam.

The camp has honed that ethic to a fine edge and now, as part of the staff, it's Walt's job to impart it. They chat for a minute about some campwide activities slated for the coming week, when something dawns on Mike: one of Walt's advisees—each counselor has three or four campers he mentors—who happened to be on the expedition Mike just led "has not one, but two autistic brothers."

Mike just found out. The kid, Craig, a twelve-year-old, is a new camper. Wondered if Walt knew. "No, he never mentioned it to me."

Mike nods. "Thought you might be interested." It so happens that Mike's one of the few guys at camp who knows Walt has an autistic brother.

It just kind of happened that way. And then Walt didn't make it un-happen. At first, back when he was twelve, he felt it wasn't anyone's business. A lot of kids at camp didn't talk much about their families. And then it felt nice not to have the whole autism thing be an issue for two months of the year. It affected so much at home— seemed to own the house.

But, up here, Walt can take ownership. It's like he can be a different person here, accepted for who he was, just like everyone else, without any special designation; it seems to make every defeat, the stuff of learning; every victory, sweet. Sometimes people would hear he had a little brother. And because there are so many generations of families at camp, they'd say, "Hey, another Suskind coming up?" And Walt would just say, "He's just not a camp kind of guy." That's all.

All part of a bigger equation—Walt can see that now: how the independence he won, or was granted, with his folks spending so much time and effort on Owen, allowed him to create a bit of a double life. In a way, that's what his mom and dad seemed to want; that his day-to-day would be as normal—whatever that means—as possible.

But hearing about this kid with the autistic brothers has made him consider something he hadn't thought much about: that his family doesn't have any really close friends among other autistic families. Walking to his cabin after the chat with Mike, he thinks it sure would have been nice to know—really know—another sibling of an autistic person. Someone who would understand.

• • •

The next week brings more rain. Usually, the camp gathers on Tree Talk Ridge, an outcropping in a grove of pines that overlooks Newfound Lake, for the weekly "Tree Talk." It's a stand-and-deliver moment, where counselors, starting their second year at the camp, step up to offer some wisdom, maybe hard-earned, that'll be valuable for the campers. Today, a hundred campers, counselors, and staff gather in an open-air hall, high atop the camp. Rain pounds the cedar shingles. Walt composes himself, and looks down at the typed pages in his hand. It's time they knew what's really been going on in his life.

I want to begin by telling you a little about the best teacher I have ever had.

He is eighteen years old, sketches cartoon characters like there is no tomorrow, and every Friday we make our ritual trip to the video store. He is my brother, Owen.

When Owen was diagnosed with autism as a three-year-old, I didn't really understand what that meant. I just remember my mom telling me that Owen was a little different than other kids. In the fifteen years since then, Owen has struggled with and overcome barrier after barrier that stood in his path.

At times, it has been tough, but having a brother like Owen has taught my parents and me lessons we never would have learned otherwise, and helped us become the family we are today. And although maybe at eighteen and twenty we are a little old to be going back to Disney World year after year, and yes, maybe our encyclopedic knowledge of the characters in Fievel Goes West *isn't quite the norm for most families, as far as I'm concerned, I wouldn't have it any other way.*

The joy my brother finds in things that most people would roll their eyes, at has helped to let my family realize what is important to us. And that makes every up and down along the way not a blessing in disguise, as some might call it. Just a blessing. When I wonder if life would have been easier if Owen was a "normal" kid, I always remember it is because of him that I am the person I am. The hard work Owen puts in day after day in taking on the myriad challenges that stand before him—and because I know he works harder in a single day than I could even imagine possible—helps me to realize that as tough as things may appear at times, it is in the face of the seemingly insurmountable challenges that you have your greatest victories and learn things about yourself you'd never thought possible . . .

He goes on to talk about the insurmountable challenges they faced on this last expedition, walking days through the downpour, and how the campers rose to the occasion.

After it's over, and the boys come up, one-by-one to shake Walt's hand, Craig approaches Walt.

"Wow, Walt, that was quite a Tree Talk."

"Glad you liked it."

"I felt like you were talking to me."

Walt puts a hand on his shoulder.

"Well, it's something that's hard to understand for most people."

• • •

It's Walt's twenty-first birthday on September 13, 2009, and we Skype to Spain, where he's starting his junior year of college abroad. It's 11:00 P.M. there—he's six hours ahead—and things are just cranking up in Seville. We all sing. He laughs. Love you guys.

Everything's good. He tells us he tried out for a Seville football team—American football in a league that plays across Europe. It's somewhere between club and semipro, mostly local enthusiasts and a few U.S. college players; and he made the team. That's a real kick. Working the huddle will certainly help his Spanish, that's for sure. Listen, got to go. Other kids in his program are calling. It's his birthday. The night beckons.

Cornelia and I watch the screen darken. We're missing him, of course, on his birthday, but watching him enter the wide world is a thrill. We try not to over-appreciate—to greet everything he does like some huge victory. As he often tells us, "don't make a big fuss over me—I'm just doing what other kids do."

And he's right. Take out the twist of playing football, and he's living the basic junior-year-abroad experience, a common feature these days of college life.

But it's hard not feel awe of the commonplace when you're thinking about how to reengineer it from scratch. Try to map, for instance, the social schema (a cognitive framework for organizing and interpreting inputs) for a night of barhopping in Seville; or finding a cab back to the dorm at dawn. How about something more basic, like getting along with a roommate. Or one level down: calling for assistance when you're lost or learning to use money. And one more step, still: not getting into a car with a stranger, or crossing a busy thoroughfare against the light.

That's what's on our mind as Walt signs off: engineering a life. Owen's starting his senior year. After that, *who knows?*

Early the next morning, Cornelia and I slip into a deli in Cabin John, Maryland, a riverside enclave atop the Potomac's cliffs north of Washington, DC. We're here for the monthly visit, a few doors away, to Owen's psychiatrist—this time just us. We do this once in a while; go to a session without Owen. That way we can talk openly, strategize, and probe a bit beyond our shared knowledge, our team of two. And there's a lot to discuss, as Owen enters his senior year.

We brought Dr. Lance Clawson in when the bullying was revealed—a year and three months ago now—and liked him. He's caring and attentive, but matter-of-fact. What do we need? What do we do? Is there a right answer? Cornelia and I have built up so much knowledge over the years, that we often get treated like colleagues. We like that, up to a point. But we're not doctors, after all. That's why we're visiting one.

We settle around the deli's wrought-iron table, with the heart-shaped chairs, and quietly spread cream cheese on our bagels.

She asks, "What do other couples do with all their spare time?"

"I don't know, golf, maybe. Bridge. Progressive dinner parties, with the fondue forks."

"I guess we'll be doing some of that next year when we're empty nesters. What fun."

Her tone is light, facetious, with a base note of resignation. We eat our bagels in silence. Her Herculean effort of Patch of Heaven was to boost him to a high school that might usher him off, well prepared, to some college program. We've looked at a few over the years: programs where kids live in collegiate environs, with added structural support and, generally, a lighter academic load. Many are small campuses that are like a college, or are situated within an existing one. The goal, most often, is not to graduate. One big school, in fact, is called CLE, which stands for College Living Experience. Some kids get degrees. But for $80,000, that's mostly what you get—the experience.

That's not going to happen. "He's not ready for anything like that," Cornelia says after a bit. "And I don't see him being ready in a year."

A few weeks before, we called parents we knew from his school to discuss the possibility of starting a transition program, a group house where a few kids—including The Movie Gods—might live next year, at least a few days a week. Cornelia sketched outlines of how we could hire someone, maybe a young man, who could mentor, coach, teach, and help them build life skills. The other parents were interested, if tentative. Of course, it'd be a huge undertaking—bigger than Patch of Heaven—where a house would need to be rented and a supervisory person hired. Plus, activities, a curriculum, would need to be developed and implemented. It'd have to be created, whole cloth, and Cornelia knows it'd mostly fall to her.

I know not to offer any easy answers—any "here's how we fix this" suggestions that, as a guy, are always within reach. After all, it's mostly been her burden to carry. Might be for quite a while.

"He's not going to graduate and settle into the basement—that's not good for him or for us." Cornelia's adamant about that, and she's right. But where does he go? Or, if he's home, what do we do with him each day?

"Look, honey, it's still a year away."

"Nine months."

A few minutes later, in Lance's office, we run through updates. His medications, mostly a very low dose of Prozac, are fine. No bad reactions. On the last visit in August, Cornelia reported there were some scattered verbalizations over the summer, where, unprompted, he'd yell out "no!" or "I hate that word!"—a residual, still, from the bullying. But she hasn't heard any in the past month.

Lance says these outbursts will happen from time to time, but the progression over the past year has been good and he thinks we should take him off a drug he's taking for OCD.

He asks if we detect any anxiety about what's ahead for him, with Owen starting his senior year. None we detect is our response.

"How about for you guys?" he says, lightly. We laugh.

Cornelia runs through some of the preliminary options, and describes the parent meeting, and the possibility of building a transition program.

Lance immediately sees what a large undertaking that'd be. "He may be at home for a while," he says. "If they have a structure, a job, responsibilities—and maybe a separate entrance. Lots of young adults thrive that way."

"It's not that we don't want him home, Lance," Cornelia says. "Over the years, we've seen him thrive when he's out of the house, when he's challenged. He rises to it."

"What's Owen think about any of this? You talk to him?"

That gives me an opening, something I've wanted to get Lance's view about since last spring when Owen told me more about his movie.

"Owen's untroubled. He thinks he's going to be an animator at Disney in California. And there he'll create a movie—about how we're all sidekicks, searching for our inner hero—that'll save the world."

"Well, he sure doesn't aim low," Lance says, with a laugh.

I talk about my uncertainty about how to proceed, how, when he first vanished into autism, we discarded parental notions of future greatness for him and never much thought about him having dreams. If we didn't, how could he? Across the years, he's developed little sense of the prevailing consensus about what society deems as worthy of aspiring to, about the big prizes, or reckoned with the traditional adolescent awakening about how distant those hopes might be, about how very large and competitive the world is.

Lance nods. Yes, of course. Owen's gaps are common features of autism. A grasp of scale, and one's measure, are all calculations of context.

I feel context is one thing I understand, and how this is a mighty tall mountain he's cast his gaze upon. When Owen was just four, I recount, and I was working on *A Hope in the Unseen* from Providence, Rhode Island, the kids at Brown University—fully realized young artists and math whizzes who could draw—were already flocking to animation. It grew after *Toy Story* came out in 1995 and spread to video games. It hasn't abated.

Cornelia steps in, broadens it. "Every parent worries about their kid being disappointed. With him, just multiply those feelings. He's still so hopeful, even as he's becoming aware of the world's judgments, how harsh they can be. It seems he's rested his whole identity on this dream. We just don't want him to be hurt."

Lance lightens it up. "So what's the book title—*A Hope in the Unseen*? This is our nature." He talks about how guys wrestle with this in their teenage years—how they realize they won't be a quarterback for the Redskins. "A boy reconciles with that. Then some girl says she loves him anyway, and they live happily ever after. It's part of life to work this out on our own."

Okay, that's the general point, but the challenge, every day, is to draw the line between what's the same and what's different, where the conventional thinking does or does not apply to those with autism. Over fifteen years as a developmental psychiatrist, he's seen thousands of teens and young adults on the autism spectrum.

"Look, I'm sure you've dealt with this before."

He has. "Some people disagree, but my policy has always been let them dream and learn what they can, or not—in their own way— about how the big, bad world works.

"We were allowed to dream," he says. "Why shouldn't they."

We all sit there for a minute.

"I'm sure many just keep dreaming," I say. "Context blind and quite content."

He nods. "They do. But there's really nothing wrong with that. So their dreams don't die. Maybe that's a path to happiness."

•   •   •

On a snowy Sunday in mid-December, Maureen O'Brien is standing in the doorway of an unusual two-story studio beside her Northwest, Washington, DC, house. This tall hut is itself eccentric—blissfully inhabited each Sunday by the giddy Maureen and five artsy teenage girls. We've been coming to this locale for most of the fall. And today, like always, there's great fanfare when Owen arrives that's led by Maureen, a wide-eyed, red-haired, late-forties, child-mom painter, photographer, calligrapher, drafter, and sculptor who runs the art program at a nearby private school.

We had been introduced to her by a friend with an autistic son, who may join our prospective transition program. And she's been the find of the year.

Maureen, as eccentric as her studio, views Owen as a creative colleague. She calls him an artist. She's one, too. So are the girls, who look up from paint-splattered tables, downstairs and down from the second-floor loft, and call out his name. It's an artists' den, with an ancient chandelier, a fireplace, artwork hanging from any surface that'll support a nail, sliced fruit and cookies, and a prized, comfy chair in the corner tucked beneath strung beads and small papier-mâché figures hanging from the underside of the stairs. That's his chair. Beside it is a small low table where Maureen sets out art supplies that seem to have shaped themselves to Owen's hands in the past three months.

On Owen's first Sunday visit, back in September, Maureen looked at his sketchbooks of Disney characters—declared them fine art—and literally walked into his head. She had him bring his thick Disney animation books the next week.

Disney animation techniques emerge from a variety of artistic traditions, different styles in different eras, that she could instantly deconstruct. She saw patterns between which characters he was drawing, and how they made him feel

After a few Sundays of this, she didn't need to draw him out. He came to her, ready to go. They'd flip through books he brought, select figures he'd redraw. She'd have him take artistic ownership, pressing him to render the figures on wild backdrops with an array of materials—charcoal, watercolors, oils—in colors he would select to accentuate mood and emotion. In other words, art. After years of working alone in the basement—compulsively perfecting his technique—Owen found a coach.

Owen shakes off the snow, hangs his coat, and settles into his desk, and starts drawing. It's like he's hungry for it. My phone rings; it's a story source I've been chasing pulling me outside for a few minutes. When I duck back in to say I'll be back in ninety minutes, Maureen has some of Owen's latest works in her arms to show me. I start to look, and then something surprises me. It's not one of the canvases, startling as they are. Owen, engrossed a few feet away in his sketch of King Triton, is talking calmly, assuredly, to a girl at a nearby desk. She's a pretty, blond girl.

This doesn't happen. When an attractive girl addresses him,

or just walks by, he literally has to turn his head. This has been going on for a few years. We've talked to Lance and Dan Griffin about it. Their explanations are fuzzy, a grab bag. Sex is a complex transaction along the autism spectrum. For typical teenage boys, when an attractive girl walks by, they get flushed, their heartbeat ticks up. For autistic teens, this is often too jarring, too eruptive and jangling to their nervous systems. They turn away or tamp down the reaction.

Others move along the steps of sexual awakening very slowly, with measured steps, and may not have a first sexual experience until they're thirty. It's hard to know where Owen fits, a mystery. But, in this warm and safe place, it seems the art is acting as a thermostat, directing certain senses in one direction—toward the emotive expressions on the page—and freeing them in another. His head down, he tells her he's drawing Triton, the father of Ariel—the beautiful heroine, whom the girl says she was raised on, just like he was. And then he asks her what she's drawing.

Now, across the room, another girl joins in—another attractive, artsy girl, in a flowing, peasant blouse—and he tells her his feelings about Ariel, about her motivations and fears, never lifting his head, his eyes finding the line for his pencil.

Maureen, beside me holding up one of his canvases, sees my attention has been drawn away, listening to the exchanges; to the way, in her lair, Owen is learning to manage his unruly senses, to harness them. She watches me watching it all, which I notice as I turn back.

"They like him," she says.

"I think he likes being liked."

She nods. "I think he likes being an artist. It's who he is. That's what the girls see."

• • •

Owen will have to do it on his own.

When neuroscientists talk of their fascination with autism, they're referring to how alterations in the way the autistic brain works—what's different about it—gives them insights into what it varies from: namely, the typical brain. There's a subtext to that interest. In the past ten years, understanding about the brain's famous functional map—frontal lobe for this, left hemisphere for that—has given way to a view that the brain is much more dynamic, adaptable, and inscrutable than we'd ever imagined, with various regions and billions of cells instantaneously connecting and carving "neural" pathways.

The humility this is inducing among some very smart people notwithstanding, there's palpable excitement about one area of powerful and growing consensus: when challenged, the brain finds a way.

In the early days, when Cornelia talked of re-birthing Owen every day, she—like countless other parents, trying anything that they could to reach their child—were experimenting with the brain's ability to improvise, what would later be called its "neuroplasticity."

Science caught up with the moms, which is actually not all that uncommon, and now has its hottest lights on autism. Because autism is pervasive, it covers almost all of the brain, putting everything on display. There is clearly a connection between the way deficits in processing language may be caused by, or create, heightened capacities for pattern recognition and certain types of memory. Those three core functions—language processing, pattern recognition, and memory—can be difficult to probe and assess in the typical brain.

But you can see the neuronal gears turn in the way those functions are heightened or diminished by autism, and the way the brain—challenged in this way—is busy discovering itself. Watching that teaches scientists what the brain is inherently capable of. Call it the discovery principle.

All this becomes important for parents in surprising ways, allowing for the notion that the autistic person isn't less, but different, carrying both thorny challenges and concomitant strengths. But knowing these whys—why a person is the way they are—is of only modest value in a daily struggle that rests on *what* and *how*; what will work to help them live better lives, and how to manage it; a parent's hour-to-hour campaign to build in our their obsolescence.

In terms of the oft-cited Heisenberg Uncertainty Principle—the energy generated by the observation of a particle in motion changes its path—there are few instances where observation alters outcomes to match that of a parent and a child. Now, multiply that constant by the special circumstances of our intense, round-the-clock observation of Owen, where—like so many ASD parents—we soon became the unmatched experts in ways to prompt him and press him, on what references worked and when, and on how to redirect him and when to let him blow off steam.

Across a decade and a half, we tried to edify professionals—teachers, psychiatrists, therapists—with what we were learning so that they could match our knowledge with their expertise. The point was that they *weren't us*. If things worked as we hoped, the need for this constant exchange of information would diminish, as Owen's ability grew, to deal productively and happily with people who may not know much about Disney movies; mixed results, there.

But there was no real choice. If he was to live in some realm beyond our home, even one with boundaries and careful controls, he'd need to be able to engage competently with people who knew little about him and were not experts in directing his path or helping him discover himself.

Owen will have to do it on his own.

Of course, the use of his affinity for Disney from his earliest days, and in recent years ever more so, is something of a proof of neuroplasticity. His brain was using Disney to get around the blockages of autism, to *find a way*. It was using Disney to discover, itself; just as he was using Disney to discover himself.

Could he develop or discover ways to carry that focus, that energy and acuity to areas—subjects, people, venues of all varieties—that were unfamiliar or uninteresting? Hence, the great struggle with trying to teach autistic kids. How do you get them off their island—of whatever affinity—and into the main.

But a bridge is being built on Sunday mornings with Maureen in her artist's den. Part of it is being constructed on the sketch pads and canvases. She is helping him loosen the reins that had tightened around his drawings as his skill level rose—an almost fierce precision. Each session, she has him start with a character sketch as a warm-up. She says, "Yes, perfect, but now let's pick another character and take him somewhere new, mess him up, have him wear some new colors and texture. Draw some things around him."

The Disney characters, his alter egos, are traveling to new places. So is their draftsman. And that's where the girls come in.

For twenty-five years, Maureen has been mixing and matching teenage artists in this studio, including a wide pallet of kids who live more vividly on their pads than anywhere else. During the two-hour Sunday session, she makes sure the kids get up to look at each other's work, say how it makes them feel.

That's what happens, as each girl stops by Owen's cozy corner and looks over his shoulder. He continues to look down, as, one after another, they place a many-ringed hand on his desk's edge and lean over him, hair falling, and tell him how his drawing makes her feel, how this character or that may have scared her as a kid, or made her sing, and what an amazing artist he is.

After a few weeks, Maureen whispers in his ear, "If you want them to come look at your work, you have go look at theirs." And he does, looking at the still lifes of fruits and flowers, charcoal sketches of bucking horses, and the muted paintings of homeless ladies and forlorn children, and then tells the girls how each picture makes him feel. He doesn't say much. But each word is one word more than he's spoken to pretty, typical girls since puberty hit.

At the same time the girls are stopping by his desk—in early 2010—he is working hard in history, a yearlong class, and a focus for his senior year. In an assessment sent home by the teacher, we see the usual mix: his conscientiousness in completing homework and preparing for tests, but also how he requires "frequent reminders to stay focused."

Other notes point out Owen "often requires encouragement to answer questions more thoroughly" and how graphic organizers were helpful in "his developing more organized and perceptive responses." The class covered all of U.S. history, the basic fare that citizens should have at least a passing familiarity with: birth of the nation, slavery, the Civil War, robber barons, the Great Depression, both World Wars, President Kennedy, right up to Vietnam.

Owen has never been a big fan of any of this. Each one of these historic passages is either a trial or a tragedy. Save some connection Cornelia or I could find to hook them to a Disney movie, he didn't see the point of any of it; it happened a long time ago and has nothing to do with his life. The ugliness of each chapter affronts him; he turns away, offering the minimum.

But at the bottom of the teacher's assessment, there's something odd. *"Owen uses his artistic talent to help him understand and remember historic events. At one point, he drew cartoons showing poor farmers and slaves, and others about factory workers. The details of the cartoons were accurate. However, of greater note were the cartoon characters' emotionally expressive faces—these, in and of themselves, provided much of the full meaning of each of these issues. These cartoons were on the bulletin board in the classroom for a period of time. Everyone who saw them commented on how moving these facial expressions were."*

Everything in the preceding paragraph represents a first. It shows the way the bridge from Maureen's art class leads to the school. There, he begins to use his art, nourished by Maureen and encouraged by those girls in her "hut," to help him make sense of the hard-to-fathom traumas and triumphs of history, even ones he finds repugnant. His brain found a way, and the rest of him followed.

And we didn't have one damn thing to do with it.

• • •

"You should grab a few chairs from the dining room," Cornelia calls from the kitchen. She's getting the coffee and desert items pulled together. I move the dining room chairs into the living room.

She slips by me carrying the cheesecake. "This is going to be one expensive party," she quips.

"Hmm. How expensive?"

"You don't want to know."

"Yup. You're right."

That's the way our life goes. I stick with revenues. She handles expenditures. Both jobs have their particular stresses, though it's fair to say the cost-side analysis drives the equation. Since Owen turned three, the daunting, never-enough demands of autism have remained inelastic, bottomless. Not knowing what really works, or helps, makes identifying the inessentials all but impossible.

You try everything. And we have: from changing his diet to gluten-free to auditory processing, where he spends hours doing high-speed computer tests while different noises ring in his ears. Lots of families run themselves into bankruptcy. Though divorce rates are no higher than the norm, families tend to either break apart or pull more tightly together. But every family knows the crush of constant pressure. Cornelia has a joke that vacations should be covered by insurance under mental health. If only. Seven trips, thus far, to Walt Disney World. Now, when we call, we get switched to some sort of telephonic concierge—I imagine in some plush office at the call center—who gushes, like someone handling high rollers in Las Vegas, "When will you be coming back!"

The vacations, though, are a rounding error when compared to about $90,000 a year we've spent on Owen. Actually, that's just a bit higher than the norm—autism organizations estimate it costs about $60,000 a year to provide adequate educational and therapeutic services to an autistic child; about half of which, in terms of school tuitions, often comes these days from public funding.

We didn't have public public funding for much of Owen's schooling and Cornelia's round-the-clock efforts, the key ingredient, are only measurable in opportunity costs. But the seventeen-year totals of both time and money are not something we think about. We just push forward, knowing this is just the way it is—and probably will be for quite a while.

But that's what we're hoping to get our arms around tonight: some sense of what the future—the long future—might look like.

There's a knock on the door and Team Owen begins to arrive. Fifteen minutes later all six are comfortable, chatting. Dr. Dan Griffin, the psychologist, is excited to see Dr. Lance Clawson, the psychiatrist; they've never met, though they've exchanged reports for Owen and other patients they share. Most everyone else knows each other, as leading specialists in the area. And all of them are linked through Owen. Suzie Blattner, the education specialist, has been tutoring Owen since he was three, right around the time Bill Stixrud first tested him. That's fifteen years. And for this six, there is another six that everyone knows—and periodically mentions—that have cycled in and out over the years.

These people, and those not present, have helped Cornelia and me parent our son. It's a humbling thought, and one that prompts a blurring of lines between hired professional and colleague and friend. That's why Cornelia's line about how much a two-hour meeting with all six will cost—in fact, about $1,500—is spoken at least half in jest. These relationships seem anything but transactional; we pay them all without a second thought, and—as opposed to the parents of Owen's friends—see some of them socially. After all, there are things we share, as members in good standing of the neuro-typical world, who carry significant knowledge of autism.

The immediate issue is what comes next—how the autistic world and neuro-typical world might be fitted together for Owen—with only five months until graduation. The discussion moves swiftly, between possible plans to set up a group house to college programs we've seen, and some we should. There's a school Cornelia has heard about called Riverview on Cape Cod up in Massachusetts that has a program for high school- and college-age kids on the spectrum. Lance is down on the place—he's known kids who've gone there. It's $65,000 a year, he says, "And three years later they're back in the basement—nothing's changed."

Cornelia's becomes impassioned. "What kind of life is he going to have? If he lives in the basement, he lives in the basement. We'll always be there, in every way for him, until the day we die, and pray God, we live a long time. We just have no sense of how this looks twenty years from now."

But no one knows. The breadth of the autism spectrum is matched by a spectrum of outcomes. Some of them get married. Most don't. Some have jobs, and live a quiet, regimented life with routines they come to rely on. Some live in group houses and do odd jobs. Many yearn for love, and are unrequited. Relationships are hard, for anyone.

"A lot of young adults—and even not so young—live at home," Lance says, "with parents—and sometimes aging parents—and they give them independence, like the separate entrance to an apartment in the basement."

I can see Cornelia's face fall any time basements are mentioned—the image of Owen watching videos in the basement at fifty is a waking nightmare. I'm with her on that.

But everyone agrees that there's been strong progress, especially since Patch of Heaven and high school.

"He'll always test badly," says Bill. "And that'll . . . hold him back. People will look at his scores and make assumptions that are wrong but hard to disprove. In terms of square pegs and round holes, kids like Owen aren't even pegs. They're spheres. They roll, often brilliantly, but on their own path and own accord. Try to test for that."

But over the hour, and into the next, Dan talks more and more about the Disney therapy, as we've come to call it. Of course everyone knows of his affinity for these movies—it's been a factor in the work of every one of them; Suzie helped Cornelia develop Patch of Heaven lesson plans, using Disney; many have sidekick drawings from Owen framed in their offices. For the first time, though, we can hear them discuss, professional to professional, what's been going on in Dan's office.

It's almost as though Cornelia and I are not there. The pointed questions fly fast; some responses are in professional jargon. You can almost hear the whir of collected consciousness—six diverse experts, with one hundred years of experience with autism spectrum disorder patients between them.

"It's not so much how he's used the movies to help with academics," Suzie says. "It's how he's used them to guide emotional growth, which, of course, is the bigger and more complex challenge."

Everyone nods to that.

Dan cites some surprising recent insights Owen has channeled, of course, through various voices: Rafiki on why change is so hard and how we manage it, Jiminy Cricket on the meaning of conscience, and how to converse with that "voice in your head."

Last week, Dan recalls, he had asked Merlin how would he advise a boy like Owen who was concerned with high school ending, and what would come next. "So, as Merlin, he says, 'Listen, boy, whistle the graduation song, a little bit every day. By the time the big day comes you'll be fine."

At that point, they all seem to notice that Cornelia and I are in the room.

Bill Stixrud turns to me, and says, "Have you ever thought about writing a book, *The Wisdom of Disney, as Told by Owen Suskind to His Father.*"

•   •   •

I'm about to respond in full, but I don't. I just say in a polite way. "Yes, well, we've thought about it."

That phrase stopped me: *the wisdom of Disney.*

Then I look around the room, face to face, take in everyone's gaze, and murmur, "I'm not sure if the wisdom is with Disney, though."

Of course, we'd thought about a book from time to time, but not until Owen was old enough, and able enough, to fully participate. And certainly not about Disney being a repository of wisdom.

But I think about the meeting—and that question—many times in the next few days, especially that moment of overhearing, when everyone was talking as though Cornelia and I weren't there. It's the kind of thing you live for as a reporter—experts earnestly trying to assess a problem and maybe finding a solution among themselves; the presence of a reporter not corrupting the dialogue. And even with their collective century of experience, and long history with Owen, no one in the room could quite figure out what they'd been seeing.

But Cornelia and I knew. It's not about the wisdom of Disney. It's about family—sometimes wise, often not—and about the power of story in shaping our lives. Disney provided raw material—publicly available and ubiquitous—that Owen, with our help, built into a language and a tool kit. I'm sure, with enough creativity and energy, this can be done with any number of interests and disciplines.

Owen's chosen affinity clearly opened a window to myth, fable, and legend, that Disney lifted and retooled, just like the Grimm Brothers did, from a vast repository of folklore. Countless cultures have told versions of *Beauty and the Beast*, which dates back three thousand years to the Greek's "Cupid and Psyche," and certainly beyond that: these are stories human beings have always told themselves to make their way in the world. It's how people embrace these archetypal tales, and use them to find their way—that's where the wisdom lies. This is just one example.

The paradox is how to make our example useful to other families and other kids, whatever their burning interest—that's what Team Owen seems to be talking about. How does this work? Is there a methodology? Can it be translated from anecdote to analysis, and be helpful to others in need. After all, they're professionals; this is what they do: see parents and kids year after year pass through their offices, looking for answers. And when the day is done, they go home to their own kids.

But there's no doubt that, in terms of autism, Disney stumbled into a strange, unexpected place. Walt Disney told his early animators that the characters and scenes should be so vivid and clear that they can be understood with the sound turned off. Inadvertently, this creates a dream portal for those who struggle with auditory processing, especially, in recent decades, when the films can be rewound and replayed many times.

The latest research that Cornelia and I came across shows that a feature of autism is a lack of traditional habituation, or the way we become used to things. Typically, people sort various inputs, keep or discard them, and then store them; our brains thus become accustomed to the familiar. After the third viewing of a good movie, or tenth viewing of a real favorite, you've had your fill. Many autistic folks, though, can watch that favorite a hundred times and feel the same sensations as the first time. Along the way, though, they'll often look for new details and patterns in each viewing—so-called hyper-systemizing—an urge that underlies special abilities for some of those on the spectrum. In a way, it's not so different from a celebrated musician spending a week working on a few chords or a filmmaker endlessly reviewing a short scene. In the autism world, this is often referred to as "over-learning;" yet in the arts, an expression of the old William Blake standard, "to see the world in a grain of sand . . . and eternity in an hour." Is that distinction a value judgment, borne of a narrow perspective? What is indisputable: lots of ASD kids have bonded with Disney movies. In recent years, at least in our circles, ASD families have been among the most regular—one might say, tireless—visitors to Walt Disney World. Some have even relocated to the Central Florida area.

Then there's the issue of ubiquity. Disney's success means everyone, worldwide, has watched these films. That's a great equalizer, that eventually spurred me, Cornelia, Walt, and every one of Owen's therapists to pose an identical question: How can he match and then surpass the deepest insights we can summon watching these very same movies? That's why the many ways he used Disney—turning it into both an analytical tool kit and emotional paintbrush—might have resonance. It shows *comparative* capability. And if he can do it there, then where else?

And he's just one kid. While our household may not be conventional, with a pair of certifiably insane parents and a fixation on stories—all of which may have accentuated and amplified Owen's native inclinations—we have no doubt he shares a basic neurological architecture with autistic spectrum folks everywhere. At the time our therapists are meeting in the living room, in 2010, there are two million autistics in the United States, five hundred thousand of whom are children, with the total expected to reach four million by the end of the coming decade. Beneath the oft-cited incidence rate of one in eighty-eight children, is a more startling one. Due to the four-to-one prevalence in boys over girls: it's one in every fifty-four boys, a number with few epidemiological precedents. Down syndrome, by comparison, occurs in one of every 691 children. And worldwide, autism incidence rates are surprisingly uniform. Globally, the numbers are in the tens of millions.

Showing how affinity reveals underlying capability may, if properly presented, lead to a reappraisal of possibility. Namely, what is possible in how so many people might be helped to discover productive lives. The alternative is federal support that runs approximately $50 billion a year in 2010, and is sure to rise exponentially.

That's more or less the calculus that's secretly running through my head in the days after our therapist meeting. That is, until Cornelia and I go out on a date, about a week later, to talk seriously, for the first time, about it. *A book.*

I'm figuring out how she'll respond, so I try to pre-empt it. I say a book would mean a convergence of competing and neatly separated parts of our lives—professional and personal, public and private—into one big headlong, heartfelt mess. She nods. Of course, she knows all this. We sit at a table in a Washington, DC, restaurant, as I go on and on about these lines being crossed, until she interrupts my monologue: "So, what's wrong with that?"

She looks at me, squarely. "It might help people, like we needed help."

All I have to do is nod.

chapter ten

THE MOVIE GODS

t's 1:40 P.M. on March 6, 2010, a few days before Owen's nine-teenth birthday, and we're in the midst of giving him his present: a day in New York City, seeing the sights, and meeting his Kennedy aunts for a pizza dinner immediately following the afternoon matinee of *Mary Poppins*.

It starts in twenty minutes. We're inside a cheek-to-jowl scrum, inching forward across the ornate foyer of the New Amsterdam Theatre in Times Square. Cornelia and I—with Owen between us—are thinking the same thing: *we've been here before.* When we saw Disney make its initial mid-1990s foray onto Broadway, we figured this would be heaven for him. A play is a conversation of sorts between actors and audience. Owen was in a dense internal dialogue with his favorite characters, almost like he was staging little plays in his head. Onstage, they'd bring his beloved movies to life. Perfect fit.

This hypothesis was first tested with *Beauty and the Beast* on Broadway in 1996. As Belle began singing her opening number, Owen, then five, slipped into a thrashing panic, like he was drowning. I hustled him out. Cornelia stayed with Walt in their seats, along with her two sisters and all their kids. We were befuddled and, at $100 a ticket, dispirited. We figured this was something all the

cousins could do together, a kind of group activity of shared enthu-
siasms, where Owen wouldn't be the outlier.

After he calmed down in the lobby, I held him up to a small
window in the swinging door at the back of the theater. Through
that glass frame, about the size of a portable-TV screen, he could
watch the distant characters of Beast and Belle, Cogsworth and
Lumiere dance about, but with the sound on mute. I held him up,
nose to the glass, until my arms began to shake.

At first, we thought it was the noise—that it was just an issue of
it being too loud in the theater: a matter of what autism specialists
call overstimulation.

In the coming few years, we began to realize it ran deeper than
that. These movies, our allies—providing a passage to our son—had
an independent power over him. They were engaged with him in
an elaborate dance; you had to know their moves, to keep a flying
elbow from bloodying your nose. For Owen, the movie *Beauty and
the Beast* was a big, comforting buddy, a relationship built steadily
across dozens of viewings and one he relied upon. To suddenly have
an impostor burst onto the theatrical stage was like flipping him into
a tornado—a profound loss of control. What was being flung about:
his precisely crafted relationships with the movie's animated characters, exactly as they appeared in the movie.

Round two of this perceptual experiment—*movies vs. plays; autistics vs. neuro-typicals*—occurred right here, at the New Amsterdam, a
grand old show house that Disney took over in 1997 to cap the city's
renovation of Times Square. They signed a ninety-nine-year lease
for the theater and poured millions into a restoration, giving the
place back its beaux arts grandeur.

But people don't come for the gold leaf cornices. They come for
a show, and with *The Lion King*, Disney finally cracked the code—
namely, how to make an animated blockbuster into a theatrical
blockbuster. *Beauty and the Beast*, very closely matching the movie,

did well commercially if not critically. With *Lion King*, they decided to make the play a truly original production, similar in plot, themes, and characters, but different in almost every other way. The play's director, Julie Taymor, originally a puppeteer, designed ten-foot tall, human-operated puppets of elephants and giraffes to walk the aisles; the actors moved easily beneath shoulder scaffolds of their animal characters; a stronger African flavor, in songs and dialogue, gave the play a feel of authenticity.

Critics *and* audiences loved it—not all that common—and Owen loved it, too. At least he did when we all saw it in the spring of 2002 and for a few months afterward. When we saw him start to retreat, we could begin to understand why. It wasn't a perceptual collision, a pileup, like with *Beast*; more of a steady push and shove across months, as the play struggled to hold its ground alongside the movie. By then we'd come to see how even slight alterations from a beloved movie were, to Owen, like nails on the blackboard. He hated knockoffs, whether badly drawn versions of his favorite characters or cinematic sequels, like Disney's clunky follow up to *Aladdin*, *The Return of Jafar*.

At that point, though, he had also acquired more flexibility, and had grown more practiced at moving between his parallel planes—the Disney world and the real world—especially in how he took the movies with him into the wider world. For instance, when Owen himself acted in a play like the character Br'er Rabbit or in *James and the Giant Peach*, there wasn't a problem—he was just playing out the movies running continuously through his head on the plane of reality.

A play, though, played by others—neither the original movie nor his expressed reality—was intrusive, wedging itself between those parallel planes. The fact that Taymor's play could coexist for that long beside his beloved movie showed real progress. He was managing the dissonance. Not surprisingly, the movie eventually won out.

The $40 *Lion King: Pride Rock on Broadway* book we bought in the foyer of the New Amsterdam ended up under Owen's bed collecting dust.

But we're feeling hopeful as we settle into our velvety seats for *Mary Poppins*. The 1964 movie is a combination of live-action and animation, with live actors—originally Julie Andrews and Dick Van Dyke—that dominate. As far as we knew, there weren't any beloved sidekicks about to be remolded by stage actors.

Most importantly, we want it to be a good birthday. That's the real point. If he likes the play—if this time things work out—it will be a successful day, one we can affectionately rehash with him for months or even years. So Cornelia and I embrace every bit of excitement we can grab. This is his day. And it is Disney's theater.

The houselights dim and rise, signaling everyone that it's time to shimmy into their seats. I see Owen, beside me, flipping intently through the playbill. To be fair, he was not all that crazy about this idea at the outset. That's why Cornelia made sure her sisters, Alice and Marita, who he loves, would come in from Connecticut for the pizza dinner.

He's still flipping through the playbill at this point. There are lots of actors in the play and he seems to be reading their credits, though they're almost all stage credits. To ease the tension, he's looking for something familiar, something to hang his hat on. I'm happy to see him reading. He flips a page and gasps.

"I can't believe it!"

"What, honey, what?" Cornelia, from the other side, asks, hoping nothing's gone haywire.

"Jonathan Freeman—he's playing the admiral!"

My brain races to connect. Yes, the admiral: the guy in *Mary Poppins* with the hat and muttonchops who fires the cannon from a nearby rooftop on Cherry Tree Lane.

Freeman?

"Dad? Jonathan Freeman is the voice of Jafar from *Aladdin!*"

I'm pretty sure Owen is the only one in the theater who knows this, or certainly who cares so much.

The curtain rises. It takes a while before Freeman appears in one of the bit parts, doing his exaggerated British captain's accent and elaborately saluting Bert the chimney sweep.

I can see Owen's face in the half-light. It's like he's spotting a famous recluse, an elusive figure he's thought about for years.

The play is fine. Owen seems to be attentive and upbeat. He hums the songs, the ones by the Sherman brothers made popular by the movie.

As the actors take their bows on the second curtain call, he grabs the sleeve of my shirt, eyes aflame.

"Can we go to the stage door to meet him?"

Which is where we spend the next hour. The lead actors pass as a few enthusiasts press them for autographs or iPhone shots. Owen pays no attention, up on tiptoes, craning his neck to keep focused on the stage door.

Then, we're pretty much the only ones left. Cornelia looks at me, eyebrows up in a "so now what?" expression.

"Maybe he went out a different door," I demur.

We both look at Owen. He's already got the plastered-on smile, his mask. "It's okay Dad. *Noooo* problem." He does the big-head nod at "noooo," like someone just punched him in the chest.

I slip under the felt rope and tap the security guard on the shoulder. He's a little startled, but I start right in—telling him we're waiting for Jonathan Freeman. The guard, a youngish African American guy in a yellow Lion King shirt, seems to know Freeman—"yeah, he's a good guy"—but is vexed. Freeman? If we were to write a note to Freeman, I ask the guard, could he leave it in his dressing room? He thinks this over for a moment. "Sure, whatever," responds the guard.

Then we talk some more and I tell him a bit about Owen, and watch his expression shift. It's amazing, really, how far we've come. All of us. A hundred years ago, what fate would have befallen Owen or some Down syndrome kid? It's unthinkable, really. Many were abandoned or worse. JFK's sister was lobotomized. Now you mention to someone that a kid with special needs has a problem, and they stop everything. Of course, I don't have what I need. The guard goes inside to find me a pad and pencil.

I tell Cornelia and Owen to go ahead to the nearby restaurant, as—a moment later—I settle on a nearby stoop, a Disney Theatrical Productions pad on my knee. If I spend an hour getting this note just right, it'll be time well spent.

The wind picks up as dusk arrives, blowing litter down the caverns of Midtown. There's a wildness about it. Garbage flying upward gives scale to the soaring vastness of the city. And to me, sitting on a dirty stoop.

It's wrong, somehow, that Owen's struggle has made me better than I deserve to be; kept my eyes clear, as long as they're focused on how to help him, restore him, though I know now this is the way he was meant to be. I'll do anything for the boys, even when it might be better for them to fail and learn and recover on their own—that's what gives us strength. And Walt, at twenty-one, is well past really needing much from me.

But Owen still needs us and may his whole life—or so we tell ourselves.

This desire to save him, an urge every parent feels when a child's in distress, has certainly become as much about me, and Cornelia, too—about what we need, what gives us wholeness and a sense of worth—as it is about him. At this point, after so many years, it's who we are. But watching the swirls of trash, I'm not sure if I haven't slipped from shameless, my usual state, to desperate.

From the mind's eye of New York, a famously ennobling and

pitiless gaze, I sure look the part. Here I am, writing a love note from my family to a journeyman actor for voice work he did twenty years ago. I consider my pitch. Cornelia often says never mention the Pulitzer. It's unseemly, she says. If other people do, that's fine. And I agree.

Hell with it.

> *Dear Jonathan,*
>
> *I'm Ron Suskind, a Pulitzer Prize winning journalist, but you, my friend, are the true hero in my family. My son, Owen, now 18, has been a fan of your voice work since he was a small boy. He is an autistic spectrum kid, who makes sense of the world through his chosen passions and works of art. We waited at the stage door and must have missed you.*
> *But next Wednesday is his birthday and if you have a minute to call him, you'd give him the thrill of his life. Jafar and Iago have been living in our house for years—Owen can recite every line and knows—lovingly—every voice work actor in 50 plus years of the Disney pantheon.*
>
> *So, even if we don't hear from you, thanks.*
> *All the best,*
> *Ron Suskind*

At the bottom I jot down the numbers for my cell and the house line, and hand it to the guard.

• • •

Four days later, we crowd around the phone, its speaker on.

"Owen?"

"Yes?"

"This is Jonathan Freeman."

I had talked to Freeman the day before. He called me on my cell. Lovely guy, sixty, single, lifelong Broadway actor and a Disney regular. After a few minutes of profuse thank-yous, I told him a good time to call was in the early evening, after Owen's birthday dinner at home—just the three of us—was over. When we hear the ring, we nonchalantly tell Owen the call is for him and all crowd around the phone on the third-floor landing, the big Motorola, with all the features.

After Owen hears Jonathan's voice, he falls silent. Just looks at the phone.

"Owen?" Freeman says.

"Yes."

"Are you there?"

"I can't believe it's you."

Then louder.

"I can't believe it's you!"

"Happy birthday, Owen. I understand you're quite a fan of Disney."

Cornelia and I stand beside him. He looks at us—eyes wide—and then at me, beseechingly.

And I see a reflection in his eyes—of us back in the bedroom of the old house; me, under the bedspread, pushing the puppet up to meet him. That was our big moment. He wants permission to replace it.

"Go ahead, buddy."

His body snaps into form, arms akimbo.

"Okay, Okay, Jafar, listen, *yoooou* be the chump husband . . ." And off he goes, exploding into Gilbert Gottfried's crazy-cake staccato.

This time, Jafar's voice comes through the Motorola. "Iago, I *looove* the way your foul little mind works."

Owen literally lifts off the ground. Bouncing, giddy, taking flight.

"My God, I feel like I'm talking to Gilbert. I mean, Owen, *I know Gilbert.* I know them all," says Freeman.

Owen asks about everyone in the movie he can think of. Jonathan does his best to give updates. Together, they commiserate over the passing of Douglas Seale, a British actor who played the Sultan and died in 1999.

"He was a very nice man, Owen," notes Freeman. Both then rejoice over Jonathan's good friend, Alan Menken. "You know Alan Menken! He's the greatest composer ever!" Owen exclaims.

"Owen, I'll tell him you said so—he'll get a charge out of that."

Then they do voices. Owen is gushing dialogue, mostly Iago, but throwing in stanzas of Genie dialogue and one of the Sultan's. Jonathan, of course, does Jafar, until he pauses, giggling. "Owen, help me . . . what's my next line?" Owen does Jafar, which is then repeated by Freeman. It's symphonic.

After twenty minutes, Jonathan winds it down. "Owen, I'm tapped out. I can't keep up. Listen—talk to me. You love this movie. What do you love about it?"

There are a few exchanges. Owen describes what he likes about different characters. Jonathan tries to bridge it into what Owen thinks the movie is about, its themes, which they begin to discuss.

Cornelia and I listen to the back-and-forth.

She grabs my arm.

"What?"

"Don't you see? Jonathan's running up our path," she whispers. "A whole decade of it, from the voices on to the themes, the deeper meanings."

Right to the present.

"Isn't it about the forces of good and evil fighting it out," Jonathan proffers. "And how in the end, good triumphs."

"Umm. Sort of. I think it's about more than that," counters Owen.

There's a look Owen gets when he does one of his deep dives, a downward gaze, like his eyes are folding inward. That's what he's doing.

Jonathan can't see him, but he must sense Owen is thinking—no one speaks—and a moment later, Owen resurfaces. His voice is soft, otherworldly.

"I think it's about finally accepting who you really are. And being okay with that."

The sound of sighs and sniffles comes from the phone. "Oh my. How is it I never saw that."

• • •

Three months later, Cornelia is sitting in the auditorium of a synagogue in the Maryland suburbs. Owen's high school uses this hall once a year for graduation day.

Walt's at her side and the extended family, both sides, fill two rows, a sizable contingent that last gathered for Walt's high school graduation three years before and, before that, the bar mitzvahs.

Cornelia looks left and right, checking that the gang seems settled and happy—the product of exhaustive planning, about flights, hotels, and the weekend's schedule of events. Now, with five minutes until the ceremony, everything's set, just so. She's grown accustomed to this chair: working, scheming, organizing, lifting, creating—across the years, for both boys—and then stage-managing the finale . . . where her husband steps to the podium. I've spoken at several of the kids' graduations, starting with Walt's graduation from sixth grade. I always feel guilty that Cornelia's not up here. She's a fine public speaker, but, by nature, private. It's a sensible division of labor. I'm good at this. She's good at just about everything else.

And she can't help but feel that this is a moment of earned rewards. After sixteen years of round-the-clock effort on her part—much of her adult life, really—he's graduating from a high school. The real deal. He'll get a diploma.

The school has been a good place—maybe a perfect place—for him. She often wonders if the nightmare with the bullies was avoidable; if the school could have, or should have, caught it sooner, or how those two kids ever even ended up in the building. But the school certainly responded forcefully and their care for him, their attentiveness, in the two years since then has been exemplary.

Especially in this last year, he's been thriving. Maybe knowing it will soon end, and being uncertain about what's ahead, has focused him. He's been embracing everything the school offers—from gym to art to his homework each night to the prom, just last week. To see him in his tuxedo—Cornelia's grandfather's old J. Press tux, which fits him just fine—is stunning, one of those moments when you see them differently, though they don't even know it. They just smile back and step forward.

She's pulling together the transition program for next year, just three children—Owen, Brian (two of the three Movie Gods), and another boy, Ben, whose mother introduced us to Maureen. Ben, a year older than Owen, already has a job, bagging groceries at a local supermarket. There's so very much to do—a huge undertaking, just now under way, including the prospect of finding Owen a job.

The high school's final assessments were painfully clarifying about the complications ahead. As Stixrud said, testing will always be a problem. Even he, a master of innovative testing, struggled to tease out Owen's uneven, well-concealed abilities.

The wider world won't be as creative or patient, or even as attentive as the school's vocational assessment office, which sends home its final report in the late spring. Under JOBS TO CONSIDER they list: COLLECTING TICKETS, ASSISTING WITH CLEAN-UP, ASSISTING WITH ARRANGING AND CARING FOR PLANTS IN A NURSERY OR GREENHOUSE, and—because of his drawing acumen—ASSIST WITH

ARTISTIC ACTIVITIES FOR CHILDREN, ADULTS AND THE ELDERLY. That last one was the only suggestion that credited Owen with having any developed skill—his drawing.

Cornelia showed me the report a month ago, at a particularly inopportune moment. All I could hear were echoes of Owen's early descriptions of the sidekicks. That they were underappreciated.

My response—if not necessarily a remedy—was to find a first-rung graduation speaker. That was my way to show the kids, to show everyone, that—whatever those tests showed—these kids had accomplished more in terms of distance traveled than any graduates, near or far. A battle over the graduation speaker had already been raging for much of the spring. I'd spoken at KTS's graduation the previous year and had figured I would just be a dad in the audience—where I hoped to be—when Owen walked to "Pomp and Circumstance." But the night after the telephonic lovefest with Jonathan Freeman, Owen forced the issue. "You talked at Walter's graduation," he said simply. "I want you to talk at mine."

Not surprisingly, the school said they couldn't have the same speaker two years in a row, and I began to look for someone I could introduce.

First call—Dustin Hoffman's office. Sorry, he's shooting a movie. Very nice, but no dice.

Two months and a hundred phone calls later, I'd worked my way down to the Shriver brothers (I'll take either one); both had schedules they thought could be changed . . . but no. Last hope, Maryland senator Barbara Mikulski, arguably the U.S. Senate's leading advocate for the disabled. She thought she could do it, but then not.

I was tapped out and outraged. "I suppose this means they shouldn't have a graduation speaker. That no one can give up an hour of their life to make this a day for them to remember!" I said to Corn.

Cornelia put her hand on my shoulder. Her voice was calming.

"Let's just think this through. These kids don't care about the Shrivers or Barbara Mikulski—the parents may know those people; the kids don't." I could see something had dawned on her. "There're only eighteen students graduating. You go to school, do a speech-writing workshop, and have each one of them write a short speech. You can be master of ceremonies—they get to be the stars."

 •   •   •

Cornelia looks over at the eighteen capped and gowned students clamoring into folding chairs, three rows of six, on the far edge of the stage, and whispers to Walt, "Wait until you hear the speeches—I saw some copies Dad brought home."

"Bet he's happy not to be working tonight."

"I'm sure your father will have something to say."

He laughs—he's now twenty-one. He's beginning to see us as we really are.

Thirty feet due east, and four feet elevated, I offer just a few words, mostly for Owen's measure of equivalency with Walt. Then, "We have eighteen valedictorians tonight."

They come, one by one. I have copies of the speeches, most about two paragraphs long, and they each have their own. A few freeze and ask me to read for them. I have to do that for only one kid. The rest step up, some with surprising confidence.

A boy named Robbie, said that at KTS he "discovered my confident stride," showing "the world, that, even though you may have your downfall, you are happy and proud to be you"—but that to "soar like an eagle you need support, love, and passion."

A girl named Tynisha spoke about being bullied at her old school, but "now I have so many friends to hug."

A boy named Mickey, who was ousted from Lab School a year before Owen, spoke of what he learned at KTS about friendship: "To me, being a good friend is being there in difficult times and helping others out when they're having trouble. I am a good friend because I'm always there."

A girl named Elena spoke as well about lessons in friendship, and that "just as important as the skills I have learned in class, are the things I learned about myself."

One of The Movie Gods, Brian, credited teachers who showed him "kindness and compassion," while his fellow Movie God Connor spoke about becoming a "fearless, intelligent, and funny person" in his "full transformation into a man," and ended with a Ron Burgundy flourish: "So stay classy, Katherine Thomas School."

The third Movie God, Owen, went with a movie reference from his own vault—intoning, in Merlin's voice, that "Knowledge and Wisdom are the real power!"—and finished with a story about a story:

A long time ago, I wrote a short story about a boy who found a magic stone. The stone was like a mirror—looking into it, he could see glimpses of the future. One day, the boy lost the stone, but he found that he wasn't sad, because he knew his future would be fine. KTS has been a little like that stone for me. KTS has helped me see into the future, and see bright things and great things up ahead. Leaving here is a little like losing the stone. But it's okay, because I know now that the future will be fabulous, and full of joy. Thank you KTS.

From where I stand, next to each speaker, I can see, most clearly, the array of expressions crossing the faces of the assembled. This is the one thing many of the speakers don't see, or can't swiftly process—and today it is their charm. It is rare for any speaker to be truly independent in front of an audience, because they all care—we all care—what the audience thinks. Why else would you be at the podium? And the shifting reactions, face to face, second to second, alters the presentation, any presentation, because every speaker plays to an audience, with some exceptions.

Today, there are eighteen exceptions. Each speaker simply says the truest thing they know. And that's why there are so many awed faces looking up toward the stage, waiting for their moment to express the truest thing they know: that, yes, each graduate is more than worthy. When the crowd gets a chance at the end to cheer, they won't stop.

They can't.

• • •

Cornelia figured that a dinner with the twenty-two out-of-town guests would be the best way to end the day.

She reserved the upstairs room at a French restaurant near our home. Owen's request—the same place Walt had a lunch for his graduation. Again, she planned it to a fare-thee-well, setting the table for everyone.

But what occurs confounds even her finely tuned predictive capacities. As dinner ends, Cornelia gives a toast. Then me. Then one of Cornelia's sisters. Owen is appreciative. But he wants more. He turns to an aunt next to Cornelia. "What do you have to say to me?" A bit surprised, she stands and speaks from the heart. He goes to the next chair. "What do you think about me today."

Then, chair by chair. All twenty-two.

Not done, though, not quite.

"And what about the people who are not here. What would they say? Can someone speak for Granny?"

Cornelia stands and speaks for her mother, the family matriarch, who died a year ago. And another of her sisters speaks for Owen's grandfather, while others talk on behalf of the lost aunt, Lizzy, and

Uncle Martin. He asks me to speak for my father, who he calls "Big Walter."

Not being able to read peoples expressions, doesn't mean you don't want to know what they feel. Especially about you.

On your big day.

•   •   •

A week later, on June 24, 2010, Owen Suskind finally makes it home.

We still live in Washington. But he's been living here in his mind and in his heart since before he knew that Los Angeles was a city, or California a state.

As the car idles, he sits silently in the backseat, breathing lightly.

The guard takes my ID, disappears into his booth, and returns with three passes: one for me, one for Cornelia and one for Owen.

"Welcome to the Disney Animation Studios," he says, rosy and cheerful. "Park ahead and to your right."

Freeman made calls. I had to travel to New York to visit former Federal Reserve chairman Paul Volcker for the next book—about the fall of the economy and rise of Obama—so I called him. Freeman, that is. I carried a large flat box to the lunch with Volcker. He looked at it, but didn't ask. I didn't offer. Inside was a two-foot square drawing of an Arabesque nobleman and his parrot. Afterward, I hustled across town to a diner, outside of which waited a man whose blue eyes and expressive eyebrows matched those of the boxed picture. Jonathan and I talked for three hours. He was deeply moved by the phone call. I told him the whole saga of Owen, and handed him the portrait of Jafar with Iago on his shoulder. He called Burbank.

Those are the mechanics of it: how we end up, here, gazing up at a cobalt blue sorcerer's hat, dwarfing the front entrance of the Roy E. Disney Animation Building.

The reality of it is more complex, having to do with a silent boy who spoke in dialogue and lived on a diet of myth and fable. Cornelia and I wrote all that up in a few thousand words—Owen's story—and sent it ahead of us.

That's so they'd know who was coming.

If it is the nature of originality to ignore consensus, he is strikingly original in his convictions. In his mind, these are the greatest people in the world; presidents and popes, step aside.

Howard Green, a longtime Disney publicist, meets us, a female assistant in tow, at the welcome desk in the front foyer. This is the guy Jonathan called, who then read our treatise about Owen and is now providing us passage. Cornelia and I are in a state of bliss that's deepening with each step. We know the issues of scale, how long a distance it is from our basement to this place. Owen greets Howard with delight—they are fellow members of the Disney family—but, without a transactional sensibility, he's otherwise focused on the people, the creators, he imagines are waiting up ahead.

I think to egg him on, to impel gratitude, Howard is making this all happen—but I bite my tongue as I turn toward Owen. Immaculately dressed in khakis, a striped polo shirt, and stylish brown shoes, he's intent and businesslike, his sketchbook under his arm. He's context-deep on visits to Walt Disney World. Here, it goes even deeper; he feels this is the place for him.

A minute later, up a flight of stairs, our delegation knocks on the open door. A dark-haired man at a drafting easel swivels around.

"You're Andreas Deja," Owen says, in a tone of disbelief. Smallish and youthful in middle age, with a wide, quick smile framed by a Vandyke, Deja crosses the room, right hand outstretched.

"You must be Owen."

"I'm so happy. I love what you do," Owen says.

Deja is gently taken aback, almost bashful. He and a handful of other senior animators, middle-aged or better, are considered the heirs to the so-called "Nine Old Men," a storied group of artists—Les Clark, Marc Davis, Frank Thomas, Ward Kimball, Eric Larson, John Lounsbery, Wolfgang Reitherman, Milt Kahl, and Ollie Johnston—who started with Walt Disney, creating the first signature hits beginning with *Snow White and the Seven Dwarfs*, and shaping the company's animated movies across five decades. Eric Larson, running the studio's training division in 1980, guided the young Deja and other animators, who then created what was soon called the "new golden age": the big four starting with *The Little Mermaid* in 1989.

"So which are your favorite characters," Deja says, warmly.

"All of them!" Owen cries, and reels off ten of Andreas's animation credits, including King Triton, the father from *The Little Mermaid*, Gaston from *Beauty and the Beast*, Scar from *The Lion King*, and, of course, Jafar.

"I met Jonathan Freeman, he's my friend!" Owen can barely contain himself. He's become an exclamation point.

Andreas nods—"Yes, Jonathan, a wonderful guy"—and then he slows things down a bit, puts his arm around Owen, and then they just talk.

Owen shows him the sketchbook. Andreas is impressed—"these are really great"—and Owen does this little shoulder swivel, an autistic tic, that he does when a heavy jolt of joy overloads his special neurology.

We all listen, intently, crowded in the doorway. "Owen," Cornelia says, "would you like to give Andreas a picture?" He nods and carefully tears out one of Rafiki.

At which point, Andreas, enlivened, skips over to the drafting table and, after three minutes, turns to hand Owen a rendering of King Triton. "Now, we're even."

Owen seems suddenly overwhelmed. He's up on his toes, like he's going to start jumping. But Andreas seems to feel it, too—the crazy vertigo of his greatest fan turning out to be an autistic kid, whose greatest joy, and talent, is relentlessly drawing characters Andreas and his gang invented. Those characters live inside the boy. Will forever.

"I really want to thank you, Owen, for coming." And they hug.

• • •

This happens several more times, as Owen visits two other senior animators in the hall—Dale Baer and Eric Goldberg. The crazy rhythm of the meetings is similar to the Deja meeting, where Owen reels off all their credits, dating back to the 1970s. They show Owen drawings, old and new, and he shows them renderings of their characters in his sketchbook. It has the feel of a reunion.

With Goldberg there's an added dimension—he's a specialist in sidekicks. He created Robin Williams's Genie, Danny DeVito's Phil, and Louis the Alligator, the signature sidekick in Disney's latest feature, *The Princess and the Frog*, which came out in 2009 to good reviews and a respectable box office. There's much talk of sidekicks with Eric, with Owen doing Phil's voice and then calling the Genie "the most powerful of the sidekicks." Howard, clustered in the doorway with the rest of us, interjects—"wait the Genie's not a sidekick"—only to have Owen correct him, with Eric's agreement: "Of course he is, Howard—stick with Owen on this." Owen does another shoulder swivel, a current of affirmation racing though his ganglia.

Finally, the delegation races toward the office of Glen Keane, who's kind of the boss of the group. It's fair to say the other animators have a childlike quality; they draw pictures, do voices, and try to make each other laugh. Keane, the son of Bil Keane, the cartoonist/ creator of *The Family Circus* comic strip, is the father of two adult animators and has been at this his whole life, managing change, and surviving it. He's Deja's artistic peer—having created Ariel, the Beast, Aladdin, Pocahontas, and Tarzan—but with the demeanor and cadence of a teacher or a pastor.

He looks at Owen's sketchbook. Like the others, he praises the drafting and precision, and asks Owen how it feels to draw.

"I can see and feel with my fingers," he says. "I feel what the characters do, if they're happy or sad or scared or lighthearted. When I draw it, I can feel it."

This is something Owen has never said, even to us.

Keane smiles and digs in. He's the only one, it seems, who has read what we sent to Howard—the write-up of Owen's story—and he's purposeful, wanting to get a sense of who's in front of him.

He takes Owen on a tour of his large office, drawings rising on the ten-foot-high walls, as we all watch, wanting Owen to have an unmanaged encounter with one of his heroes—maybe a once-in-a-lifetime moment. But overhearing a question about how long it takes Owen to draw one of his pictures, I detect the deft, probing tone of a job interviewer.

My eyes refocus and pulse quickens. Of course on the first night when we saw the first pad of sidekick drawings we dreamed of him maybe becoming an animator at Disney—the kind of dream/fantasy that we once embraced for both boys, as they ran around the yard in Dedham.

That was eight years ago—eight years in which we saw the episodic nature of his path; one step forward, two back; though, of course, all of it is progress. But not enough, not nearly enough, to imagine such a thing and again begin harboring dreams for him. We'd given that up. It was about living day to day, and making the most of these moments.

But in this moment, those embers started to glow. What if? Who can say? Miracles occur. A few feet away Owen is kicking into one of his standard lines—"I want the return of traditional, hand-drawn animation, especially by Disney, to start a new golden age." When he said this an hour before, Andreas—a fellow hand-drawn purist— cheered.

Glen, though, steers Owen over to a large computer in the far corner. He beckons us all to come over. There's an animated figure on the screen, mostly in outline. He hands Owen a thick stylus and asks him to change the shape or draw in features, right on the screen, telling him that a computer, inside the screen, will reshape the figure to meet his drawn line. It's a hybrid, where the computer is guided by the artist's pencil. Owen bears down, but everything's wrong. He needs to be looking at a picture from a Disney book to draw his version; he needs the tactile feel of a pencil in his fingers, the bond paper sliding across the pad of his hand. Beyond the technical issues, he's deeply unsettled by computer animation.

He can't draw anything of quality—a mess of lines—and puts down the mechanical pencil. My heart sinks.

Cornelia turns away—she can't watch.

But then Keane grabs the mouse and clicks. The screen fills with an unfolding scene, of Rapunzel spinning, as her famous hair—blond in Disney's version—flows in a swirling cascade. It's a snatch from the movie *Tangled*, the Rapunzel story, four years in the making, that's due out in November.

It's Keane's baby. He's executive producing it along with three others including John Lasseter, who left in the early 1990s to launch Pixar, which Disney ended up buying in 2006. They are working on a project to merge hand-drawn's artistry with the ease and flexibility of CGI (computer generated imagery). This software, produced by Disney at a cost of nearly $20 million to bridge these warring camps, will be on display in *Tangled*.

As he reduces the screen, Keane tells of showing those few seconds of Rapunzel's hair to his mentor, Ollie Johnston, the last surviving member of the Nine Old Men, just before he died in 2008. "I told him to look at the hair, the way it flows like a moving painting, the best of both hand-drawn and computer," Keane recounts. "Ollie looked at it. And said, that's very nice, 'but what I'm interested in is what's she feeling.'"

The mention of Ollie Johnston activates Owen's hyper-focus.

"It's not about the animation," Glen says intently. "In terms of the animation, we can do anything now on the screen. It's about the story."

He looks intently at Owen.

"Remember, all the great movies all begin with a story. It's the stories that we need. "

Owen drinks it in, nodding vigorously. "I understand."

Glen swiftly draws a picture of Ariel, signs it, gives it to Owen, and they hug. We profusely thank him, and we're off, as Owen begins to vigorously pace and gesticulate in the hall. Cornelia can see he's flagging. An hour of interactions, especially of this intensity, is like ten hours for a typical person. This is another little recognized feature of autism—how much energy it takes to engage with another human being.

But there's one more stop in the building. After a few turns, Howard ushers us into a round striped room with a high-domed ceiling. The room is; cool and pristine like still a shrine. Owen drifts in and turns, arms out, eyes carried upward on the stripes.

Cornelia and I watch the slow spin, palms up, like a pilgrim in ecstasy.

Disney was a driven man. His first cartoon studio failed after just one month while he was still a teenager, and he later had a difficult time with two distributors who tried to steal his characters away. The vast majority of cartoons released in the nascent days of the animation industry, were like moving comic strips: goofy, exaggerated, played for gags. With *Snow White and the Seven Dwarfs*—called "Disney's folly" and almost bankrupting his still modest-sized studio—he experimented with the presentation of complex human feelings. To help the animators understand what he was envisioning, he would tell them the stories, sometimes acting out the parts. Their job was to draw it so people could feel it. Audiences, startled to experience joy and sadness while watching moving artwork, cheered. They literally stood and applauded in theaters.

He'd taken a crafted image, hand-drawn in a way anyone could on a pad—albeit drafted by professional artists—and turned it into a verisimilitude of life that carried basic human emotions. That was his real innovation—presenting lifelike emotions on the screen to draw forth real emotions.

And that's really why Owen's here—emotions. It's unsettling to see him set reverently, blissfully, on the striped room's lone couch, as though he's sitting in the lap of God. The man started a company that makes movies, sells things, and runs theme parks.

There are times when we felt like Walt Disney kidnapped him; that Owen lived in his world more than ours. Along with the joy of discovering that Disney products provided a way to meet him, to be with him, there were times when there was real resentment about the important role these characters had assumed in our lives. Some of that was eased today. Hearing Owen talk to the animators—and seeing them moved, and often surprised, by how he had to rely on their movies—reminded us that this was always a dialogue: Owen, since his earliest days, talking to the screen. What the lifelike emotions presented in these movies drew from him, and still do, are *his* emotions, *his* deepest feelings, from his life as our son. Not Walt Disney's.

•　•　•

Cornelia almost rear-ends the car in front of her.

Hearing the screeching brakes, the driver—a woman stopped at a four-way intersection—turns in the driver's seat to see what sort of idiot nearly hit her. Cornelia offers a "forgive me" shrug, swiftly parks, and leaps out of the car.

She can't believe there's a FOR RENT sign on the lawn of a house just six blocks from where we live, what looks like the perfect house: one story, maybe three bedrooms, an enclosed backyard. She jots down the rental agent's number on a grocery-store receipt and whispers to herself, "Please God, let this work."

She has just one item to complete her setup of the transition program—a place to house it. Everything else it set. A former Pasquaney camper with Walt, who worked with autistic young adults while getting his college degree in psychology, will be the program director. He'll manage, teach, job coach, and guide Owen, Brian, and Ben through a year of independent living skills. She's been working all summer on creating the curriculum and an array of activities. And she just bought a used van on eBay, for Tyler, the house manager, to drive the trio where they need to go. She'll be in charge, supervising him, and all three families will share the cost.

She told all of this to a realtor for the apartment she saw a month ago in late July in Bethesda. They had already agreed to the rental. They were talking logistics for the paperwork, when she said it would be three autistic young adults and a supervisor. Sorry, no. End of discussion. Cornelia explained they won't even be sleeping there most nights. It'll be a place they'll be working on skills, like cooking and cleaning, traveling on buses and subways. Sorry, we can't have "a group" here.

She was beside herself. "But how is it functionally any different than three guys sharing an apartment?" She got no response. The matter was not negotiable.

At the next apartment, when they said it was against policy, she demanded to see where this prohibition is found in the lease. We'll get back to you, was the evasive response.

The third apartment was less ideal. But it was mid-August, so she couldn't be choosy. The landlord said he had nothing against autistic people, but he'd need to check with the owner. When that "no" came back, we did some online research and found that the building was owned by a rabbi. I spent half a day digging up Talmudic references in drafting an impassioned letter. He turned us down—the Talmud says nothing about rental properties in multiunit structures—prompting me to write a terse follow-up letter, beginning, "And you call yourself a Rabbi?"

We've already begun paying Tyler. The kids are ready. I said I'll give over my office/studio behind the house. It's one big room—tight for four people—but it would suffice. I can see about renting an office elsewhere or working in the house.

The morning after seeing the rental sign, Cornelia and I go out for breakfast, out of Owen's earshot.

"We can't get turned down again," she says after we order.

I tell her I'm willing to offer my office. She swats that away. "That's utterly ridiculous. You're finishing a book. Where are you going to do it? On the front lawn."

"No . . . I'll manage."

This is a typical exchange. Call it "The Sacrifice Games." Who can sacrifice more. It's difficult for both to sacrifice simultaneously—so there are strategic issues, of move and countermove. No prize money attached. But the deification points are redeemable for periodic gifts and regular trips to the moral high ground. Cornelia generally crushes me here, but I'm making a run with the office.

She dismisses the whole subject—it'd be a disaster—and switches tact.

"Today's basic question," she says, "is do I lie?" For her this is a massive moral sacrifice—*nice move.*

Cornelia hates to lie and isn't very good at it. But these are special circumstances. We begin to work through rationales. I spend a fair amount of my life trying to understand the "good enough reasons" for why sources or subjects do what they do. It helps me to better able render them "in full context"—that's what I tell them—in a way that undercuts judgment.

Cornelia has firm codes of conduct. She wants me to try to help her get around them. So, the problem, I tell her, are the misimpressions people have of autism. The unknown scares them and, even if they know someone with autism, the spectrum is so wide they can't be sure what they're getting. At noon today, you just don't tell them that these four young men—the three guys, plus Tyler—are any different from any other group. Tyler can speak for the quartet.

Eventually, when they meet the other three and recognize they're mildly challenged, they'll also see that they're gentle, happy, and compulsive rule-followers. The owner will never have better tenants and she'll have met her first autistic spectrum people. It's ignorance that causes fear. That's how it'll be conquered.

"Ends justifies the means," Cornelia says, ruefully, as the omelets are served.

"We could also do breaking eggs and omelets," I say, drawing a small laugh, but enough to seal it.

Three hours later, she's completed the house tour. The owner, an African American woman in her fifties is beginning to ask if Cornelia has questions, including does the house fit her needs. It's perfect. Three bedrooms, living room, dining room, kitchen, backyard. Not cheap—$2,500—but manageable, split between the families. She then starts to ask a few questions about the guys. Cornelia's ready. She's rehearsed. *Three college guys, one just out of college and . . .*

"Listen, I have to tell you, it's three autistic guys and a supervisor." She describes them, how they're really no trouble, and that she's been turned down at three different places.

The owner pauses for a long minute. "Because you told me the truth, it's yours."

•   •   •

Based on a series of bargaining agreements over the decades between Actors' Equity and The Broadway League (producers), New York stage actors tend to be off from Sunday afternoon until the Tuesday evening performance.

It also so happens that Halloween in 2010 falls on a Sunday.

The combined result of this virtuous confluence means that Owen, sitting in his corner nook of Maureen's artist's den, drawing a picture of the Genie in a wild pastel montage, has the voices in his head replaced by something more real.

"Owen, are you in here . . . ?"

"Oh my gosh, it's Jonathan Freeman!"

Owen leaps up, arms out and looks quickly at me, Freeman's chauffer today—I nod a yes, hugging is fine—before he throws his arms around a smiling, well-coifed baritone, who took a personal day for his Sunday afternoon's performance and caught an early-morning train.

Of course this touches off celebration in the matriarchy. Owen effusively introduces "one of the greatest actors of all time and my good friend" to Maureen and all the girls.

This is exciting for all concerned: the female artists having witnessed many versions of Jafar drawn over the past year, as well as for Jonathan, an actor meeting an appreciative audience. He does not disappoint, turning the praise after a moment on Owen, and queuing him gently. "Owen, isn't something happening tonight?"

It takes him just a second. "Yes, I'm having a Halloween party tonight at my clubhouse and everyone's invited."

That's what the rented house is called—"the Clubhouse"—which is fitting in that the young men rarely sleep there. It's officially named Newfound Academy, after the New Hampshire lake that's next to Walt's summer camp, and—in ways both conscious and subconscious—there's a desire to bring to Owen's life some of the self-reliance that has been instilled in his older brother.

Tyler, the program director, carries the camp's old-world, energetic optimism (the cultural norm during Teddy Roosevelt's presidency) to great effect. The three young men, after all, are without cynicism, the attitudinal currency of much of the developed world. It simply doesn't exist in autism, like lying, but with fewer attendant complications. Take away jaded, world-wise appraisals, distancing and disdain, and you're left with appreciation and participatory vigor. Tyler directs this readiness to tasks, like lessons in cooking and balancing checkbooks, travel training (riding subways and busses), and bike outings or regular hikes on woodland trails. There's a lot of role-playing in the house, with Tyler acting one day like a distracted job interviewer, and the next like a frustrated customer. If the young men are to succeed in the workplace, they'll have to deal with the uncooperative and the impatient.

Ben already had a job working at a local supermarket—a place where Owen is now trying to get a part-time job. So, in the week leading up to Halloween, Tyler worked with Owen in the clubhouse's kitchen on speed, technique, and customer courtesy while bagging groceries.

A "practice bag"—filled with dry goods like cans and cleaning supplies—is still on the counter as Owen and Jonathan string cobwebs in the kitchen and then move to the living room to prepare for the party.

Once the room seems well webbed, the two of them sit on the couch. Owen says he just wants to look at the room, make sure the webs are hung just right. After a moment, Jonathan suggests they keep moving—it's already late afternoon, and there's much to do for the event—but Owen says just a couple more minutes.

When asked a few years later what he was feeling that day, he mentioned that time on the couch. "It was Halloween and Jonathan

Freeman was there. It was the greatest day of my life and it all was going so fast. I wanted to slow it down. To just be in this day for as long as I could."

• • •

We wake up, little by little, throughout our lives. There are signature days that are like thresholds crossed. They reveal a before and after.

This was a day like that for Owen.

After several years, when he was told high school kids don't dress up for Halloween, he wonders why the edict is lifted now that he is of college age. As we unload food from the car, he asks me why. I have no real answer. College Halloween parties, I tell him, are the stuff of legend.

"I'm glad Halloween's back," is all he says, and soon he's slipping into the costume of Jack Skellington, the treacherous and romantic Pumpkin King from *Tim Burton's The Nightmare Before Christmas*. We all worked on it with him in the late afternoon, stitching rubbery bones on his dark gloves. Once he's snug in it, Jonathan—with a hand seasoned by decades in theater—deftly applies the makeup in the bathroom of the clubhouse.

For so many years, it was Owen and his autistic friends, often dressed as Disney characters, who carried later than most the magical realism found in small children, as they knock on each door with a smile that says, "Look, who I am tonight. I am what I imagine."

They ran into the high school prohibition and, as for Owen, he didn't understand why. The reason kids don't dress up and knock on doors when they're in the tenth or eleventh grade is because those are the years their basic architecture—the foundations of their personality—begin to settle. Their inner, private selves start to take shape, as does their sensibility of how everyone—parents and teachers, included—offer a face to the world. They begin to feel deeply the divide between how they feel and how they behave, and are forced to recognize the consequences, for better or worse, that rest on drawing that line just so.

Once kids get to college, they've come to accept that our inner life—a place of restricted access—is where we live and love, and that we all wear masks in public; masks they joyously discard for a grown-up Halloween and replace with some mask of their choosing, also crafted for presentation and effect.

How much Owen senses these shifts is not clear. Though tonight, much is reversed: the masked people come to Owen. Girls from his art class come—Maureen, too, and her husband—mixing with his clubhouse mates, their families, and friends from school: Connor, of course, but quite a few others from high school, too. Laura, Owen's same-aged first cousin, and now a Georgetown University freshman, also stops by with her friends.

The three-bedroom ranch, with its tag sale furniture, is soon filled with people from many parts of Owen's life, enjoying each other's company, drinking, eating, and listening to music. In the center of the swirl is Jonathan, greeting an array of kids from Owen's school, who know quite a bit about him, and not just from Owen.

Certainly, he's deeply appreciated by a fellow Movie God like Connor, who treats him with giddy deference. But Owen tells everyone who he is, and even the unaffiliated already knew the movie and the character, if not who did the voice work. He also claims another IMDB credit, favored by a certain subset of aficionados: he was the voice of Tito Swing, the jazz piano player in the band that lives inside a jukebox on PBS's *Shining Time Station*. Brian, dressed as Jack Sparrow from *Pirates of the Caribbean*, is at his side much of the night, having a cathartic moment not unlike Owen's first sighting of Freeman at the New Amsterdam Theatre. Jonathan welcomes the attention—"now Brian, which episode was that, number 162"—as, hour by hour, he wades into this upside-down world. Here, he leads the marquee. Special needs kids mix easily among their so-called "typical" peers. *Tim Burton's The Nightmare Before Christmas* runs in one room, rock and roll—and rap—blares from another, and a gangly autistic young man in skeletal whiteface moves about with an affectionate attentiveness and flexibility that runs counter to his neurological profile.

He just wants to make sure everyone has a good time.

The next morning, Jonathan—sleeping in Walt's bedroom—awakens to a thrumming on the door.

"Who's there?" he calls several times. No answer. It's the wagging tail of our dog, Gus, who's nose-up to the door of Owen's bedroom as his heavy tail pounds Walt's door. The reason Owen can't hear him is that "A Whole New World," the inspirational ballad from *Aladdin*, is blaring in his room.

A few minutes later at breakfast Jonathan asks, "Did you play that for my benefit, Owen?"

Owen looks up quizzically from his bowl of cereal. "No, I play that every morning." *Why?* If he was able to articulate it to Jonathan, he'd say that it clarifies and nourishes his inner self, and helps him navigate the threshold between how he feels and how he behaves. Basically, it grounds him, like so much of the Disney fare he carries, giving him the strength to face the world—a whole new world it seems each morning—which is particularly difficult when it's hard to read how people see you.

But he's managing it. He's recognizing—and accepting—who he is, both in his own eyes and the eyes of others

We didn't really understand what was going on until he explained it to us a few years later. Not surprisingly, he did it by using a scene from a movie. Surprisingly, it wasn't a Disney movie. He'd periodically use a non-Disney movie as archetype, relying on the architecture of plot and character to tease some truth from himself.

In this case, it was *Monty Python and the Holy Grail*. It was one of the live-action films he seized upon in his senior year in high school. The 1975 movie by the Monty Python troupe spoofs King Arthur and the Knights of the Round Table. It's a cult classic, quite durable over the decades. It was one of my favorites. I'd watched *Monty Python's Flying Circus*, a BBC import that was a hit on PBS in the mid 1970s.

When the movie came out, I was a sophomore in high school. I rediscovered it with Owen, who was drawn to it, initially, because John Cleese (who plays Sir Lancelot) and Eric Idle (who plays Sir Robin) had both done lots of voice work for the animated movies he liked.

We watched it together and swapped dialogue. One scene that he couldn't get enough of involved a father, a medieval lord, talking to his fey and feckless son from the tower of the family's castle.

FATHER: ONE DAY, LAD, ALL THIS WILL BE YOURS!

HERBERT: WHAT, THE CURTAINS?

FATHER: NO, NOT THE CURTAINS, LAD. ALL THAT
    YOU CAN SEE! STRETCHED OUT OVER THE HILLS
    AND VALLEYS OF THIS LAND! THIS'LL BE YOUR
    KINGDOM, LAD!

HERBERT: BUT, MOTHER—

FATHER: FATHER, I'M FATHER.

HERBERT: BUT FATHER, I DON'T WANT ANY OF
    THAT.

FATHER: LISTEN, LAD. I'VE BUILT THIS KINGDOM UP
    FROM NOTHING. WHEN I STARTED HERE, ALL
    THERE WAS WAS SWAMP. ALL THE KINGS SAID I
    WAS DAFT TO BUILD A CASTLE IN A SWAMP, BUT

I BUILT IT ALL THE SAME, JUST TO SHOW 'EM.
IT SANK INTO THE SWAMP.
So, I BUILT A SECOND ONE.
THAT SANK INTO THE SWAMP.
So I BUILT A THIRD ONE.
THAT BURNED DOWN, FELL OVER, THEN SANK INTO
  THE SWAMP.
BUT THE FOURTH ONE STAYED UP.
AN' THAT'S WHAT YOU'RE GONNA GET, LAD—THE
  STRONGEST CASTLE IN THESE ISLANDS.

Owen would do the scene, often wanting to do the father. And then laugh uproariously. Could barely make it to the end.

And, after one such bout, with Cornelia and I present, he said, matter-of-factly, "That's my life."

We leaned in, and he explained:

The first castle I built at the Lab School and it fell into the swamp when I had to leave. The second castle I built at my next place, at Ivymount, which I liked, but that fell into the swamp when I had to get homeschooled. The third castle I built when I made it to high school. That burned down, fell over into the swamp when I met those bullies. The fourth castle, I started building when I got that call from Jonathan Freeman. And my life as a great Disney animator and expert began. And that castle stood, the strongest in these islands. That's because it's built on all the fallen castles.

It was humbling and hard to hear that—to hear how he placed our efforts, both in victory and defeat, as part of a sunken foundation. The homeschooling, which we saw as such a triumph, didn't register that way for him. He wanted to be with other kids, not in some room with his mother.

And, of course, it all ranks behind the moment Jonathan called. Why should we be surprised? It's hard to remember that Owen—like all kids, and all of us—is . . . *different yet the same.* His differences are so striking, that when you hit that sameness—that we are all essentially identical in our urges and needs and joys—it's still a surprise.

When he was a tiny kid, fallen silent, I wrote that scene in the *Wall Street Journal* article where Cedric gets the acceptance letter from M.I.T., a letter directly to him, affirming his worth and capacity, and—pressing to his chest—says, "This is it. My life's about to begin." When he gets the letter, his ticket out of the ghetto, his mother reaches out to touch him—it's her triumph, too—but he turns away, already gone, looking to the horizon.

Loving and letting go. It happened with Walt, and now it's happening with his brother. His crafting of the four castles into a life metaphor, with Jonathan at the center, throws both Cornelia and I backward, to see that first phone call for what it truly was.

When Jonathan asked from the speakerphone what Owen thought *Aladdin* was about, he said, "It's about finally accepting who you really are. And being okay with that."

That was really Owen talking about himself, though he was using Aladdin as his surrogate.

That was the moment he saw it. Now, we could see it, too.

It was his inner hero, beginning to emerge.

•   •   •

A few days after the Halloween party, Owen is sitting in the kitchen with Cornelia. I'm off working. She makes dinner for the two of them. It's been the two of them for so long, so many hours and days. She can talk to him more frankly nowadays. And she does, about ideas she has for Newfound Academy, about how well he's done and will, she's sure, in the days ahead.

He meets candor with candor, looking at her intently, waiting until she meets his gaze.

"I've decided I want to go away to college, like Walter."

chapter eleven

TO DO IT ON HIS OWN

Define *emergence*. From where, toward what?

The only thing we were sure of was what we'd learned long ago: it only works for our son if it's self-directed. He'd have to lead—there was no other way. And we'd have to work off of clues to support him, just as we had been since he was a small boy speaking his invented language. Now, though, the stakes were so much higher. We're helping him plot a path away from us.

The night of his grand pronouncement about going away to college like his brother—we begin our usual effort of deciphering: is this a lark, an uninformed notion based on what Walt, his only role model, has done? Is there some other desire tucked within, of being free to go his own way, watch as many videos as he wants, have gatherings like the Halloween party, and be liberated from the pressures of the transition program, or is it just the natural passage of a child needing to leave his parents to find himself—to *become* himself?

Is it simply wanting to be like everyone else?

Maybe all those things.

What was indisputable: in an eventful six months, from Freeman's call to graduation to the trip to Disney Animation and the Halloween party, he is edging out into the wider world. Each instance, gives us a chance to see how others reacted to him, in a first encounter, and how he responds. Our long-held concerns, that he would be off-putting and incomprehensible to the uninitiated, the non-expert, the stranger, and then treated poorly—are easing. The bullying and his regression set him back a year; he still carries the scars. But the intervention of his own internal voices—an ongoing conversation with his wise sidekicks that, once revealed, we could gently guide—help him charge back. Though he was just beginning to master the divide between feelings and behavior, he seems to be rising, ever more, to the challenge of presenting himself to people he does not know.

The complications are still vast, with him not being able to hedge or fudge in these encounters. He can only show who he is, his essence, and hope for a favorable response. But the responses are good—better than good.

And now he wants more.

Cornelia and I begin scheduling visits to college programs in something of a frenzy. This is what Owen wants—one of the first things he's ever really requested. *How can we help him achieve it?* That is the only question. If he's going to get accepted into some program, and be able to successfully attend next fall, many things need to improve—and fast. His expressive speech is strong, whether giving the graduation speech or talking to Disney stalwarts. Successful social interactions—something we'd been working on for years—are a whole other game. It's the difference between monologue and dialogue, between shooting foul shots and actually playing basketball.

The big opponent: the self-stimming Owen's been doing since he was three. It's been reduced dramatically, of course. But it's still there, especially when he's not in a one-on-one situation with an ardent interlocutor, or when he's stressed and his mind wanders. He's made progress; he can now attend to a task, even one of little interest, for five minutes. But then he'll break into quickstep, doing a little hand flap or throw out his arms, a bit like Jackie Gleason in that "and away we go" move from "The Honeymooners," or Jim Carrey in a full, cartoon-character gesticulation in *The Mask*. Keeping his attention focused and reducing stim are clearly linked—and, beyond one-on-one interaction, there's been some success in very structured settings, like classrooms. But most workplaces and all college dorms are free-for-alls, as are shopping malls, busy sidewalks—most anywhere.

Cornelia consults with Dan Griffin, tells him the clock is ticking. Owen will probably have to visit schools for evaluations early next year, just three or four months from now.

Dan starts visiting Newfound Academy once a week, in addition to his group session with the boys. Together, he, Cornelia, and the program manager, Tyler, begin to institute various behavior modification programs, some already tried, some new, all urgent. The first feature is a "stim meter," which rates everybody's stims from 1 to 5 on the degree of disturbance it might cause. This is matched with something of a stim-replacement therapy, identifying an imminent outbreak of a high-disturbance stim—like Owen jumping up and pacing, clearly a code 5—and replacing it with a still satisfying but lower-disturbance stim—a code 2—like clenching fists over and over.

The satisfaction issue is important. The reason autistic kids do the stimming is it feels good reintegrating senses or settling a jangled nervous system. But it's also related to attention. To keep it from drifting, Cornelia and Dan create a system of prompts, using the vibrate function on Owen's cell phone. In an e-mail asking for Dr. Lance Clawson's assistance—especially in reviewing Owen's mix of medications—Dan writes that, "in this little Manhattan Project," we "would love to have someone come up with a Google app that emits vibrations at random intervals that can be tweaked from afar by a computer or smartphone." Cornelia searches far and wide for one; there's none to be found.

But, immediately, this behavior-modification machine starts

running on the high-octane fuel of desire. Owen's desire. Through many years, and the many efforts to reduce stim and heighten social engagement, Owen's stated goal was always "to be popular." It was often heartbreaking to hear. He'd say it when he, literally, hadn't a single friend. Most of his interactions were with extended family—that didn't count. He had two friends at school, an insular trio with little social clout. But he was starting to understand how *popular* felt; like that warm wash of applause at graduation; like the girls from art class hugging him at the Halloween party, or him introducing the guests, many of whom were acquaintances or friends of friends, to his Disney mentor, Jonathan Freeman. Making those introductions felt just fine.

The operative word, now, is volition. In Webster's definition of "an act of making a choice or decision," it lists this example: *Tourette's syndrome is a neurological disorder marked by recurrent tics and vocalizations that are beyond the sufferer's volition or control.*

That would apply to many people with autism, especially those who are—in the therapeutic term of art—heavily "involved" with little or no speech. Many behaviors are beyond being controlled. And maybe they shouldn't be. For Owen, too. But his mix of capacities and dawning aspirations have hit a point where, in more and more areas, he can be volitional.

The word Owen decides will work is *bingo*. Not a word you hear every day, but not one that draws special notice. It's a code word. As Dan tells Lance in his e-mailed progress report, when Owen hears the word, he has recently learned to assume a "volitional calm facial and body posture that replaces a class 5 stim."

This explains why, in the weeks leading up to Thanksgiving, shoppers at the Giant Foods Supermarket near Chevy Chase Circle (in nearby Maryland) feel like they've wandered into a bingo parlor. Owen is trying out for a part-time job there. He's in uniform—the Giant Foods yellow shirt, black apron, and cap—helping in the checkout lines. Ten paces away, Tyler fingers magazines on the rack or fumbles with change in front of the coke machine, muttering "bingo." Owen's heightened hearing capacity for certain sounds— any word used by Disney, Cornelia and I whispering—now includes *bingo*. He knows he needs to get *stim* under control. How you feel . . . is who you are. But how you behave . . . *gets you what you want*. He's beginning to make choices. His own choices. Not ours.

• • •

Cornelia hears from a friend about a documentary she's got to see that aired briefly on Showtime during the summer. In a coincidence, another friend knows the filmmaker, has his contact information, and, by mid-November, she's opening an envelope with a disc and slipping the film, *Dad's in Heaven with Nixon*, into our DVD player. It's a late-night viewing—Owen's asleep. This is for us. The main character is an adult autistic man, just a year younger than the two of us.

Respect denial? It asserts itself at every stage. For years, we wouldn't use the word autism. We came around. But, even now we had never gazed upon a fully grown and mature man with autism. Ever. Couldn't bear to.

It's not as though I hadn't seen Owen as an adult. I had . . . in my sleep. It's painful to admit, even to myself, but starting a year or two after the autism's onset, I started to have dreams of meeting Owen at some later age, as though nothing had changed. He was typical. In the first dream, I picked Owen up from soccer practice. He jumps in the car, ruddy from exertion and a little sweaty. He was a few years older than his real age—right about Walt's age—but it's him. Curly hair, same face, slim, there in the jersey and cleats, telling me how he scored a goal and asking me what Mom's making for dinner, all very nonchalant. We chat as I drive, just like I talk to Walt.

In another dream—one I had a few times when the boys were both teens—Owen had just driven home from a dance. He flips me the keys, says it was a great night, and smiles a rosy-cheeked grin, hinting at some unmentioned teenage discoveries. Each time I'd wake up feeling guilt, like I've betrayed him, the real Owen. But that doesn't stop the dreams.

And in one, around the time of the bullying, I finally met him as a man. I was my current age, but he was in his early thirties, flying into Washington after a business trip. He looked great—in a suit, dapper, wry, quick smile, the curls trimmed close and his face starting to look a bit like my father's. He alluded to a wife, a baby on the way, and asked about how my mother—his grandmother—was doing. I told her she was a few years along with the dementia and we planned to move her up from Florida—which is what was actually happening at the time of the dream—and he said that that would be good, and he'd be able to see her more often. I woke up from that one, the last of these dreams, feeling pathetic, remorseful. I blamed it on my mother (I could find a way to blame her for just about anything) and how I was raised under her motivational methodology: that I'd be loved more if I were successful, with her withholding praise and setting up one specter after another of future perfectibility, ever beyond my reach. Part of me resented that, even if I knew it had always quickened my step out of the starting blocks. And, here, I was doing the same thing, conjuring unattainable avatars for Owen, despite being fully aware, and at least consciously accepting, that he would never be anything like that curly-haired man, filling me in on his busy life.

But what would he be like?

A few minutes into the film we're looking at someone who seems to be a reasonable extension of Owen's line, cast forward thirty years. Cornelia and I are on the sofa in the basement, and she grabs my hand when we hear fifty-year-old Chris Murray say, "I'm a very great artist and I'm very talented," in a man's voice a touch more routinized than Owen's, but close. It's like a wave crashes over us; we struggle to get upright before the next one hits.

The filmmaker, Tom Murray, the subject Chris's older brother, narrates a montage of passing photos, home movies, and recollections from his mother and six siblings about Chris. They basically describe our life with Owen—as though Walt is the guide. In the film, the two Murray brothers, both now in middle age, meet in New Haven, Connecticut, where Chris lives in a small apartment there, works at a health food market, and creates intricate urban landscapes, every window on every building and always on sunny days. It was an artistic affinity he suddenly embraced after a heavy blow: the death of the family's angry, bipolar father in middle age. Chris's paintings sell in galleries; they carry the same expressive—and relentless—precision as Owen's sketches.

The connections are eerie, from the way Chris took up art after a setback, like Owen, to Chapel Haven, a school Chris went to that Cornelia and I are due to visit next month. We're not only glimpsing what may be Owen's future, but our own. This is really the portrait of how Chris's autism affected each member of a large, wealthy Irish Catholic family who ran in the same circles as Cornelia's family, led by a mother "who never stopped believing" in Chris. The eighty-two-year-old woman even bears a unmistakable resemblance to Cornelia's mother, creating a wrenching video mash-up, as though Cornelia's mom—a woman who always believed in Owen with unflinching fervency—is the one raising the autistic child, speaking directly to the woman now holding my hand on the sofa.

By the movie's finish, the white-haired Janice Murray—after a half-century caring for Chris—is trying to prepare him for the day when she won't be there. "Don't . . . don't die Mom, please," Chris says, his voice cracking, as Cornelia is overcome. I am, too. Does love die? It's a question Owen might ask. No, often not, I'd tell him. But everything else does. And you miss them terribly when they go. You turn, though, to other loves that hopefully you've found, and friends, and the call of life, however you've filled it. But I know what Cornelia's thinking, her face wet beside mine. Who will care for him? Who will know that he's not angry, just confused? Who will be there, to remember which voice he's doing and then offer the next line?

Then we hear what the film's title means. The father hated Nixon, among his many wrenching animosities. "He's in heaven with Nixon," Chris says, near the film's end. "They're hanging out. Playing poker and eating up meals and watching TV." Improbable wisdom—or maybe not so improbable—so much like Owen and his sidekicks.

Cornelia and I don't sleep much that night—we just talk. At a very late hour, we've worked our way across the many characters, to the filmmaker's final insight about how, in terms of happiness, his autistic brother "has much of that stuff all figured out;" and "is guiding me," Tom Murray concludes, "by just being who he is and living his life the way he does."

Bleary-eyed, we slip into a conversation about how all the studies show that happiness is a comparative issue, at least once the basics of food, shelter, and clothing are handled; a calculus of identifying one's peer group, and one's rank within it (often an equation of more negatives than positives), or finding a place within a community, people you connect with. We agree that Owen has done that for us. Or we've done it for ourselves. And then agree it doesn't matter, even if we could draw that line—a welcomed respite of the incalculable that ushers in sleep.

• • •

A week later, Walt trundles up to our bedroom for a forced viewing of the movie.

Cornelia's extended family has crowded into our house for Thanksgiving and she's decided they should see it. Her two sisters and their spouses settle in, along with Walt and a few cousins. They're all attentive, though Walt is the only one who, like us, can step into the shoes of the characters; in his case, the main character, Tom, the filmmaker. What's on-screen is an unfolding nightmare. He looks over at us, trying to gauge our reaction.

He's a college senior, just turned twenty-two, home for turkey during a tough semester. He worries plenty that, someday, it'll be him taking care of Owen and a pair of aging parents. He doesn't need this movie to paint a picture for him. After twenty minutes, he looks for an opening to slip out.

The one person who's not been asked to attend the bedroom screening is Owen, who's in the basement. He's watching *Pocahontas*—part of his annual Thanksgiving viewing. He has a lineup of movies for each holiday: Halloween (*The Nightmare Before Christmas*, Tim Burton's *Sleepy Hollow*), Christmas ("Charlie Brown's Christmas," "How the Grinch Stole Christmas," *It's a Wonderful Life*, *Home Alone*). Wouldn't be a holiday without them. It's not just the themes. He once explained to Walt that it connects him to each holiday across the years—all their Thanksgivings, since he was little—where he was, what he felt.

"Hey, Ow."

"Hi Walter. Want to watch *Pocahontas* with me?"

"Sure, but pause it for a minute." Owen sometimes likes to talk when one of his movies is running, but only about the movie.

Walt came home from Penn State for the weekend a month ago, and picked Owen up from Sunday art class. Something dawned on him on the drive back to State College, Penn State's home.

"So, Owen—you know those girls from art, that pretty blond one that's always talking to you."

Owen nods.

"She's at Sidwell. I know who she is. And here's the thing—*she drives.*

Owen looks at him. Nothing registers.

"So here's what you do. Once you get to art next Sunday, tell her you may need a ride home. And ask her if she'd give you a lift. And if she says yes, slip outside for a minute, call Dad, and tell him one of the girls is driving you home. Dad'll get it immediately—he'll love that."

Owen's excited to see Walt excited, but he's not sure why.

He's running through the arithmetic—ask the girl for something he doesn't need, and Dad will be happy?

"Does Dad not want to pick me up?"

"No, no—Dad's happy to drive. This is about getting what you want."

Owen looks at him quizzically. "What?"

Walt pauses, regroups.

"Wouldn't it be fun if that really pretty girl, who seems to like you, drove you home. Just the two of you in her car. Wouldn't that be fun?"

Now, he sees. "Yes, it would be!"

Walt feels a surge of victory. Owen is not going to be that lonely fifty-year-old man in the movie, hanging out with his mother.

"And, listen. You and her in the car. Who knows where it'll lead?

Owen smiles—he knows this answer.

"Home!"

· · ·

Owen told us long ago, that the sidekicks' role is to "help the hero fulfill his destiny." As he works at defining destiny, we settle ever more into the role of sidekicks.

Cornelia takes easily to it, still holding onto a bit of the shy kid she once was, never comfortable being the center of attention. I was raised thinking the role of hero was the only role you'd ever want; spoon fed it from the start, with mother as coach: hero isn't everything; it's the only thing.

But I've been taught otherwise, by parenthood and our special circumstances, with the lessons ramping up when Owen was three. But that period—nearly two decades, stretching back to our days as young marrieds, raising two small boys—is coming to an end.

It's early April 2011, and Owen has been accepted into Riverview School, an innovative secondary school/college program on Cape Cod with two hundred kids, a campus near the beach, a full run of facilities and activities. He'll be in a program called G.R.O.W. (Getting Ready for the Outside World), which goes all the way up to age twenty-two. The usual college calendar of holidays and breaks will apply. Roommates. Dining hall. Requirements and electives. A real college experience.

In just four months, we'll be packing him off and having that moment at the dorm, where we make up his bed, give him the teary hug, and get in the car.

But every day now feels like drop-off day, carrying that immersive sensation of a big river, cool and strong, rushing around you.

Which is why we're in California.

Owen wanted to come on one last trip to the dreamscape of Los Angeles. He now says, like a chant, that someday he'll move here to be a Disney animator. We told him that what he'll learn in college over the coming years will—if he works hard—make the possibility of a Hollywood ending that much more real. He asked if we could go one last time for "inspiration"—that's the word he used.

Cornelia wanted to visit her best friend from childhood, who's living out there, and who she so rarely saw. So it was set. We still controlled his schedule, without worrying about when he'd be off for Christmas vacations or spring breaks. It was a matter of volition.

Sidekicks, after all, have choices, in carrying forward their purpose.

Where Owen's self-definition currently rests, within this construct of his own making, remains unclear. It's something he's been working through for years, in the deepest of the deep wells. He was clearly settled into the role of sidekick at eleven, drawing furiously in his pad and—and, as "the protekter of sidekicks"—ensuring that "no sidekick gets left behind." At fourteen, he cleanly stated the starting point of his movie, wherein twelve sidekicks, he among them, would face obstacles that would force them to find the heroes within themselves.

I think it's fair to say that he could have scarcely imagined the challenges that awaited him in the coming years, or how he would come to rely on certain sidekicks to advise him—to guide him, a fellow sidekick, just as they tend to direct the hero—to get him this far.

In some ways, further than even he could have imaged. As of the morning of April 7, that distance traveled is about to include a second trip to Disney's animation headquarters, and an office one step above where he ventured the previous year.

The "Sidekicks" write-up—basically, Owen's life story along with a few finishing paragraphs suggesting it be made into some sort of a movie using animation mixed with live action—had made its way to the office of Don Hahn. He's one of the most successful producers on the Disney lot—the producer of both *Beauty and the Beast* and *The Lion King*, two of the biggest movies in the company's history. He also produced *The Hunchback of Notre Dame*, in 1996; was associate producer on *Who Framed Roger Rabbit*, in 1988; and, most recently, produced a series of award-winning feature films under the banner Disneynature.

We're here for a few days and spent yesterday at Disneyland. Tomorrow, Owen will go to Universal Studios. We'll do a few other things he prizes in the gritty mecca, like go to the Hollywood Wax Museum on Hollywood Boulevard and drive up the twisting roads to get as close as is allowable to the famous HOLLYWOOD sign in Griffith Park.

Today we meet Don Hahn, though it's not clear what kind of meeting it is. After our visit last summer with the animators, Don Hahn read a copy of the sidekicks write-up. He agreed to meet with Owen and me on our family trip west. But is this a social call or a pitch meeting? Owen has become a curio around Disney. But since Owen told us of the "four castles"—revealing how central the first encounter with Jonathan and last summer's lovefest with the animators was to his budding identity, his *personhood*—our view is that any encounter with a Disney honcho, for any reason, is a golden moment. He'll live off of it for years. Maybe forever.

In the rental car, driving onto the Disney lot on Alameda Avenue, I'm thinking of the conversation we had after that session with Dan Griffin, the one where Owen told me how his sidekicks were doing in the dark forest, and how—in that secret story, as well as the parallel story of his life—the inner hero emerges. He said it clearly that day: the making of "a movie that saves the world."

But describing the concept of a pitch—of selling oneself and one's idea—is like chatting with him about quantum physics; grasped or not, it's a transactional engagement that affronts every chromosome in his being.

I fall back on Owen's lexicon: "You know, he makes the movies— he helps decide which ones. Maybe you could tell him more about which sidekicks are in the forest, and what they're up to. He might be interested."

"I'm working on that," he says.

"But I'm really excited to meet him!"

●　　●　　●

And he certainly is.

Owen shouts out his name and hugs him as Hahn, a big, bearded guy, with large, soft eyes, enters his outer office. He tells his assistant it'll just be a few minutes—indicating it'll probably be a short meeting—and leads us inside.

He first looks at Owen's sketchbook and seems genuinely impressed. "You've got a little bit of everything in here; wow, good for you, these are really good," he says with a sincere tone. Every time he looks at a sketch, he adds, "That's a very good Rafiki," or "This is a strong Sebastian"—that character's voice, care of Owen, comes from the couch.

And soon, they're doing voices. Or, mostly, it's Owen's doing them while Don laughs. Soon, both Don and I are egging Owen on.

My anxiety fades; my pushiness, perhaps? *Pitch?* Who cares! Owen's telling his story in voices. I tap a reference, or Don does, and out one comes, sidekick after sidekick, from Iago to Rafiki to Merlin. Owen does voices from all of Don's movies and at one point sings, "Witchcraft, nothing but witchcraft" in Frank Sinatra's voice—a scene from Roger Rabbit that Owen loves. By the time he gets to "although, I know, it's strictly *tabooooo*," Don is singing with him.

At my prompt, Owen talks about his first call with Jonathan, how he told him *Aladdin* was about "accepting who you really are, and begin okay with that," and Don tells him that for each movie, they post the main idea above the drafting rooms to inspire the animators: "Don't Judge a Book by Its Cover" for *Beauty and the Beast*; "Remember Who You Are" for *The Lion King*. All I can think of after this exchange is how Owen's interpretation, what he sees, goes so much deeper.

"You've figured us out—it's not fair," Don laughs. But, in a moment, he sees it, too: "You see so much more in these stories than most people."

Which bumps things right along to the deeper meaning of Owen's idea—that one line, about a band of sidekicks searching for a hero and, not being able to find one, they have no choice but to summon heroism from within themselves.

"I love that idea," Don exults. "It's an everyman idea. You can actually walk in the shoes of the sidekicks," as they search. "It's just so cool."

I'm feeling a little light-headed. We're actually talking about the concept and its possibilities. Don's working it—"it's so much the way life really is—we might be a hero for one day; then it's back to being a sidekick. Or not even a day."

Alright, I think, *now we're getting somewhere.*

"Can I ask you a question?" Owen interjects. It's about Mary Wickes, who voices one of Quasimodo's three gargoyle sidekicks, and died during the final days of production for *Hunchback*. "She was replaced by Jane Withers, wasn't she?"

Owen knows this answer, knows everything there is to know about these two old ladies. Wickes, who he bonded with when he embraced this character as a young child, died right as the movie was being finished in 1996. She was replaced by Withers, who was mentioned in a mysterious nonspecific credit. Once he discovered what happened, he fixated for years on which lines were done by Wickes, and which were handled by Withers. And he thinks he knows based on the slightest vocal variations. But he wants confirmation from Don, who marvels at Owen's factual knowledge—"almost no one knows that Owen"—not realizing it's the edge of a cliff.

What I realize, sitting next to Owen, is that there is a God and he's having some fun on his lunch-break: let's put the salesman-father in a pitch meeting with his autistic son, and—what the hell—throw a thousand pounds of pressure on the nape of his neck. *Oh, what fun!*

I tamp down panic. If we go down the Wickes/Withers rabbit hole, they'll call Disney security in a half hour and drag us out. I've been down there—Uranus Trench. There's no bottom. Owen will run through the movie, line by line—which line he thinks is

Wickes's, which ones were done by Withers, and opine whether Mary Wickes should have gotten mostly full credit for doing the voice. There are deeper issues driving it: how this unanswered question, of who did what and who deserves credit, undermines his confidence in the veracity of a few thousand credits he's cataloged in his head and weighted with emotions. If this one is imprecise, which others are as well? It's like Ben Bernanke buying groceries and realizing the bills in his hand are counterfeit. Should he keep spending or call in federal marshals?

As Owen and Don plow through the Mary Wickes filmography, Don mentions that she was friends with Bing Crosby.

Did he say Crosby?

"Owen, do a little of the Binger for Don!" I say, urgently, and Owen leaves behind the Wickes/Withers vortex for several lines of Crosby doing Ichabod from Disney's *Legend of Sleepy Hollow.*

Don and I jump back to the sidekicks, and Hahn seems grateful.

But Owen has another question, and moves like a "Jeopardy" champion to a *Hunchback* "Daily Double" about how the movie's theme song is sung one way during the movie, proper, and a different way during the credits.

"Well, Owen that's a little complicated," Hahn chuckles. "Can I get back to you on that?"

Then something dawns on Don. "Wait, Owen, I have a book for you that I can sign," and he pulls out a large, art book about *Beauty and the Beast.*

Owen looks at it, unimpressed. "I already have that one."

"But you don't have one signed by Don Hahn!" I crow, a desperate man.

"Oh . . . right."

The assistant ducks in his head—we've been there an hour. Hahn waves him off; Owen—*thank you, God*—opens the book. Don and I quickly pick up the thread, the conversation jumping swiftly between the dynamism of a hero emerging from within a group of sidekicks to cross-platform marketing of iconic sidekicks to a new audience, until some invisible threshold is crossed. He begins to do what a producer does, which is to fit the key components together: who might help with a script; who at Disney should be involved—"Eric Goldberg's the king of sidekicks"—and where we might go from here. He said he'd try to dig up some development money for a young screenwriter to come east and flesh out concepts.

Everybody rises. Owen tears a picture of Rafiki out of his sketchbook and hands it to Hahn, who then draws him a Cogsworth—the clock from *Beauty and the Beast*—to return the favor.

After warm farewells, and assurances to be in touch soon, we're out in the hall and then the car, driving through the Studio's gates.

I'm not sure I know what just happened.

But, for Owen, it's a huge moment—an unmistakable breakthrough, as he explains it to me after we drive off the lot.

Something about sitting with the definitive *Hunchback* authority created an epiphany: "It's not about the voice actors," he says, dreamily, like a prisoner savoring freedom. "It's about getting the voices right, so you don't even notice—and the characters can live forever!"

• • •

To engineer a life, you have to cover the basics.

Shelter. *Check.* The clubhouse fills the bill, outfitted with minimum requirements: a sofa, a TV, two comfy chairs, four throw rugs, beds, bureaus and desks for each bedroom, standing and desk lamps, bulbs, plus the cleansers, pails, rags, cleaning implements for the kitchen, a separate set for the bathroom, vacuum cleaner, garbage cans and bags, broom, mop, dustpan, and a key for the door.

Transportation. *Check.* There's a DC Metro bus that passes outside the clubhouse's front door every thirty-five minutes during peak hours that connects to plenty of other buses and the subway that runs through Washington, DC, and Maryland.

Job. *Check.* Owen is now an employee of the Giant Foods Corporation (or at least one of their entities) in Bethesda, Maryland. As he was learning on the job, his hours were modest. Two hours a day for two days per week. Four hours. At $7.25 an hour, that gave him a gross income of $29.00 a week. He is also now a member of the United Food and Commercial Workers International, the union that represents food workers, retail clerks, and farm workers. His monthly dues for the UFCW are $25. That makes Owen arguably the most selfless labor activist in America, with 86 percent of his salary going to support his union.

Cornelia thought that the first check would be a good time to do a budgeting lesson. Instead, she and Owen go to the computer as she pulls up photos of Samuel Gompers and John L. Lewis and tries to explain how, over a century, rights had been won by workers.

"Like me!" Owen cries before looking quizzically at a photo of Wobblies being whacked by Pinkerton guards.

"That's right," Cornelia says, reducing the screen. All you need to know.

The *Owen Economy*, meantime, is worthy of some study. A country of Owens would halt rampant consumerism. He still doesn't watch television, and ads on the Internet, where he trolls sites for movie-related memorabilia, have no effect on him. Their come-hither tone, that some purchase will make the buyer a better person, or at least more content, wash right over him. The equation that someone could be changed or enlivened by what they buy—a birthright of just about everyone except Burmese Buddhist monks—never took root.

Needs, he knows—they're modest and covered by us. *Wants?* Barely any. His only consistent desire is to rent two videos each

Friday night at Potomac Video, not far from our home. Because he is also immune to the siren song that some new movie will be better than all those that have preceded it, he's happy to have discovered, over many years, various genres of old movies in modest demand— mostly animated—that are the cheapest to rent in the store. And the oldies tend to be VHS tapes, which suits him. In the early days, he'd rewind the tape and play a short, favorite passage almost frame by frame, then rewind and repeat. Until recently, that slow-play option was impossible with DVDs. Beyond function, there's familiarity: the old VHS tape is in a format, albeit grainy and less precise than its DVD cousin. But that spells comfort for him.

Final tally: at $1.25 per VHS tape, he has $1.50 to spare, from his $4 take-home pay. Unlike his parents or brother, he always returns the videos promptly—rules are meant to be followed—so there are no late fees. He's a prudent, young man.

Cornelia grabs the car keys in the front foyer. She has to drive to Giant Foods on a Monday evening—April 25, 2011—to pick him up. His hours have gone up to four hours a day, two days a week. He's banking $30 a week. As she races out, she checks her watch and wishes me luck on a phone call I'm about to have with Don Hahn.

After we left California, Don sent me a heartening note, but— once returning to Washington—I was being assiduous about tamping down expectations. Having gone through two full scripts and three options on *A Hope in the Unseen*—none of it amounting to anything—I had no illusions about the distance between an interesting idea and anyone hoisting a camera or, in this case, a CGI stylus. Projects that spend an eternity in development hell are as numerous as the stars in the Milky Way.

But those long shot odds are almost beside the point I think as I slip out to my office for tonight's call. Something deeper than scripts and treatments is under way. We've spent more than a decade wandering in a hall of mirrors—between Owen's rich imaginary world and his terrestrial life of daunting challenges. Now, those mirrors are shifting as he bends more and more toward interactions and experiences in our world that he finds satisfying.

His stated desire to someday turn that internal story into a movie—as a way to bind him to others like him, ostensibly creative autistic kids like Connor and Brian—is a way of integrating his inner self with his growing needs; refitting what he knows best into a kind of conveyance, a vehicle for his escape from a life spent too much alone, trapped in his head. His emergence as a healthy, self-aware adult—that's the goal.

Don is a particularly valuable visitor to this hall of mirrors. He's both an expert on Owen's source material and on the common urge to craft stories as a mirror to life.

We pick up right where we left off in California. "I keep thinking about it," Don says on the phone. "To have the sidekicks, themselves, searching, changes the model of the hero being identified early and everyone slotting into their expected role. This turns it on its head. It allows for more ways to enter the story, for both the kids and their parents."

He wants to know more about Owen, what's he up to? What's his life like, now? I tell him a bit about him having his first real job, working at the supermarket, and about him going to a college program in the fall. "I'm sure he'll be bringing his sidekick advisers with him," I say, half in jest.

"Does he rely on them now?" Don asks.

"I'm sure he does. It's part of his internal voice."

"You mean, like Jiminy Cricket and conscience?"

I hear the car pull into the driveway.

"Look, he's just back from work. I'm going to talk to him. I'll call you right back."

A moment later, I see Owen slumped on the couch in the

sunroom, just off the kitchen. He's in his black GIANT FOODS cap and his apron.

"Hey buddy."

"Hi Dad."

"You look bushed."

"I'm *exhaaaaausted*," he says, a flourish he picked up from his mother.

We talk for a minute about how much harder he finds the four-hour shift. The energy he needs to expend to stay focused, to stay on task, is daunting, as his mind is being pulled in many directions.

"Let me ask you something—you bringing any of the sidekicks along? You know, to help."

He nods. "Two of them." He says it casually. This is common-place to him.

"Which two?"

"Well, I bring along Phil," he says. "When I'm getting tired, he says, 'Listen Kid, it's not enough to be your best for a minute or an hour. You've got to be at your best . . . *for every minute of every hour of your shift!*'" Of course, he does it in Phil's voice and, with a little laugh, brings up the volume for the "every minute of every hour" exhortation.

"And also Sebastian."

Phil, I get. *But Sebastian?*

Owen sees I'm perplexed. "Well, Dad, when people are coming through the line, and I'm bagging the groceries, Sebastian says to me, 'A smile can go a long way, when you don't got a lot to say.' And it reminds me to smile at them, all of them, even if I have nothing to say." This is an elegantly altered line from the movie.

He pauses. "But I do talk to them sometimes!" and laughs, hopping up and doing a little twist/turn with his hand, a jolt of energy, *sidekick energy*, running through him.

I slip out back to report these latest findings about Phil and

Sebastian to Don. I paint a picture of Owen on the couch in his uniform, what he says, and the way he says it. It is what I do—tell stories. Don does too. Mine have to be factual, crafted from real lives, and often, of late, get weighted down by having to sift through heavy, self-referential analyses by sources and subjects that are often designed to conceal rather than reveal. He and his team do stories, as well—ones they make up. But I have no delusions. You often find more subtle truths in a pure, powerful story—fictional or real, but borne from the heart—than in reasonable, logical, and fact-heavy versions of reality.

As we talk, I look over at a quotation I've tacked to the wall next to the phone; it's a favorite line from G. K. Chesterton, the British novelist: "Life is not an illogicality; yet it is a trap for logicians. It looks just a little more mathematical and regular than it is; its exactitude is obvious, but its inexactitude is hidden, its wildness lies in wait."

I'm using the quote as a guidepost for the book I'm writing, almost finished, about the misplaced confidence of Wall Street in its seemingly logical models of the way the world worked; and how Obama, struggling to reset the nation's course, may have relied too much on his own powerful faith in logic and bloodless reason. It's the wildness, lying in wait—inexact and startling—that deeply animates our lives and that of the nation. And we carry it, sloshing this way and that, in our stories. Obama knows this as well as anyone alive: he told a redemptive story of his life and then lived it as a candidate—before people's eyes—such that they lifted him to the presidency . . . against all reasonable and exacting expectations.

As president, though, he told me in an interview in February 2011, that he lost his "narrative thread"—sinking into policy combat with powerful political and economic interests, each wielding their self-interested analysis and irrefutable metrics; he forgot, he said, that "what the president can do that no one else can do is tell a story to the American people about where we are and where we need to go."

I'm ever-more sympathetic to his struggle. Owen has done that. Those metrics are a language, of sorts, a lexicon of analyses that form the so-called *meritocracy*, which allocates money and power in society, and judgments about human worth. Meanwhile, stories— interpretive and hard to control—are dangerous and disruptive, creating humility, self-recognition, an opening of the pores. That's where the deeper answers often lie.

As Don thinks over what Owen just said—seeing an image of him on the couch with his black cap—he gets philosophical: "This is about all the people who work so hard, every day, to make the hero—the chosen one—look good. People who are never thanked and easily forgotten. That's just about everyone in the world. This is a global movie . . . Hell, it'll start a new labor movement."

When he says that we laugh, but I can't help but think of Owen inside in the apron. What of him? As a young adult, he's entering an ever more exacting, logical, mathematical world, that's discounted effort, alone, in favor of analytical abilities he'll never summon. Those who can will be the victors in his lifetime. He'll bump into plenty of them, I'm sure, as he grows. He doesn't register in their meritocracy. A nonperson. That means he should be happy and grateful to wear that uniform for the rest of his life.

• • •

I wait five days, until Saturday afternoon, before I approach Owen. He's hanging around the house, nothing scheduled. Cornelia's seeing a friend. It's quiet.

He's in the kitchen, just having finished his lunch. Makes it himself, always the same—peanut butter and jelly on whole wheat, three Oreos, an apple, and a glass of orange juice.

Whenever I approach with a serious look on my face, he always says, "Is Everything okay?!"

I always say, "Everything's fine!" with a little punctuation for emphasis. It gives me a glimpse into how much anxiety he wrestles with, but I hate him thinking that something's always wrong.

This time I don't punctuate. I want him to sense that yes, everything's fine, but there's something important to discuss.

Before I hung up with Don, we talked about schedules. Owen's off to college in September, which is also when my book on Obama comes out. Don's soon to vanish into his next project, a stop-action animated film he's doing with Tim Burton called, *Frankenweenie*. If he's going to dig up some development money, and maybe find a screenwriter to assist us, this is the time. He wondered if I had any more specifics on what happens to Owen's sidekicks in their journey.

I get right to it. "Owen, Don Hahn's is asking for a few more details about the plot, you know, what happens in the forest with the boy and his gang of sidekicks."

He's on one side of the kitchen island, and I'm on the other.

"I'm working on it."

I figured he'd say that, so for the past few days I've been thinking about how I'd respond. All his leaps forward he's managed alone—from the first sketchbook and its inscriptions to the rewriting of the scripts to the story of the magic stone. The one exception was when Walt pressed him after the Halloween rescue—that's where he first said it, about the sidekicks searching for a hero. But Walt has a channel into Owen's deepest places, the place where his desire to be like his brother, surprisingly strong, resides.

Or maybe it's not so surprising. Belly up to the bar, I'm standing on the fault line where Cornelia and I stood much of our lives. On the *same versus different* conundrum: wondering how he's like other kids and how he's not. And no teenager wants to be pushed into something by a father. But then again, most teens wouldn't need a parent to draw this line for them: between their stated dreams and maybe their one and only shot.

"Owen, if you have something in there that you've been thinking through, this is the time." Then, I figure, what the hell. "Listen, if you want me to help, try out ideas on me. You know, I'm pretty good with stories."

He nods. Looks down.

"No, Dad, I know. You're the story guy. But I'm okay."

An hour later he seeks me out. He'd gone up to his room and now he's back—again in the kitchen—with a drawing he's made. He hands it silently to me.

It's from a famous sequence, where the newly released Genie—explaining his powers to a startled Aladdin in the Cave of Wonders—makes a run of transformations from William F. Buckley to Arnold Schwarzenegger to Jack Nicholson, proving that Robin Williams was meant to be an animated character. In the midst of them, to show he's the original Genie—and Aladdin should "accept no imitations!"—a blue puppet genie, a ventriloquist's dummy, appears on the Genie's lap and is then discarded.

Owen has drawn a precise rendering of the Genie, with the puppet genie on his lap.

I look down at the picture.

"I can be the Genie," he says, softly. "Not the puppet genie."

Same, not different. This is Owen's version of adolescent rebellion. Quite pointed, actually.

"Okay buddy. Got it."

• • •

The moment has arrived.

As a new student, Owen will need to attend the summer program at Riverview School, where we'll drive him right after the Fourth of July from our Vermont lake house. That means, on June 26, he'll be leaving his home in Washington for college.

Ask him to find which mathematical function applies to a straightforward word problem, and you're liable to get a blank stare. But add one key element—the date June 26—and he reverse engineers an equation matching the number of available viewing days with the number of videos he simply must see one last time in the beloved cave to prepare for, well, his future.

Of course. How else could it end, except with a twenty-four-day movie marathon?

Every day, there's a movie. All the Disney favorites and a few— like *An American Tale Fievel Goes West* or *Quest for Camelot*—that have nudged their way into the pantheon. Most times he wants company.

Cornelia and I are more than glad to oblige. It doesn't take more than a few viewings to feel a strange grip envelop us all.

We might as well be watching home movies.

When a child leaves for college, parents are usually hit hard on drop-off day. When we dropped Walt off at his dorm at Penn State, we got there a little early and left him in what was all but an empty dorm. We hugged him and told him what he already knew—that we loved him and were proud of him. Cornelia wept as she embraced him, now reaching way up.

He's a tough kid at this point—prides himself on it. He smiled his, "got this covered" smile. But the image of his standing alone in the dorm hit Cornelia hard once we began the drive home. "He was forced to grow up so fast, always ready to be on his own, and there he was."

All I could say is that it's made him strong; cold comfort to Cornelia, to say the least.

For Owen, we watch his movies with him. This has really been a big part of our life with him, since we sat on the bed in Georgetown and wondered if the flicker in his eye, as one scene passed to the next, meant that our son was in there somewhere.

In this basement, we got to meet our son, bit by bit. And, as a family, we danced and sang and took on the life of his characters, until they began to take on our lives and join us in the noisy, sunlit world above.

There were years when Cornelia and I resented Disney, couldn't bear another viewing of *Peter Pan* or *Dumbo*. But, over time, that's mostly changed. We love the movies because we love our son, and the movies are a part of him.

The day we watch *The Lion King*, well along in the movie marathon, he jumps from his chair and stands before the screen for the part he's been waiting for—when the teenaged Simba tells Rafiki how difficult it is to change.

"Change is hard," Rafiki responds. "But it is good."

Soon, Rafiki tells him to learn from his past, as a guide to his future, and sets him off to fulfill his destiny. The baboon raises his arms in triumph—"go, go"—and Owen does to. And, as he turns, we can hear him whisper, "Thank-you."

It's not to us.

The Lion King is in the final quartet. He seems to have scheduled viewings in reverse order of his early discovery. Which means next is *Aladdin* and then *Beauty and the Beast*. For that one, Cornelia excuses herself, beckoned by an enormous checklist to prepare for Owen's departure.

As *Beauty and the Beast* ends, he's up, singing the finale. And I'm up with him. He waits, as always, until the credits have run—reading all the names like he's checking on the whereabouts of old friends—before he flips it off.

I stop him at the base of the stairs.

"Owen, can you help me understand something. You've been watching this movie nonstop since you're three. . . ."

"Actually, I've been watching it nonstop since I was one."

I'm caught up short about how we see him differently before the autism hit and after. He doesn't. It was him before. It's him after. I smile, happy to stand corrected.

"No, you're right. Since you're one. So, help me understand what you see when you watch this movie. What's it look like through your eyes."

I can instantly see that a gift is coming. Maybe it's the time and place, or maybe something that has come to fullness in him, as he prepares to go. But his voice goes soft, letting down a register.

"The movie doesn't change. That is what I love about it. But I change. And each time, it looks different to me. It was scary when I was small. And then I understood that it was about finding beauty, even in places where it's hard to find. But now I realize it's about something else. A bigger thing. It's about finding beauty in yourself, because only then will you really be able to really see it in others, and everywhere."

He rolls his shoulders and head once, resettling himself around having given voice and shape to this feeling.

"And now I can see beauty everywhere."

• • •

Finally, he finishes. *The Little Mermaid* was the first movie for him—the first one that became a lifeboat when he so needed it.

Retracing his steps, it comes last.

And he's ardent about both of us watching it with him. We'll be leaving the very next morning. Checklists are checked. A new array of items—college stuff—is packed into suitcases.

We're on the sofa, he's on the black leather chair. The room gets quiet when Ariel loses her voice. I'm about to say something. What he said about *Beauty and the Beast* last night is all I can think about—I want more—but Cornelia stops me with a squeeze of my hand. "Let him watch," she whispers.

He does. And we do. More quietly than usual. Right until the end, where King Triton looks upon to the forlorn Ariel—safe finally, as is her love, Eric, but still a mermaid—as he considers whether to turn her into a human:

> TRITON: SHE REALLY DOES LOVE HIM, DOESN'T SHE, SEBASTIAN?
>
> SEBASTIAN: WELL, IT'S LIKE I ALWAYS SAY, YOUR MAJESTY. CHILDREN GOT TO BE FREE TO LEAD THEIR OWN LIVES.
>
> TRITON: YOU ALWAYS SAY THAT? THEN I GUESS THERE'S JUST ONE PROBLEM LEFT.
>
> SEBASTIAN: AND WHAT IS THAT, YOUR MAJESTY?
>
> TRITON: HOW MUCH I'M GOING TO MISS HER.

Owen hits PAUSE and turns his head toward us, his face pensive. "Are we okay?" he asks.

We both tell him we are. "We're going to miss you terribly, Owen," Cornelia says. "But that's the way it should be. It's a good thing. It's because we love you so much that we'll miss you so much."

He nods, requited, and rolls the credits.

chapter twelve

THE ANIMATED LIFE

Owen is opening the microwave in the galley kitchen when we arrive.

"Should I put in the Orville's," he calls to the dorm counselor out in the suite—gets the A-OK—and then emerges to help us lay out cups, juice, and M&M's on a table in the TV lounge. The students trickle in.

It's the Sunday night meeting of Disney Club in mid-April 2012. Owen decided to start the club not long after he arrived at Riverview eight months ago. It's been a fine first year thus far in the college program: he's getting a mix of academic and social challenges, has made one good friend, and is building independence.

Starting Disney Club has been a highlight—he's never been in a club, never mind the president of one. About a dozen students come to Owen's dorm each week, settle in to eat popcorn, chat a bit, and watch their favorites. They don't do much. A few times across the months he described club meetings to us and we tried to suggest activities over the phone. Then a few weeks ago, he asked if we could come out as Disney Club's parent advisers.

We always knew there were other autistic spectrum kids who focused intently on Disney—we'd met several, after all, over the years. But by starting this club, Owen has drawn together a roomful of them.

Cornelia and I arrive well armed to meet this group. We bring refreshments. We stopped at the Disney Store to pick up a trivia game with questions to help us facilitate discussion. Of course, we've been preparing for this much of our lives.

Tonight's selection is *Dumbo*—a fertile tale of self-recognition and emergence. With Cornelia feeding me questions, I move right into familiar terrain. Dumbo is ridiculed because he's different.

"Ever happen to anyone, here?" I ask the kids, spread across couches and chairs in the dorm lounge. The room gets quiet.

The students begin to discuss when they've been ridiculed and bullied. Everyone has a story. It's clear some have never spoken about this before.

"I've been bullied, too," Owen says, joining in. A girl named Tess says that when it happened to her, "it made me want so much to be normal."

It becomes immediately clear that these students have rarely, if ever, had their passion for Disney treated as something serious and meaningful. There're so many avenues to walk with *Dumbo*. After they watch a bit of the movie, we freeze it and talk about how the thing that makes the little elephant a pariah, his huge ears, ultimately allows him to soar.

I ask each of them about their "hidden ears," the thing "that makes them different—maybe even an outcast—that they've discovered is a great strength."

One girl talks about how her gentle nature, something that leaves her vulnerable, is a great strength in how she handles rescue dogs. Another mentions, "my brain, because it can take me on adventures of imagination."

A boy named Josh, speaking in a very routinized way, with speech patterns that closely match the *Rain Man* characterization, asks me a question: the date of my birthday. I tell him—November 20, 1959. His eyes flicker. "That was a Friday." Does the same for Cornelia, a Monday. *What are his hidden ears?* "I can do the birthdays!"

When I ask the group which character they most identify with, Josh, now enlivened, says Pinocchio and talks about being "born with wooden eyes." He goes on to articulate his choice more clearly: "I feel like a wooden boy, and I've always dreamed of feeling what real boys feel."

A dorm counselor who told me ahead of time that Josh has disciplinary issues and an unreachable emotional core, compliments him—"that was beautiful, Josh," she says—and looks at me with astonishment. I shrug. He'd already bonded in a soul-searching way with his character. I just asked him which one.

Owen, handling the remote, fast-forwards to the key scenes. When Dumbo lets go of the magic feather he's been told he needs to fly, Molly—a girl with a pad of intricate Disney drawings on her lap, just like Owen—says that we all need that feather "sometimes because we don't have confidence in ourselves." Other kids echo that.

It's that way for an hour. Like a broken dam. Students—many of whom have very modest expressive speech—summon subtle and deeply moving truths.

When I ask, "What villain do you identify with when you're having your worst day?" we even learn something new about Owen.

"Hades," he says, softly. Hades from *Hercules*? Cornelia and I exchange perplexed glances, as I ask him why.

"Because Hades is always disappointed he's not invited to any parties and celebrations. And he wants revenge on Zeus, who banished him from Mount Olympus," Owen notes. Of course, Hades, Zeus's brother, lived in paradise until he was cast down to an underworld he came to rule. "Is Zeus super popular?" I ask.

He nods, "Yes. Hades is *not popular!*"

After the meeting, we press the dorm counselors looking on— several are now observing—and they tell us Owen's been more isolated and alone than we'd imagined, still at a loss for friends and feeling it acutely. In fact, the dorm counselors, who see these students every day and night, are perplexed. "Many of these kids barely talk," one says. "And never like this."

. . .

Cornelia and I are conflicted. Part of us is ecstatic about what we found at Disney Club. Part of us feels we shouldn't have come. This is the long-awaited year of transition—for all of us. A time of endings and beginnings. And everything had been going according to carefully laid intentions.

We had an empty nest in Washington—just two parents on the third floor—and it felt just right. We checked in with Owen, regularly, of course. We visited Cape Cod for Parents Weekend last fall. He came home for Thanksgiving, like other college kids. Cornelia began to think about projects—a book she's long been wanting to write, a class to take to become a florist, helping more with a clinic in Haiti run by a friend.

I was offered a six-month appointment at Harvard's Kennedy School. We rented an apartment in Harvard Square in January 2012, to start the semester not far from where Walt was born. All our old friends were waiting for us. There and back again. It felt like a fresh start.

It was comforting to be just an hour away from Owen on the Cape, and convenient to get to Riverview for things like the school's Transition Weekend in late February.

It was sort of like Parents Weekend for the second semester, but jammed with programs about where students go after they leave the school.

A few minutes into the first session, we realized why there were two hundred Riverview parents sitting pensively, even grimly, in a

RON SUSKIND

hotel ballroom in Hyannis, including many, like us, still years away from a child's graduation.

It's clear many of us had misused the term *college*. It's a word loaded with connotations of earned rewards and bright futures, the start of a young person's journey away from parents and into the wider world. Everyone in the ballroom recognized we were all on a different path, but that didn't change the way you felt when you'd tell someone that your kid—*that's right, that's the one*—is in college in Massachusetts. It felt good that you'd managed to give them the same experience that other kids had, the big right-of-passage through college. And what after that? Well, we'll figure that out when it's time.

At a long raised table in the banquet hall, a panel of parents of Riverview alumni, brought it all into stark relief for us. They told us that the years at this school are over before you know it, and then described how their kids, between their early twenties and mid-thirties, were faring. The parents of a couple that had met at Riverview, and had each just turned thirty, told us about sterilizing them both (because who would raise their children if they had them) and how their "wedding" was a small religious ceremony, because they'd lose federal disability benefits if they were legally married.

Others talked about their kids being in group houses, sometimes lonely and full of yearning, and many of them unemployable. The message, nonetheless, was "moving back home is not good for them or for you," as one parent said, but be prepared to be involved in their lives forever, even if it may not be the lives you want or they want.

Another parent talked of how isolated the kids can be when they leave Riverview, and how this was a short oasis in a community of the like-minded before embarking on a long journey of the disabled adult, where services reaching the growing wave of autistic folk dry up. Someone raised the question of what happens in old age, when we die.

The day of pain had begun. Parents moved room to room, many of them, like us, in a bit of a daze. Cornelia and I sat in a breakout session led by a lawyer, a disabilities specialist, going through the basics of legal guardianship, where our kids wouldn't be permitted to make decisions for themselves—financial or medical—but they'd be protected against fraud, medical mishaps or, God forbid, trouble with the law. Legally, they'd be children forever.

Some of these things wouldn't apply to Owen, or so we still felt. But they might, so we took notes, or Cornelia did. I looked over at the side of her face as she intently jotted pros and cons on the pad in our welcome packet and thought of that young mother packing up our house in Dedham; how far we were from those days. Now we could both see something we'd looked away from for so long: just how long the road still stretched before us. The rite of passage at hand was not so much the arrival of college life—it was much larger: a transition, with vast complications, into adulthood.

However much our kids' childhoods were different from that of their typical peers, their adult lives seemed destined to be even more so. I guess I'd figured otherwise and didn't even realize it. I felt a last parental expectation, hiding there, so inconspicuously, pulled from my chest and smashed in the corner.

Looking around the room at the faces of parents just like us made me realize that this was where we belonged, at long last. And many of them, like us, seemed as though they'd rather be anywhere but in this room, even though there was plenty of company. There was even more unease in the room that followed, where a psychologist gave a keynote about how we need to talk to our kids about sex, even if it's uncomfortable for us. She then tried to lead thirty tables of shell-shocked parents through desensitization exercises—"okay, now everyone say vagina!"—and I felt like we were back with Owen and the curse cards. The bully today was a life we'd tried so hard to avoid.

• • •

And that's why, two months later, when Owen called about us coming to the Disney Club gathering, we didn't demur, as we should have. This was his time to try things on his own, succeed or fail on his own, in the controlled and protected ecosystem of this school. He was lonely. He went with his strong suit and started a club. Whatever happened, or didn't, in that club was up to him.

But after Transition Weekend, we felt a final gasp of that old urgency to do whatever's necessary to make it right for him—to plow the road—and a sense that these few years was our last shot, really his last shot, to make friends, build skills, find a home in a community of kindred.

So we jumped in our car in Harvard Square to go watch *Dumbo*. It's so convenient after all. Just an hour down the road.

Then we go again the next Sunday night to watch *Beauty and the Beast*. Again, Cornelia and I lead, using all our acquired knowledge. And it doesn't take us long to see we're witnessing something of real worth: the club members are "talking Disney" to each other as a way of talking about themselves and their deepest feelings. There are heartfelt testimonies again—beyond anything most folks think these kids could manage—and singing. They all sing the songs, every lyric, like their lives depend on it. At the end, Owen and Molly, his closest peer in Disney expertise, slip into an impromptu duet to finish the theme song of today's movie selection.

"*And for once it might be grand,*" she sings,

"*To have someone understand,*" he responds.

And together, "*I want so much more than they've got planned. . . .*"

Cornelia and I find ourselves singing with all our might.

• • •

Just doing whatever you want, whenever you want—your time mostly your own—is what people look back on fondly, wistfully, when they think of youth; something the youthful don't much notice until it's gone.

Or is about to be. Which is what Walt's feeling on the last week in May as he drives across the Sagamore Bridge onto Cape Cod. He's back from a postgraduate year in Spain, where he taught English at a high school and strapped on the football pads for the last time. He just applied for a job in Washington with the new Consumer Financial Protection Bureau. Real world.

But not quite yet, which is why, on a whim, he can just jump in our car, drive down to the Cape, and take Owen out to lunch.

Owen's waiting at Riverview's student center, filled at midday with students having lunch, and he introduces Walt around like a dignitary.

There's an eagerness in the handshakes—"Owen, is that your brother!"—that Walt well understands. For many kids here, like Owen, a brother or sister is among the only neuro-typical, same-aged person they know intimately. A visiting sibling is a friendly representative of the wider world. Someone who *gets* them.

And Walt's attentive, too, trying to quickly size up how college life is going for his brother. The place is smallish for a college—more like a boarding school—with boys and girls mixing and matching in a very nice cafeteria. Owen eagerly introduces Walt to a girl named Emily, who tells him she's in the Disney Club with Owen. As the three of them talk, another boy enters the conversation, a gregarious kid named Charles, who introduces himself to Walt and then says that Emily's his girlfriend.

"Back off, Charles," Owen says—not threatening, but firm—and the boy does before Walt and Owen bid Emily farewell and get into the car.

"Wow, what just went on there?"

"He says he's her boyfriend, but he's not. She doesn't have one."

"Would someone in this car like to be her boyfriend?"

"She's really nice and pretty and gentle," Owen says.

By the time they're sitting down to lunch in Hyannis at Friendly's, the restaurant and ice cream chain, he has a pretty sound take on Owen's first year. Sounds like he's not having much trouble with the school-work; loves his art teacher, Nate Olin, and has two private lessons a week beyond a studio art class; he has one good friend in his suite, John, and another suite-mate who bangs on Owen's dorm room door a lot, complaining that he's playing his Disney songs too loud. Sounds like what you'd expect. Walt's first year at Penn State wasn't all that great either.

Disney Club's the bright spot, and so is Emily.

Walt knows to go slow—relationships are hard for everyone; so much about picking up subtle cues, of knowing things about each other without having to ask. But Owen is very literal—says what he feels. Maybe she's that way, too.

"Have you told her that you like her?" he asks, poking at a decidedly subpar chicken Caesar.

Owen looks at his grilled cheese sandwich for a moment, shakes his head. "No, I haven't. Should I?"

Then Walt does what we all do—try to size up what's different and what's the same about Owen, and draw that line precisely in offering advice. "Just coming right out and saying, 'I like you.' No girl's going to want that."

By the time Owen gets to his hot fudge sundae, they've worked through the basic logistics of dating. He needs to ask her out on a date. Okay.

Maybe invite her over to his suite for dinner. He can make spaghetti for her—and they can watch a movie. Does she have any friends? Yes, and one of them—Julie—is someone his friend John likes.

Now we're talking. *Double date.* Invite both girls over to the dorm for dinner and a movie.

But there are only three weeks left in school. "Now's your moment, Ow. You gotta hustle." Though Owen's listening carefully, he's been saying—"I know, I know"—to most of Walt's suggestions. Now he looks at him intently; a look which says, *what else do I need to know.*

Walt measures his words, wanting to get it just so. "I know this doesn't make much sense. It'd be easier to just walk up and say, 'I like you. Do you like me? Okay then, off we go'. But that's not the way it works. You've got to show the way you feel by what you do. And the guy has to make the first move."

"Okay Walter . . . I know."

Driving back to Cambridge late that afternoon, Walt feels a surprising burst of optimism. As he thinks about career paths, how many suits he'll need, what leads then to what—and all the choices of adult life, when things start to count—he replays their discussion in his head. It was a real conversation about relationships; the kind he can imagine having with Owen ten years from now, or twenty.

And the best part: They didn't talk about Disney even once.

•   •   •

There's a mix-up on the double date. Either it's a miscommunication between the dorm counselor and Owen, where Owen didn't know how many days' notice he needed to give the counselor in his dorm to call the counselor in Emily's dorm; or he knew, and didn't act; or the dorm counselor didn't make the call. There have been problems here before, and relationships and dating are one of the thorniest problems these kids face. Some of them are sexual. Some are not. Some marry and have kids. Most do not. But most want to be in relationships. It's the area that makes Riverview most different from a typical college.

The mating dance is heavily managed. There's lots of counseling, classes on relationships, sex ed; and innovations, like a "cooling off" period after couples break up—no dating for two weeks. The kids, who like Owen, tend be rule-followers, are known to walk around checking the calendar for the next "start-dating" date. When it comes to the physical issues, the school takes no chances. Public displays of affection are discouraged, under the proviso that it makes other kids uncomfortable. The policy, as we were told at a parent gathering, "is kissing should only be done in private . . . and then we make sure couples don't have much private time." In terms of romance, the killer provision is that all dates need to be planned by the dorm counselors. A real bucket of cold water, but obviously essential for their safety and to ease parents' concerns.

The practical effect for Owen—the miscommunication means there's only one weekend left in the school year to, as Walt says, "make his move."

On Saturday morning, May 26, he rouses John, his suite mate, with a plan. They'll take a Riverview bus that makes scheduled trips to the mall in Hyannis, about twenty minutes away. They'll get haircuts, have lunch, and then buy flowers for the girls. They'll have the girls meet them on the track of the athletic field. "We'll give them the flowers," Owen says, "and walk them around the track."

All goes according to plan. They catch the bus, called the Conga Line. They get lunch at Panera. Then they both get haircuts. It's a big mall. Lots of everything. But after several walks from one end to the other, it's clear: no flowers.

Owen and John board the bus to go back.

"You've got to help us," Owen pleads with the driver. "You have to take us somewhere we can buy flowers."

The bus driver says it's against regulations to take the bus off the scheduled route.

"Let me try to explain," Owen says, trying to keep his voice even. "It's the last weekend of school. This is our last chance to show the girls how much we like them. "

It so happens this driver—a woman—is enough of a romantic to explain to the other passengers that this is an emergency and that they'll be taking the long way home.

And so it happens the girls are waiting on the track, right on cue, as the boys approach. Owen's holding a dozen long-stemmed red roses. John goes with purple ones.

Owen hands Emily her bouquet. John hands his to Julie. Then the two couples kiss.

A few hours later in a phone call, Owen says, "It was our first kiss, a real kiss." They didn't walk around the track, he adds. The girls wanted to go back to their dorm to put the flowers in water.

"So John and I walked back to our dorm."

I asked him how he felt when they walked back.

The line went quiet for a good twenty seconds. He was doing a deep dive. A first kiss, after all, is a big deal, at any age.

"We felt really good about ourselves."

•   •   •

The DISNEY CLUB YEAR-END PARTY e-mail goes to all the kids: be in the music room on Thursday afternoon, the day before students are permitted to leave for the summer.

But we get the return e-mails from parents.

Can they come?

Absolutely, Cornelia e-mails back. We're as anxious to meet the parents as the students are to celebrate their newly discovered community.

On a Thursday afternoon, June 1, they come in force, each kid with at least one parent in tow.

Cornelia has gone overboard for the finale, with enough food to feed an army—high-end finger food, pizza, drinks, a sheet cake, large sugar cookies in the shapes of Disney characters. And, minutes along, we break naturally into groups: parents and kids. The students have been telling their folks about the club all year. Every Disney Club parent is ready with stories about their family's fitful, often reluctant, relationship with Disney movies: some explain how their child's only comfort in the early, difficult days, when many did not speak, were these movies, which they endlessly watched; how the nonspeaking kids often bonded with nonspeaking characters, like Dumbo and Pluto, who expressed a wide range of emotions without speech; how, as they grew, doctors and therapists often echoed the parents' frustration—"will we ever get beyond Disney"—and some recommended a control or cutoff of viewing.

Many parents did. Others swung to and fro. But none of the kids seemed to abandon the passion. What was rare was for parents to see it, or use it, as a tool. The exception is Molly, whose mother, Nancy, arriving from Arkansas, is a therapist. Molly's acuity and use of the narratives matches Owen's.

Kids are mixing, picking through Owen's video collection as music plays—Owen's also brought his Disney CD collection—as he and Molly huddle in the corner.

There's seems to be a philosophical debate under way. The topic: competing interpretations of *The Fox and the Hound*. The particulars are important. Something of a departure for Disney, the movie closely follows two characters—Tod (also the term for a baby fox) and Copper, a bloodhound puppy, who become best friends, running with other small animals, until they grow and are pushed apart by both instinct and societal dictates. But the film does not have a classic fable's resolution. After they save each other as adults, the bloodhound and fox must part, leaving a final scene of Tod looking down at Copper from a distant hill, thinking of their long union, now ended, as the hunter and his dogs make their way home.

Owen and Molly's debate is about the nature of friendship. And neither of them know crucial subtext about the other: as Molly's mother later explains, this was a movie Molly and her sister, who's two years older, watched often as her marriage to their father was breaking up. Molly was four at the time and, very much like Owen, was heavily involved with autistic behaviors and largely unreachable. But the movie got through. It hit home so squarely on painful issues of separation that, after their father left, the girls agreed to stop watching it.

For Owen, he's worried about losing his friends in Washington. We're thinking of moving permanently to Cambridge. There are many reasons, including from wanting to be close to Owen for his two years at Riverview and have him eventually be a resident of Massachusetts, which has the country's richest benefits for autistic adults.

Harvard's Center for Ethics has created a position, senior fellow, where I can write my books, and many of our closest friends are still in Boston. At a dinner a few weeks ago, we told Owen that if we did move, he'd still get to visit his friends in DC. Cornelia said, simply, "Owie, always remember, that home is where the heart is." Owen nodded, said that he understood—he believes us when we say things like that—but he's afraid his friendships with Connor, Brian, and a boy named Robert may be in jeopardy. It was so hard for him to make friends, to find The Movie Gods, to have someone to share his passions with, to laugh. He sees himself as Tod, looking down from the hill.

As I fuss with the cake, I overhear their debate arrive at its closing arguments.

"It's a bittersweet ending Owen—that's what they call it," Molly says. "But it's really sad. Tod and Copper will never again be together. And that's just sad. There's not another way to see it."

"It's more sweet than bitter," he says, his brow furrowed. "They'll be apart, but they'll always have their friendship, and their memories. No one can take that from them."

A few feet away, next to the boom box, I see Josh sitting, vexed. I walk over and ask if he's all right. He says he wants to ask Elizabeth to dance. I know there's subtext here, too. He's sweet on Elizabeth, who regularly brushes him off. Saturday is his last day at school—he'll be moving on. His last chance is right now.

"Mr. Suskind. If I ask her to dance and she says yes, will I feel less like a wooden boy? And what if she says no. Then what."

I rummage through my pockets for some guy advice, and offer a few bare scraps. "Either way, Josh, I think, you'll feel more like a real boy."

Music fills the room. Kids begin to get up and move, dancing, gesticulating, each playing out images in their heads that match each sound, while they sing the lyrics. Everybody here is singing. And that's the way this year finishes for Riverview's Disney Club, with young adults holding tight to their youth, moving to a song about beauty and how it lies within. Among them are *Dumbo* fans, who've found their hidden ears, and a very real boy, not the least bit wooden in his soft steps, who just found a dance partner.

I hear Owen cry out, "Emily!" who has just arrived. Molly may be a match for him in so many ways—they're so similar—but it is Emily he's drawn to in ways that make him feel renewed and alive and, right now, far from Tod's melancholy hillside.

As he moves swiftly across the room toward her, and she toward him, Cornelia and I move to meet her mother, Gabrielle—our first encounter. We reach her as Owen and Emily fall into an embrace, and we all watch, thunderstuck, as the two of them passionately hug and nuzzle each other. It's one thing to hear about it, another thing to see it. We stand there, dumbly, hands fumbling. Then all together—in a moment of spontaneous parental choreography—we slowly turn our backs to them. Give them their privacy. It's their life now. Not ours.

• • •

Driving to a Cape Cod hotel that night—with Owen back at the dorm for his last night—Cornelia and I struggle to set boundaries.

There are a dozen students in the Disney Club. Interest for next year is already growing as word spreads.

"The idea is for Owen to run the club," she says, as I check my iPhone's directions.

"Yes, that's the goal," I say tersely. She knows that Owen and I now have a call before each meeting. With activities, like charades or ten questions, and the all-important discussions, there's time in a ninety-minute club meeting to watch about five key scenes. Owen chooses the scenes and explains to me his rationale, in relation to each movie's big idea, which he explains to the group at the start of every meeting. He controls the remote. But, she's right, I'm mostly in charge.

"Right now he and I will run it together. And my hope is eventually he'll take it over."

"Just want to be clear about that."

"Clear."

"And we went completely overboard with this party," I say. "No one was expecting that."

She nods. She goes overboard. That's what she does. A woman who does not compromise.

"We just have to keep it in balance," she says, after a bit. "Do what we need to do to support him, and give him as much independence as we can."

"Clear," I repeat.

But it's not—and not likely to become any clearer. We've caught a wave, a new one. We and Owen are sitting at its crest. We felt it today. The ardor and enthusiasm of the parents; the complex relationships of the kids, all playing out. Owen and Emily, nuzzling in the thick of it. After countless hours watching Disney movies celebrating romance, the two of them are discovering what the fuss is all about. And, beyond that, we've reentered Owen's life at a time when he needs to separate from us.

So we hash it out, running the old calculus of *same and different,* of where the conventional playbook of parent-child relations becomes different because of autism.

And, for that matter, where it's made our marriage different than it might have been.

It made Cornelia and me a team in a kind of holy war, where we've lived and loved side by side. You create a life with what's in front of you. Hopefully, by animating it with love. Owen did it. Walt, certainly as well. And we did it, too. We've never been much on the future. Gave that up, long ago. We just hold on tight, thankfully, to each other.

As the station wagon loaded with hors d'oeuvre trays and half-full juice bottles bumps along through Hyannis—just now waking to the start of summer—we sit silently, with half-smiles of resignation. She reaches over to grab my free hand. And we ride the wave.

•   •   •

Owen is up at an unreasonably early hour for a mid-July day. He's had breakfast, showered, and, by 8:00 A.M., is dressed, going with a pair of khaki shorts, mesh belt. He tries on a few polo shirts before choosing one; ties on his sneakers, over high white socks, because, why not.

The sun is burning off the last mist of morning from the lake, when he settles onto a porch chair with his pad and a sharpened number two. He looks out through the birch trees rising by the porch for a few minutes. And then:

> *Dear Emily,*
> *Thanks for a great ending year at school. You have meant so much to me. You are the most wonderful, beautiful girl I have ever met, and the sweetest one, too. When we look at each other, it's like a dream. You were so kind to me, I can't help but feel good about myself. I'm so glad you and your*

family have come to our summer house in Vermont.
I hope it's been a great summer for you like it has
been for me. Thank you very much. I love you with
all my heart.
  Love,
  Owen

She'll be here today by noon. Or so that's been the plan for almost a month. This is the long awaited midsummer visit. She lives in Scarsdale, outside New York City, but her family has a place up in Smuggler's Notch, Vermont, about two hours north of our locale. He checks the time on his cellphone, but he doesn't need to.

He goes upstairs to his room for the coup de grâce. An hour later, as noon approaches, he emerges with an illustration for his card: a precisely rendered version of the spaghetti kiss from *Lady and the Tramp*.

He has a whole day planned. Bike to his favorite place, the Whippy Dip, for grilled cheese sandwiches and ice cream. Maybe a ride around nearby Fairlee's tiny downtown, and a stop at Chapman's General Store. He's hoping they'll swim in the lake.

Walt knows this is the long-awaited day and calls in. "I know you haven't seen her in a month, but her mother's bringing her. Don't just walk up and kiss her. You've got to be cool."

Owen nods. He gets this, though he's more concerned about her father. He mentions to Walt that in Disney "it's very complicated with the fathers and daughters," and ticks off a few—King Triton and Ariel, the Sultan and Jasmine.

Walt doesn't disagree. "I know Ow—the fathers. But it's not that different with the mothers."

At eleven forty-five, Owen's standing at the top of the driveway, pacing. Fifteen minutes later, the car pulls up.

"Owen, I missed you!" Emily calls from the open window.

He's unspeakably happy to see her. But he hears Walt's voice in his head. After a quick hug, he turns his attention to Emily's mother and shakes her hand. "Hi there Missus Jathas. Welcome to our Vermont house!"

And once Gabrielle and Cornelia enter the house, leaving Owen and Emily outside, he turns to her and they kiss.

Now, he's even unspeakably happier. Hand in hand, they walk into the kitchen where he gives her the card. It'll speak for him.

•   •   •

Rainy days can be good days for autistic young adults in old wooden houses.

This finding is based on what we conclude a week after Emily's visit to our thin-walled, 1889, asphalt-shingled lake house. Owen has a very good day, safe inside the dry house during a summer storm, where he tells us things we'd been waiting a long time to hear. Other variables may be in play, such as when this sort of weather occurs in conjunction with significant life events, but we see a pattern.

Because the same thing happened a year before, in late August 2011, in a torrential downpour a few days before Owen left to start his first year at Riverview. He sat down and mapped out our whole life over a few hours. Cornelia and I could see a moment of clarity had arrived and we broke out notepads. His guideposts were the movies, mostly by Disney, that he was using at various times to make sense of the world. The animated world and the real one—those parallel planes we'd discovered when, at six, he first talked to Iago—were, in essence, laid flat on the table that day in Vermont, revealing an intricate machinery.

Very matter-of-factly, he detailed all the ways they connected. The precision was astonishing, including the debut dates of a few dozen movies, when he saw them, which theater, who attended for what were often multiple viewings, release dates for the videos, and, more broadly, which animated videos from his library were helpful at key moments. Much of this we'd pieced together, bit by bit, across the years. Now, he offered a glossary of answers. But what surprised us was that everything real was just as carefully filed and slotted into place: family trips, what Walt was doing, where holidays were celebrated, schools, friends, therapists, and citations of particular challenges and victories.

As rain pelted the roof (that was the stormy August of Hurricane Irene), he recounted our first days in Washington in 1993, when the autism hit full force and this whole apparatus began to form. He said he couldn't understand anything we were saying—it was all "blabbering," he said—and couldn't tell us what he wanted. Cornelia asked if this was scary and frustrating. He seemed to turn inward. Living minute to minute as they do, autistic folks can sometimes go back to an instant and live it over. It was "weird," he said, haltingly, and "also worrisome." And that the only things that remained the same before and after the terrifying change were the Disney movies. With his auditory processing gone haywire, I asked him if could he understand any of the dialogue in the movies. He said he could over time, because the movies were "exaggerating" everything. Then he reeled off his dozen favorite animated films. Without those movies, "there would never have been me," he said, and "I would have never talked a lot."

Now, a year later, we sit in the same room on another rainy summer day. Over Cornelia's grilled cheese sandwiches (his ultimate comfort food and maybe another sensory variable), he talks about Emily's visit, like he does most days, about how they rode bikes and waded in the lake. Again, underlying life events are at play—that he's excited to start the second year of his college program. He loves his "funny and crazy" art teacher, and is excited to soon see his friends in Disney Club. His life—the one he wanted—is taking shape.

Then, rather suddenly—unbidden—he begins to tell us what

happens to the sidekicks in the dark forest.

"There is a boy who is like other boys," he begins. "He is happy and playing, with a mom and a dad, an older brother and friends. Until one night sees from his window a storm on the horizon. He is small, just three years old, and he's scared." Cornelia tells him to stop while I run to get legal pads, fearful, that he'll say it just once and vanish. But he doesn't. He's settled—not going anywhere. After a few minutes, as we both take it down, it's clear he's ready, now, in some way. He describes how the boy—he calls him Timothy—gets lost in the storm, can't return home, and is raised in a forest, a land of lost sidekicks.

Why are they lost? "Their heroes have already fulfilled their destiny. They have no purpose." They are, of course, the ones that have been important to Owen at various times of his life. "But there are villains in the forest, and they'll have to face them without heroes," he says, before describing a villainous trio, each corresponding to what he's faced: a mischievous lord that "breathes fire into the boy's head," marking those early days when he lived deep in a fog of autism; a monster that freezes people and discards them, matching the difficult days when he was thrown out of Lab School; and finally a clever beast, "who tells lies so real that you can't tell what's true." That would be his ordeal with the bullies.

Other parts emerge, bit by bit. But easily, cheerfully—something he's ready to unveil. "It is time!" he says—the line Rafiki utters upon discovering the long-lost Simba is alive as an adult lion, ready to fulfill his destiny—"time for the return of traditional hand-drawn animation!" He says that's the way he wants his movie made, the old-fashioned way, though he knows both things—the making and the method—are long shots.

Don Hahn, busy with many projects, has moved on. It doesn't seem to matter to Owen. He's lighthearted about it. As to the issue of hand-drawn being better, it's both a philosophical and personal position. He explains in detail that you have "to feel the line to draw it right" and that when he began to draw he realized he could "see and feel with my fingers." He'd once told us that animators used to use mirrors. Now, he goes upstairs and gets an old animation book to show us a picture of a Disney animator from the 1940s with a mirror on his desk. "They would make the expression in the mirror that they had to draw for the character," he says. "It was to make sure it was right. They had to feel it to draw it. Like me."

This helps us see everything a bit more clearly: just how important mirrors have been to him his whole life. It wasn't just metaphor. It was quite real. Those animated films were the mirror in which he found a way to eventually see himself. The movie concept is the logical next step—a mix of characters he borrowed from those movies to create an original story that reflects the true complexities of his life, right up to present tense. There's even a character, he calls Abigail, modeled after Emily.

Cornelia suggests that he write some parts down, and he does. But, over the coming days, it's clear he likes to pace and gesticulate when telling the story, and asks us to take turns as his stenographer. He's finally turned the imaginative lens fully on himself. A joy to watch.

And it becomes obvious why he's been "working on it," as he'd often said, for so long. He had to live it, first. His story, like any story, had to arrive at this moment of closure and clarity; a retrospective view, which now—as a young man—he's beginning to finally assume. Or, in the familiar parlance, you can't write a coming of age story until you've come of age.

• • •

Owen and I are driving over to Dan Griffin's office for a rare visit. He saw Dan once on last year's Thanksgiving break and Christmas break.

And he may not see him again for quite a while. Cornelia and I have been swapping houses at the end of the summer. While she packs up the DC house—for either rental or sale—I care for Owen and work either at our Vermont house or in Cambridge. This week in August we flip, as she heads north to welcome a few summer guests to the lake and Owen and I return for his last few days in Washington, DC.

And ours, too. Nineteen years ago, we arrived with headlong ebullience, a young family on an adventure. I'm not sure where those people went. Owen vanished the moment we arrived and, soon enough, we did, too.

The people that grew to replace them are the ones who are now moving on. We would never have wanted Owen to face what he did, of course, but, as for the rest of us, we don't miss those people, that discontinued version of us. Not anymore. As Walt said in his Tree Talk, Owen shaped us all. Not a blessing in disguise. Nothing disguised about it.

As Owen and I drive through town, I'm full of citations—this happened there and plenty of "remember whens." But, soon enough, he takes over the citations. And it's not just because of his strong memory. He's fitting together the details of his life, looking for the patterns that make it clear to him, pointing them out as we move.

That's where he and Walt played at the elementary school. This is where he learned to ride his bike. That's where he went each morning to Patch of Heaven school. We drive by the Lab School, on a circuitous route—I need to run an errand—and he doesn't just offer a few safe memories of this friend or that play. "I felt like I was in a kingdom, there, and I was banished," he says, but with little emotion, far from it now.

•　•　•

After we pass the Lab School, I can't help but think of that replacement of terms—"learning differences" rather than "learning disabilities"—that we first heard at those glittering galas. Though it prompted Cornelia and I to roll our eyes about politically correct talk—we shifted quickly, seeing all those dyslexic and ADHD superachievers step to the podium. It was all about finding their hidden strengths.

Lab, though, didn't see Owen as similar to those storied achievers and, at the time, neither did we. Cornelia and I figured we'd never discover or help him develop abilities to counterweight his deficits, as so many of the learning disabled achievers could manage, with their less weighty challenges.

But we've come around on that—a gradual acceptance, across years, that Owen is different, not diminished, capped by the debates over nuanced issues of villainy and virtue with him and his Disney Club members. It has affirmed for me and Cornelia the conviction that Owen, and so many folks like him, are, in essence, exactly like the rest of us, *only more so and less so.*

The *less so* parts for those like Owen with autism are conspicuous characteristics that separate them from the wider world, and bring swift judgment about their limitations; the *more so* parts are often subtle and opaque, hidden. With Owen and the other kids in his Disney Club, we've learned that each person's chosen affinity, their passion, no matter what it is, can be a pathway to reach them.

Among the most surprising things we stumbled across was how important it was to Owen to accord respect to his affinity—no matter how seemingly narrow or arcane it may be viewed by the wider culture. It affirms his worth. To treat it only as a handle, to grab and pull him into something of our choosing, or twist his interest into an elusive reward, is demeaning.

There's a reason—a good enough reason—why each autistic person has embraced a particular interest. Find that reason, and you will find them, hiding in there, and maybe get a glimpse of their underlying capacities. Authentic interest will help them feel dignity, and impel them to show you more, complete with maps and navigational tools that may help to guide their development, their growth. Revealed capability, in turn, will lead to a better understanding of what's possible in the lives of many people who are challenged. *Affinity to Capability to Possibility.*

As the Disney Club members now say, it's about "finding the hidden ears" and soaring past judgment—in their own mind and, hopefully, in the view of others. It's not all that different from what Sally Smith did by celebrating her learning disabled achievers. Views changed. The learning disabled were seen as different, not less.

As Cornelia and I were driving home from a Disney Club meeting back in late May, we discussed how angry we were at Smith—and remain so about Owen's expulsion—but how we better understand her *going public* strategy.

If the world could visit a few meetings of Disney Club, Cornelia said, it would alter the view of autistics, and so many others who've been discarded. They'd be seen, she said, with new eyes and that could change everything.

• • •

As we enter Takoma Park, Maryland, and close in on Dan's office, Owen says, let's do "that love business."

Lately, we've been doing this at least once a day.

"Okay, you do Merlin," I say, which means I can do the young Arthur, who, thankfully, has only one line.

"You know, lad, this love business is a powerful thing," he says in Merlin's reedy, old man's voice.

"Greater than gravity?" I respond as Arthur.

"Well, yes, boy, in its way." Owen pauses, considering it all, just as the wizard does in, this, probably his favorite of all passages. "Yes, I'd say it's the greatest force on earth."

Romantic love. It's running through him, first and fresh, which is what he tells Dan as they sit again in the magic office. "I've fallen in love with a wonderful, kind, beautiful, soft, and gentle girl, who likes the same things I like—animated movies, mostly hand-drawn, and mostly from Disney."

Dan is giddy. He wants to know everything about Emily, and Owen lays it all out: the tale of how they met, their first kiss, her visit to Vermont.

For so long, in this cozy office and others around Washington, DC, we spoke with professionals on Team Owen about motivation. Whether it's learning to read, understanding general and required knowledge, or engaging with peers, he has *to want it*; to feel enough satisfaction or affirmation in the effort—or the reward, just up ahead—that he can harness those self-directed energies. Again, just like all of us, only more so and less so. Who hasn't struggled with deferred gratification? But we usually do what we have to, work hard each day in often a numbing or thankless effort for a distant goal. Our social interactions, though, don't feel so much like work. We engage instinctively, with sensations and often satisfactions freely harvested in the search itself.

For Owen, much of that remains hard work. Despite him often saying to Dan his aim is to be popular—a catchall for the joys of connecting with other people—that goal, largely theoretical, has been like watery fuel in his sputtering engine.

Now, it's high-octane. That's what a first kiss can do. Again, like any of us, sure, only more so. His ability to hyper-focus, to system-ize moments he remembers precisely, poring over them again and again, teasing out clues, means he's been thinking about that day in Vermont every day since—maybe fifty times a day. Every look that was exchanged. Every word Emily uttered—and she can be quite talkative when she's comfortable. The way they kissed. And they kissed often through the day, something they can't do at school.

Emily didn't bring her bathing suit, but they waded in the lake, nonetheless. On the dock, as she sat on a chaise lounge, Owen tenderly dried her feet. She didn't have to ask.

The specific therapeutic yield of this awakening is an intense focus, at long last, on what most people do instinctively—social engagement—but at its very highest peak: the mysteries of how two people can be like one.

Again, he finds plenty to work with in his chosen affinity. He tells Dan that Aladdin and Jasmine have been helpful. "I need to give her space. That's what Aladdin learns. Jasmine needs to make the choices for herself. She has to choose and he needs to know what she wants, with her asking."

Dan, presses forward on his chair, his face close to Owen's. "But how can you know what she wants?"

Owen nods immediately. He's on it. "I have a song."

He explains it is from a movie called *Quest for Camelot*, an Arthurian romance a few Disney expats produced for Warner Brothers in 1998, during the same summer as *Mulan* from Disney and *A Bug's Life* from Pixar.

Okay, got it, Owen, Dan says. *The song?*

"Oh right. The song is called 'Looking Through Your Eyes.'"

Dan doesn't know it. Owen sings a few lines he likes the best.

I see the heavens each time that you smile.
I hear your heartbeat just go on for miles.
And suddenly I know why life is worthwhile,
looking through your eyes.

He explains that he listens to the song every morning, "to make sure I don't forget to see the world through her eyes."

For nearly ten years, he's been coming to see Dan in this basement office, trying to decipher the subtle patterns of how people connect with one another. It's clear Owen is now well along in doing that for himself, in his own special fashion.

"Owen, my good friend," Dan Griffin says, his eyes glistening, "it's fair to say, you're on your way."

Owen stands up, that little curly-haired boy, now a man, almost Dan's height, and smiles, a knowing smile of self-awareness.

"Thank you Rafiki. For everything."

· · ·

"Is friendship forever."

"Yes, Owen, it often is."

"But not always."

"No, not always."

It's later that night, and we're driving down Connecticut Avenue after seeing the latest from Disney (and Pixar), *Brave*. What better way to spend our last night in DC.

The movie was fine, ending—like most of them—with an array of morals, precepts about faith and family.

I think I understand, now, from a deeper place, how he—and some of his Disney Club friends—use the movies and why it feels so improbable. Most of us grow from a different direction, starting as utterly experiential, sorting through the blooming and buzzing confusion to learn this feels good, that not so much, this works, that doesn't, as we gradually form a set of rules that we live by, with moral judgments at the peak.

Owen, with his reliance from an early age on myth and fable, each carrying the clarity of black and white, good and evil, inverts this pyramid. He starts with the moral—a whole diverse array of them—which, year by year, he's been testing in a world colored by shades of gray. That tension of his journey, testing whether these ancient principles (most Disney movies end with one) are real.

This is the reason he watches his favorites so regularly. It refreshes him in the daily conversation between black and white and shades of gray, between moral precept—*beauty lies within, be true to yourself, love conquers all*—and messy life. It's the many sidekicks who help him navigate that ongoing and eternal debate, as they often do for the heroes in their movies.

I let the exchange about whether friendship lasts forever hang, unresolved. "I know love lasts forever!" he says, filling the silence.

We're approaching Chevy Chase Circle, five minutes from the house. I'm seeing some patterns now, too—how we're always five minutes away from our street, moving in a quiet, vibrating car when his breakthroughs occur. This time I'm ready. I need to touch upon the fear, if gently, that making friends or finding love entails risk. There's no guarantee of forever. There may be heartbreak. But we do it anyway.

I drop this bitter morsel into the mix, folding around it an affirmation that he took a risk when he went to an unfamiliar place on Cape Cod, far from his friends and home, and found love. The lesson, I begin, is, "To never be afraid to reach out."

He cuts me off. "I know, I know," and then summons a voice for support: it's Laverne, the gargoyle from *The Hunchback of Notre Dame*.

"Quasi," he says, in the voice of his beloved Mary Wickes. "Take it from an old spectator. Life's not a spectator sport. If watchin's all you're gonna do, then you're gonna watch your life go by without you."

He giggles under his breath, then does that little shoulder roll.

"You know, they're not like the other sidekicks."

He's jumped ahead of me again. I scramble.

"No, how?"

"All the other sidekicks live within their movies as characters, walk around, do things. The gargoyles only live when Quasimodo is alone with them."

"And why's that?"

"Because he breathes life into them. They only live in his imagination."

"Okay, I get that. But still they're wise and they guide him, like the other sidekicks."

He nods. I do too. Everything goes still.

"What's that mean, buddy?"

He purses his lips and smiles, chin out, like he got caught in a game of chess. But maybe he wanted to.

"It means the answers are inside of him," he says.

"Then why did he need the gargoyles?"

"He needed to breathe life into them so he could talk to himself. It's the only way he could find out who we was."

"You know anyone else like that?"

"Me."

He laughs a sweet, little laugh, soft and deep.

And then there's a long pause, giving space to the moment of clarity.

"But it can get so lonely, talking to yourself," my son, Owen, finally says.

"You have to live in the world."

SIDEKICKS

(A story with lots of scenes and characters I left out,
but this is most of it for now)

By Owen Suskind, with drawings by me, too

There is a boy who is like other boys. He is happy and playing, with a mom and a dad, an older brother and friends. Until one night, he sees from his window a storm on the horizon. He is small, just three years old, and he's scared. He calls for his parents and hears nothing. He thinks he's alone and runs out into the night to find them and gets lost in the terrible rain and wind and lightning. He crosses a bridge that collapses behind him. There's no way he can get home.

He finds himself in a dark forest. He wanders, all alone. Then he sees something in the woods and hears a voice.

"Hey there, son." He knows this voice and turns to see a character. It's Jiminy Cricket, who says, "Well, you seem to know me, son. Who are you?"

The boy says his name is Timothy and he's lost and can't get back home. "Where am I?" he asks.

Suddenly, a crab appears. The boy knows him, too. It's Sebastian from *The Little Mermaid*.

They tell the boy this forest is the Land of the Lost Sidekicks.

"Why are you lost?" the boys asks.

"Because our heroes have already fulfilled their destiny," Sebastian answers. "We have no purpose."

Jiminy says that there are many sidekicks like them, wandering in the woods. But there is also evil in the forest. "There are villains, real villains, and we have to face them without heroes," he says. "What we do is tell the stories of what was—our adventures past—to try to find the qualities of the hero within ourselves, or within each other, though we're still sidekicks."

Timothy says, "I'm a sidekick, too!"

And they take him in as one of their own.

In time they meet a villain. He's Lord Fuzzbuch. He's mischievous, in a destructive way. He wears a cape, has a small scepter. He can breathe noise and fire into your head. It leaves you foggy and confused and spinning in circles.

Jiminy and Sebastian try to protect Timothy from Fuzzbuch. He's still small and they're a type of sidekick—the protective sidekicks—that defend the small and the weak. When Fuzzbuch approaches, they have the boy look intently at them and sing songs, one after another, that makes him relaxed and full of joy. The power of the music blocks Fuzzbuch's fire. Unable to breathe his fire into the boy's head, he finds it backing up inside his black cape until he spins off into smoke and confusion.

But soon the sidekicks meet another villain, a large, clumsy beast, who wears armor that's cold and steely. He's called Graytron. He

freezes whoever crosses his path. It's
hard to tell people apart when this happens. Their vivid colors vanish as they're
trapped inside this ice. That's when he
walks among them, seeing whether their
shade of icy gray matches his shade,
while he decides whether to shatter
them with his sword. Which is what
happens to the trio. As Graytron walks
among them, trying to decide, new sidekicks emerge from the forest. They're
goofy and fun, and live for the moment,
singing their songs, "Bare Necessities"
and "Hakuna Matata." They create

confusion around Graytron and tell the frozen sidekicks that fear
is what gives Graytron his power; that thinking of the simple joys
of the moment—as many moments as they can—will restore their
vividness, their true colors, and melt the ice. Which is what happens
just in time, as Graytron prepares to swing his shattering sword. The
warmth they create is so great that Graytron himself melts.

There are now five sidekicks, including Timothy. They figure
things out among themselves—the protective ones and the goofy
ones—trying to find in each other the
qualities of the hero. Then they meet a
villain sidekick—a parrot—who says he's
turned from evil to good. At first they
don't believe him, but he's very funny
and Baloo says, "anyone with a sense of
humor has to have some good in them."
His name is Iago and, before he leaves
them, he tells the band of the fearsome
Goretezzle, the most powerful villain in

the forest, who can change form at will, and does. He can become anything, instantly. He's a shape-shifter. He lies, but it's impossible to tell what is true and what is not, especially when the lies become horrific monsters and scenes that seem to be happening all around you.

The stories are so scary the boy searches for sidekicks who can train him for battle, and finds two new ones in this Land of the Lost Sidekicks: Phil, who once trained Hercules, and Lucky Jack, the wily jackrabbit from *Home on the Range*. They're training sidekicks, the type that prepares you to meet the challenges of the world, by building strength and skill. They train the group—finding hidden strengths in each of them. But in a terrible struggle, the Goretezzle is too much. Timothy and the other sidekicks are overwhelmed. They flee in fear, running and running.

That's when they meet Rafiki, who asks "what are you running from." The sidekicks, a roving team of seven, are now far from the Goretezzle, and don't have an answer. Rafiki says they're running from "the truths within," and introduces them to his partner, Merlin. The final pair of sidekicks—the wise sidekicks—has arrived. Those are the four different kinds of sidekick: protective, goofy, training, and wise.

To help Timothy find "truths within" the wise sidekicks introduce him to a girl who also wanders in the forest. Her name is Abigail. She's just like him. Lost, with no way home, and accompanied by her own pair of sidekicks, Timothy Mouse, from *Dumbo*, and Big Mama, from *The Fox and the Hound*.

The group is completed—now ten sidekicks. With Timothy and Abigail, there are twelve. Twelve sidekicks searching for a hero. It's Rafiki, meditating over the past—"trying to learn from it"—who asks Merlin, "How did you actually become so wise?"

Merlin responds angrily, "You should never ask a wizard the source

of his powers. Surest way for him to lose them!"

But Timothy says to wait. He says that he and Abigail are alike. "We both remember too many moments, every moment. But we keep running through them in our heads, because some of them hold clues about who we are."

Merlin is convinced. He digs into his book of spells, conjures one that will allow him to remember "the first moment I opened my eyes."

In a swirl of fire, he returns to that very moment.

He sees himself taking shape on the animator's drafting table and he sees a mirror. "There was a mirror on the table," the wizard says. "In it, I could see a reflection of the creator."

The sidekicks gather and consider Merlin's words. They're facing a villain of overwhelming power, but they're just sidekicks.

"If we can find that mirror," Rafiki tells the group, "maybe we can find our creators and have them redraw us as heroes."

And so the group goes, searching. Soon, they find themselves in a magical but ruined place. It's dusty. The wind blows through it. They find Merlin's mirror on an abandoned desk. The pencils and pads are discarded in piles. The creators are gone. All seems lost.

Abigail grabs the mirror and puts it in her satchel as the Sidekicks return to the forest, dispirited. As they walk, she talks to Timothy Mouse, asking him to tell her what was. He tells her about how Dumbo discovered what made him different—those ears—helped him soar.

"But sidekicks don't soar," Abigail says.

"Of course, we do, my dear," Big Mama tells her. "What allows us to soar is discovering that each of us has a gift. The gift of what makes us who we are. And a gift we can give to others.

"What's my gift?"

She smiles. "It is one of those things you've got to learn on you own. Why don't you ask the boy? See if the two of you can figure it out."

In the forest, the Goretezzle awaits. As he approaches, spinning monstrosities, Timothy turns to Abigail, trying to protect her. He sees in the edge of the mirror, poking out of her satchel, that the Goretezzle has no reflection. Just data, ones and zeros, rows of coded numbers. He turns to the sidekicks.

"He's computer generated, made by a machine. That's why he can change shape so swiftly, so effortlessly. But there's no heartbeat. We're more real than he is."

"But what good will that do us?" Sebastian shouts.

"He's stronger, too strong," cries Phil.

The Goretezzle creates an enormous swirl of fire, a flaming mountain rising from the forest that begins to topple on the band. A weight that will crush them.

Timothy tells them to hold hands, in a circle.

Close your eyes, don't look! Abigail cries.

"Merlin," Timothy shouts. "Is there any force greater than gravity?!"

"Only one . . . Love, my boy—it's the greatest force on earth!"

Abigail hears this, grabs the mirror and holds it up.

"Timothy, quick! Look in the mirror!"

The boy opens his eyes and for the first time, sees himself. It's his face—not animated, but real. As he truly is.

He's startled. "That's me, isn't it? Has it always been me in here?"

As Abigail lowers the mirror, he sees the same reflection—his reflection—in her eyes.

He gently takes the mirror from her, and holds it up to her. She sees her face, beautiful and real, for the first time. "Is that really, me?" And as he lowers the mirror, she sees her reflection in his eyes.

"That's it, boy." Merlin says. "That's what's real. The only thing that's real. What you see in each other's eyes."

"And each other's hearts," says Big Mama.

And, suddenly, it is as though the world begins to dissolve around them, starting with the flaming mountain, ready to crush them, and then Goretezzle—who dissolves into computer code—and then the darkness of the forest itself. Timothy turns and sees a bridge—the bridge that collapsed so long ago—taking shape behind him.

And when he turns, he sees that the characters themselves are changing, shape-shifting: Big Mama, into his mother. Baloo, into his brother. Rafiki, into his friend and therapist. And Merlin, into his father.

"Has it been you all along," he says to them.

His mother smiles warmly. "But it's been you, too. It's you who helped to create us. To animate our lives with a special love."

He looks at the bridge, leading back toward home.

"Where do I go now?" he asks her.

"Wherever your heart leads you. Home, after all, is where the heart is. Maybe you should ask your friend."

He turns to Abigail.

"I know where my heart is," she says.

And they kiss.

"But what about our sidekicks?" Abigail says suddenly. "Can we take them with us?"

As the two turn, the sidekicks are smiling, back as animated characters alongside the real boy, his family, and the real girl.

"Well, I certainly hope we'll be coming along, boy," Merlin says.

"We've got lots to talk about it. First off, this business about sidekicks acting like heroes . . ."

"No, a sidekick finding his inner hero, that's me," the boy says, with a laugh. "Maybe that's the sidekick's destiny. You know, sidekicks can dream."

Rafiki interjects, "Wrong again—sidekicks *must* dream! (This chatter, with sidekicks talking to each other, is the final scene, as the troop, animated and real, walks off together debating the great issues of how the hero emerges).

"You too, Merlin," the boy says. "You, Big Mama, and the others certainly *acted* like heroes."

"Well, I suppose. We're all sidekicks, searching for our inner heroes—*and I'm not about to get redrawn at my age!*"

Acknowledgments

This book is a family affair. As the designated writer, I'm mostly a facilitator of expression—the voices and feelings and insights of my wife and sons. There is pressure in any work of nonfiction to be true to the sometimes-elusive hearts and minds of subjects and sources. In this instance, that desire was deeply intensified, as were the complexities of turning private experiences into a public manuscript. I've lived much of my life in public. The central characters of this book—the most important people in the world to me—have not.

But we plunged into the bright lights together, with my wife—thankfully, a skilled writer and editor—in the lead. She helped structure our life so this book would be possible and then steeled us for the rigors of emotional inquiry and research. Soon enough, we found ourselves floating across the past twenty years like a pair of ghosts, looking down at our little family, a quartet of confused actors, with a mix of intimacy and distance. It was wrenching—having to basically live difficult moments of our lives over again—but, at day's end, deeply affecting.

We needed a map, and the pile of source materials—neuropsychological tests and school reports, home movies, cards and letters, audiotapes and notebooks, provided one. We have often used our journalistic skills to document the unfolding events so that, at the very least, we could be well informed in our consultations with teachers, therapists, artists, coaches, and, of course, medical professionals.

We traversed two decades with this close community, and several were key consultants for this book. For that, and so much more, we're thankful to the following: Dr. Alan Rosenblatt, Dr. C. T. Gordon, and Dr. Lance Clawson; our testing guru Bill Stixrud and therapists Christine Sproat, Sharon Lockwood, Jennifer Bilyew, and Debbie Regan; an array of artists, musicians, coaches, and counselors, including Ruthlee Adler, Tony Rheil, Maureen O'Brien, Tyler Ostholohoff, Karen Soltes, DJ Butler, Jeremy Jenkins, Ronde Baquie, Frank Scardino, Fallon Nickelsen, and Megan Holland. And, finally, the dedicated educators: Lucy Cohen, Stephanie deSibour, Jan Wintrol at Ivymount School; Susan Whitaker, Colleen Bain, and Cathy Parker at NCRC; Pamela Knudson, Jennifer Owen, and Lydia Kepich at Lab School; and at KTS, Rhona Schwartz, Jonathan Davis, Audrey Achmed, Lisy Holloway, and Dustin Hartwigsen. A special note of thanks as well to Nate Olin, Owen's brilliant art teacher, and all the folks at Riverview School, led by the inimitable Maureen Brenner. And to our coconspirators, Gabrielle and George Jathas, thanks for all your trust and good humor.

There are two people who have worked closely with Owen for years and to whom we owe the greatest debt of gratitude for all that they have taught us and the doors that they helped open to our son: Suzie Blattner and Dan Griffin. Thank you from the bottom of our hearts.

A turning point, early on, was our encounter with a villain who acted like a hero. That would be a gentle, large-hearted actor, Jonathan Freeman—the voice of Jafar—who came into our orbit and has since become our dear friend and the brightest star in Owen's constellation. Our gratitude extends to all the animators Owen has met over the years who were so generous with their time—along with the voice-work actor, Jim Cummings. These folks have helped our son appreciate his talents and believe that anything was possible.

There are too many friends to thank—our Dedham buddies, the "farm friends," the Boston college gang, our beloved Washingtonians.

During the period of this book and its writing, the constancy of these friendships have sustained us.

A new friend and assistant at the Kennedy School, Greg Larson, stepped in with strong early research. Our beloved Greg Jackson, a former assistant of mine, who has since become an established fiction writer, brilliantly edited the first third of the book, and helped in structuring the rest. And then there is a writer that the world already knows—the novelist Howard Norman—who has long been my indispensible shtetl chum and counsel on both living and writing. He was my guide from the first days of this project and helped shepherd it to its finale, reading it chapter by chapter and standing ready for calls, day or night. I really cannot thank him enough.

Every book is a journey, and this one took us to the Rockefeller Foundation's Bellagio Center in Italy, where we worked for a month, outlining the book and writing, with Cornelia delivering long memos each day about our life for me to shape into narrative. At this moment of inception, we were graced with a very talented community of fellows, friends all, who are kindred in this project, as are the foundation's Rob Garris and the Bellagio Center's elegant director, Pilar Palacia.

There were supporters in Cambridge, from my friend Alex Jones at Harvard's Kennedy School Shorenstein Center, where the project formally began in 2012, to Larry Lessig, director of the Edmond J. Safra Center for Ethics, where I've spent two years as the senior fellow.

We traveled quite a bit to test our ideas and experiences against expert perspectives. To try to understand what we'd observed and place it in the context of the latest research, we met with David Amaral and his colleagues at the MIND Institute at the University of California, Davis; Hazel Sive at MIT; Simon Baron-Cohen at Cambridge University Autism Research Centre in the UK; Ricardo Dolmetsch at Stanford University; Tom Insel, director of the

National Institute of Mental Health (NIMH); Gerald Fischbach at the Simons Foundation in New York; and Margaret Bauman at Harvard. All were tremendously helpful and generous with their time.

Wendy Lefkon, Kingswell's editorial director, saw the potential in this book from the very start, championed it, and enriched it with her skillful editing. She has been my trusted partner and friend from day one. Thanks also go to Ellice Lee for her creative art direction, Seale Ballenger for his strategic efforts, Arlene Goldberg for her endless patience with our last-minute fixes, Marybeth Tregarthen for her production wizardry, and all the rest of the talented Kingswell team.

Thanks to Lori Slavin, for her inspiration on the title, and to my intrepid agent Andrew Wylie, always a sober judge of projects and a master at seeing them to completion.

And it all circles back to family . . .

The Suskind/Kennedy clan of cousins, aunts, uncles, and grandparents has always been there for Owen and for us, every step of the way, with support and faith and love. "Without you, there'd be no us."

Walt, our eldest son, just starting out in his adult life, didn't exactly have a book figured into his busy schedule. But, like everything else he's ever done, he stepped forward with his generous spirit, great memory, and wonderful sense of humor to add so much to these pages, as he does to our life. Thanks, Walt.

And, finally, there's the person who inspired and guided this project. He is now very much a young man. We wouldn't have proceeded with this book if Owen had not arrived at the maturity and self-awareness to say, forcefully—as he did—"Yes! I want people to know me for who I am, and to know people like me for who they are."

He trusts the world, even while knowing it so often falls short. His story is far from over; in some ways, it is just beginning. But his faith in the power of story, and our capacity to believe in one another and show kindness, lights every page of this book. Right to the end.